FREE Test Taking Tips DVD Offer

To help us better serve you, we have developed a Test Taking Tips DVD that we would like to give you for FREE. **This DVD covers world-class test taking tips that you can use to be even more successful when you are taking your test.**

All that we ask is that you email us your feedback about your study guide. Please let us know what you thought about it – whether that is good, bad or indifferent.

To get your **FREE Test Taking Tips DVD**, email freedvd@studyguideteam.com with "FREE DVD" in the subject line and the following information in the body of the email:

a. The title of your study guide.

b. Your product rating on a scale of 1-5, with 5 being the highest rating.

c. Your feedback about the study guide. What did you think of it?

d. Your full name and shipping address to send your free DVD.

If you have any questions or concerns, please don't hesitate to contact us at freedvd@studyguideteam.com.

Thanks again!

AP Economics Macro & Micro Prep Book

AP Microeconomics and Macroeconomics Study Guide with Practice Test Questions [Includes Detailed Answer Explanations]

TPB Publishing

Written and edited by TPB Publishing.

ISBN 13: 9781628452358
ISBN 10: 1628452358

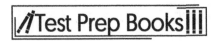

Table of Contents

Quick Overview

As you draw closer to taking your exam, effective preparation becomes more and more important. Thankfully, you have this study guide to help you get ready. Use this guide to help keep your studying on track and refer to it often.

This study guide contains several key sections that will help you be successful on your exam. The guide contains tips for what you should do the night before and the day of the test. Also included are test-taking tips. Knowing the right information is not always enough. Many well-prepared test takers struggle with exams. These tips will help equip you to accurately read, assess, and answer test questions.

A large part of the guide is devoted to showing you what content to expect on the exam and to helping you better understand that content. In this guide are practice test questions so that you can see how well you have grasped the content. Then, answer explanations are provided so that you can understand why you missed certain questions.

Don't try to cram the night before you take your exam. This is not a wise strategy for a few reasons. First, your retention of the information will be low. Your time would be better used by reviewing information you already know rather than trying to learn a lot of new information. Second, you will likely become stressed as you try to gain a large amount of knowledge in a short amount of time. Third, you will be depriving yourself of sleep. So be sure to go to bed at a reasonable time the night before. Being well-rested helps you focus and remain calm.

Be sure to eat a substantial breakfast the morning of the exam. If you are taking the exam in the afternoon, be sure to have a good lunch as well. Being hungry is distracting and can make it difficult to focus. You have hopefully spent lots of time preparing for the exam. Don't let an empty stomach get in the way of success!

When travelling to the testing center, leave earlier than needed. That way, you have a buffer in case you experience any delays. This will help you remain calm and will keep you from missing your appointment time at the testing center.

Be sure to pace yourself during the exam. Don't try to rush through the exam. There is no need to risk performing poorly on the exam just so you can leave the testing center early. Allow yourself to use all of the allotted time if needed.

Remain positive while taking the exam even if you feel like you are performing poorly. Thinking about the content you should have mastered will not help you perform better on the exam.

Once the exam is complete, take some time to relax. Even if you feel that you need to take the exam again, you will be well served by some down time before you begin studying again. It's often easier to convince yourself to study if you know that it will come with a reward!

Test-Taking Strategies

1. Predicting the Answer

When you feel confident in your preparation for a multiple-choice test, try predicting the answer before reading the answer choices. This is especially useful on questions that test objective factual knowledge. By predicting the answer before reading the available choices, you eliminate the possibility that you will be distracted or led astray by an incorrect answer choice. You will feel more confident in your selection if you read the question, predict the answer, and then find your prediction among the answer choices. After using this strategy, be sure to still read all of the answer choices carefully and completely. If you feel unprepared, you should not attempt to predict the answers. This would be a waste of time and an opportunity for your mind to wander in the wrong direction.

2. Reading the Whole Question

Too often, test takers scan a multiple-choice question, recognize a few familiar words, and immediately jump to the answer choices. Test authors are aware of this common impatience, and they will sometimes prey upon it. For instance, a test author might subtly turn the question into a negative, or he or she might redirect the focus of the question right at the end. The only way to avoid falling into these traps is to read the entirety of the question carefully before reading the answer choices.

3. Looking for Wrong Answers

Long and complicated multiple-choice questions can be intimidating. One way to simplify a difficult multiple-choice question is to eliminate all of the answer choices that are clearly wrong. In most sets of answers, there will be at least one selection that can be dismissed right away. If the test is administered on paper, the test taker could draw a line through it to indicate that it may be ignored; otherwise, the test taker will have to perform this operation mentally or on scratch paper. In either case, once the obviously incorrect answers have been eliminated, the remaining choices may be considered. Sometimes identifying the clearly wrong answers will give the test taker some information about the correct answer. For instance, if one of the remaining answer choices is a direct opposite of one of the eliminated answer choices, it may well be the correct answer. The opposite of obviously wrong is obviously right! Of course, this is not always the case. Some answers are obviously incorrect simply because they are irrelevant to the question being asked. Still, identifying and eliminating some incorrect answer choices is a good way to simplify a multiple-choice question.

4. Don't Overanalyze

Anxious test takers often overanalyze questions. When you are nervous, your brain will often run wild, causing you to make associations and discover clues that don't actually exist. If you feel that this may be a problem for you, do whatever you can to slow down during the test. Try taking a deep breath or counting to ten. As you read and consider the question, restrict yourself to the particular words used by the author. Avoid thought tangents about what the author *really* meant, or what he or she was *trying* to say. The only things that matter on a multiple-choice test are the words that are actually in the question. You must avoid reading too much into a multiple-choice question, or supposing that the writer meant something other than what he or she wrote.

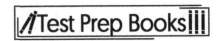

5. No Need for Panic

It is wise to learn as many strategies as possible before taking a multiple-choice test, but it is likely that you will come across a few questions for which you simply don't know the answer. In this situation, avoid panicking. Because most multiple-choice tests include dozens of questions, the relative value of a single wrong answer is small. As much as possible, you should compartmentalize each question on a multiple-choice test. In other words, you should not allow your feelings about one question to affect your success on the others. When you find a question that you either don't understand or don't know how to answer, just take a deep breath and do your best. Read the entire question slowly and carefully. Try rephrasing the question a couple of different ways. Then, read all of the answer choices carefully. After eliminating obviously wrong answers, make a selection and move on to the next question.

6. Confusing Answer Choices

When working on a difficult multiple-choice question, there may be a tendency to focus on the answer choices that are the easiest to understand. Many people, whether consciously or not, gravitate to the answer choices that require the least concentration, knowledge, and memory. This is a mistake. When you come across an answer choice that is confusing, you should give it extra attention. A question might be confusing because you do not know the subject matter to which it refers. If this is the case, don't eliminate the answer before you have affirmatively settled on another. When you come across an answer choice of this type, set it aside as you look at the remaining choices. If you can confidently assert that one of the other choices is correct, you can leave the confusing answer aside. Otherwise, you will need to take a moment to try to better understand the confusing answer choice. Rephrasing is one way to tease out the sense of a confusing answer choice.

7. Your First Instinct

Many people struggle with multiple-choice tests because they overthink the questions. If you have studied sufficiently for the test, you should be prepared to trust your first instinct once you have carefully and completely read the question and all of the answer choices. There is a great deal of research suggesting that the mind can come to the correct conclusion very quickly once it has obtained all of the relevant information. At times, it may seem to you as if your intuition is working faster even than your reasoning mind. This may in fact be true. The knowledge you obtain while studying may be retrieved from your subconscious before you have a chance to work out the associations that support it. Verify your instinct by working out the reasons that it should be trusted.

8. Key Words

Many test takers struggle with multiple-choice questions because they have poor reading comprehension skills. Quickly reading and understanding a multiple-choice question requires a mixture of skill and experience. To help with this, try jotting down a few key words and phrases on a piece of scrap paper. Doing this concentrates the process of reading and forces the mind to weigh the relative importance of the question's parts. In selecting words and phrases to write down, the test taker thinks about the question more deeply and carefully. This is especially true for multiple-choice questions that are preceded by a long prompt.

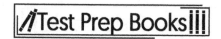

9. Subtle Negatives

One of the oldest tricks in the multiple-choice test writer's book is to subtly reverse the meaning of a question with a word like *not* or *except*. If you are not paying attention to each word in the question, you can easily be led astray by this trick. For instance, a common question format is, "Which of the following is...?" Obviously, if the question instead is, "Which of the following is not...?," then the answer will be quite different. Even worse, the test makers are aware of the potential for this mistake and will include one answer choice that would be correct if the question were not negated or reversed. A test taker who misses the reversal will find what he or she believes to be a correct answer and will be so confident that he or she will fail to reread the question and discover the original error. The only way to avoid this is to practice a wide variety of multiple-choice questions and to pay close attention to each and every word.

10. Reading Every Answer Choice

It may seem obvious, but you should always read every one of the answer choices! Too many test takers fall into the habit of scanning the question and assuming that they understand the question because they recognize a few key words. From there, they pick the first answer choice that answers the question they believe they have read. Test takers who read all of the answer choices might discover that one of the latter answer choices is actually *more* correct. Moreover, reading all of the answer choices can remind you of facts related to the question that can help you arrive at the correct answer. Sometimes, a misstatement or incorrect detail in one of the latter answer choices will trigger your memory of the subject and will enable you to find the right answer. Failing to read all of the answer choices is like not reading all of the items on a restaurant menu: you might miss out on the perfect choice.

11. Spot the Hedges

One of the keys to success on multiple-choice tests is paying close attention to every word. This is never truer than with words like almost, most, some, and sometimes. These words are called "hedges" because they indicate that a statement is not totally true or not true in every place and time. An absolute statement will contain no hedges, but in many subjects, the answers are not always straightforward or absolute. There are always exceptions to the rules in these subjects. For this reason, you should favor those multiple-choice questions that contain hedging language. The presence of qualifying words indicates that the author is taking special care with his or her words, which is certainly important when composing the right answer. After all, there are many ways to be wrong, but there is only one way to be right! For this reason, it is wise to avoid answers that are absolute when taking a multiple-choice test. An absolute answer is one that says things are either all one way or all another. They often include words like *every*, *always*, *best*, and *never*. If you are taking a multiple-choice test in a subject that doesn't lend itself to absolute answers, be on your guard if you see any of these words.

12. Long Answers

In many subject areas, the answers are not simple. As already mentioned, the right answer often requires hedges. Another common feature of the answers to a complex or subjective question are qualifying clauses, which are groups of words that subtly modify the meaning of the sentence. If the question or answer choice describes a rule to which there are exceptions or the subject matter is complicated, ambiguous, or confusing, the correct answer will require many words in order to be expressed clearly and accurately. In essence, you should not be deterred by answer choices that seem excessively long. Oftentimes, the author of the text will not be able to write the correct answer without offering some qualifications and modifications. Your job is to read the answer choices thoroughly and completely and to select the one that most accurately and precisely answers the question.

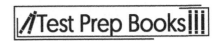

13. Restating to Understand

Sometimes, a question on a multiple-choice test is difficult not because of what it asks but because of how it is written. If this is the case, restate the question or answer choice in different words. This process serves a couple of important purposes. First, it forces you to concentrate on the core of the question. In order to rephrase the question accurately, you have to understand it well. Rephrasing the question will concentrate your mind on the key words and ideas. Second, it will present the information to your mind in a fresh way. This process may trigger your memory and render some useful scrap of information picked up while studying.

14. True Statements

Sometimes an answer choice will be true in itself, but it does not answer the question. This is one of the main reasons why it is essential to read the question carefully and completely before proceeding to the answer choices. Too often, test takers skip ahead to the answer choices and look for true statements. Having found one of these, they are content to select it without reference to the question above. Obviously, this provides an easy way for test makers to play tricks. The savvy test taker will always read the entire question before turning to the answer choices. Then, having settled on a correct answer choice, he or she will refer to the original question and ensure that the selected answer is relevant. The mistake of choosing a correct-but-irrelevant answer choice is especially common on questions related to specific pieces of objective knowledge. A prepared test taker will have a wealth of factual knowledge at his or her disposal, and should not be careless in its application.

15. No Patterns

One of the more dangerous ideas that circulates about multiple-choice tests is that the correct answers tend to fall into patterns. These erroneous ideas range from a belief that B and C are the most common right answers, to the idea that an unprepared test-taker should answer "A-B-A-C-A-D-A-B-A." It cannot be emphasized enough that pattern-seeking of this type is exactly the WRONG way to approach a multiple-choice test. To begin with, it is highly unlikely that the test maker will plot the correct answers according to some predetermined pattern. The questions are scrambled and delivered in a random order. Furthermore, even if the test maker was following a pattern in the assignation of correct answers, there is no reason why the test taker would know which pattern he or she was using. Any attempt to discern a pattern in the answer choices is a waste of time and a distraction from the real work of taking the test. A test taker would be much better served by extra preparation before the test than by reliance on a pattern in the answers.

FREE DVD OFFER

Don't forget that doing well on your exam includes both understanding the test content and understanding how to use what you know to do well on the test. We offer a completely FREE Test Taking Tips DVD that covers world class test taking tips that you can use to be even more successful when you are taking your test.

All that we ask is that you email us your feedback about your study guide. To get your **FREE Test Taking Tips DVD**, email freedvd@studyguideteam.com with "FREE DVD" in the subject line and the following information in the body of the email:

- The title of your study guide.
- Your product rating on a scale of 1-5, with 5 being the highest rating.
- Your feedback about the study guide. What did you think of it?
- Your full name and shipping address to send your free DVD.

Introduction

Function of the Test

This AP Economics guide includes two AP exams: Macroeconomics and Microeconomics. Test takers complete the AP exams in order to earn college credit at their specified university. In order to take both Macroeconomics and Microeconomics, students must have a full one-semester introductory college course in each subject. The AP exams are taken around the world, but students must check with their particular school to see if the AP exam is offered there. In 2019, 146,091 students took the Macroeconomics exam, and 58.9% got a 3 or higher. In 2019, 91,551 students took the Microeconomics exam, and 69.6% got a 3 or higher.

Test Administration

The AP Macroeconomics and Microeconomics Exams are offered at various testing sites on a specified date once a year. Students who don't do well on their exam will have to wait until the next year to retake the exam. Both scores will be reported, although you do have a choice to have one score canceled or withheld. Students with disabilities must be approved for accommodations by the College Board Services for Students with Disabilities office.

Test Format

The exams will be given at high schools and exam centers. Students are allowed one ten-minute break between the sections, but they cannot bring food or drink into the classroom. Both AP exams are two hours and ten minutes long. Both exams also have two sections: one multiple-choice section with sixty questions, and a second free-response section with three questions. The multiple-choice section takes one hour and ten minutes and is 66 percent of the score. The free-response section takes one hour and is 33 percent of the score. Two tables below depict the subject matter in the Macroeconomics and Microeconomics Courses.

Macroeconomics Exam
Unit 1: Basic Economic Concepts
Unit 2: Economic Indicators and the Business Cycle
Unit 3: National Income and Price Determination
Unit 4: Financial Sector
Unit 5: Long-Run Consequences of Stabilization Policies
Unit 6: Open Economy—International Trade and Finance

Microeconomics Exam
Unit 1: Basic Economic Concepts
Unit 2: Supply and Demand
Unit 3: Production, Cost, and the Perfect Competition Model
Unit 4: Imperfect Competition
Unit 5: Factor Markets
Unit 6: Market Failure and the Role of Government

Scoring

Scoring for the AP Economics Exams is on a five-point scale. Individual colleges will decide which number on that scale qualifies for credit and placement, so there is no pass or fail. The score is a weighted combination between the multiple-choice section and the free-response section. The multiple-choice section is graded by a computer that marks incorrect and correct answers. The free-response section is graded by college professors and AP teachers. Yourself, your designated colleges, and your AP teachers will receive your scores. In 2019, the average score for AP Exams was 2.91, and 60 percent of students received a score of 3 or above.

Basic Economic Concepts

Scarcity

Resources and Cause of Scarcity

Scarcity is the fundamental building block of economics. It is the reality that there is a limited amount of resources to meet unlimited wants and needs. In the study of economics, resources are known as **factors of production**. Imagine placing on a table the resources you would need to bake a wedding cake. It would require flour, water, eggs, sugar, a bowl, a recipe, a spoon, a mixer, and likely a host of other items. Each individual item is one factor, or resource, required to produce the final product. Each one is a factor of production.

There are four distinct categories in the factors of production: land, labor, capital, and entrepreneurship. **Land** is any natural resource unaltered by humankind. This includes lumber, minerals, stone, and petroleum. **Labor** refers to the effort exerted by a worker. **Capital** refers to any manufactured good used to create other goods or services, such as saws, computers, and manufacturing machinery. The final factor of production is **entrepreneurship**. It requires the combining of all the other factors of production by using organization, risk, innovation, and calculation to produce a final product.

In the process of determining how to use resources, a choice must be made to do one thing and neglect to do something else with these resources. This concept is known as a trade-off. A **trade-off** is the alternate decision one could have made with their resources.

Take the egg in the wedding cake example. Let's suppose the person baking the cake only had one egg left but wanted to eat breakfast prior to baking the cake. With a scarcity of eggs in the refrigerator, the baker must choose between baking the cake and eating an egg for breakfast.

Let's consider more examples you face on a regular basis:

- With this last hour before bedtime, should I study a little longer for economics or play Fortnite?
- Should I spend my last $20 on iTunes or eating at my favorite Italian restaurant?

Each of these scenarios is an example of a trade-off. Because of the scarcity of resources, a person must sacrifice one thing in order to gain another.

Three Basic Questions

Just like human beings, countries must make decisions about how to use their scarce resources. Should they provide more money for the poor or invest in the military? Should they create more federal courts or allocate more money for intercity housing? Regardless of the option they choose, there are trade-offs to their decisions.

But before making these decisions, a nation must design an economic system. When designing an economic system in a nation, there are three fundamental questions that are integral to determining how the resources of a nation will be allocated:

- What goods and services should be produced?
- How should these goods and services be produced?
- Who should consume these goods and services?

A **market economy** is one that is guided by the free choices of individuals and corporations, answering the three questions as they choose. These individuals and groups choose what goods or services are produced, how they are produced, and who to sell them to. There is little government intervention in a pure market economy, and no central authority determines how these individuals and groups should make their decisions.

On the opposite side of the continuum is a **command economy**. In this economy, a central authority (the government) owns all of the factors of production and chooses which ones are produced, how they are produced, and who can consume these goods and services.

The drive to make a profit is known as a **positive incentive**, or a reward that motivates particular behavior. Profit is an incentive that motivates people to use their entrepreneurial skill to combine the factors of production in a way that simultaneously makes a profit and satisfies the wants and needs of consumers. A **negative incentive** is a punishment that results from making a particular choice. Those making economic decisions should always consider the positive and negative incentives involved before making their final decision.

A **mixed economy** is a combination of a market economy and command economy. Most nations today have a mixed economy. This means that individuals and businesses are given a substantial amount of liberty to combine the factors of production how they see fit, but the government regulates certain industries or business practices.

Production Possibilities Curve

Production Possibilities Curve (PPC) and Related Terms

As we consider the idea of trade-offs, it is important to realize that some are measurable and tangible, whereas others are intangible and therefore unmeasurable. For those trade-offs that are measurable, there is a visual representation known as a **production possibility curve (PPC)**. It is illustrated below.

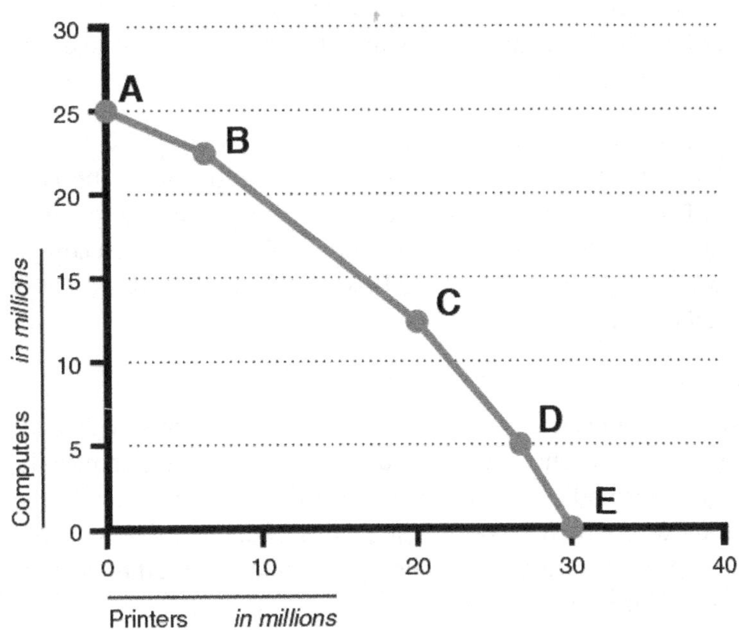

In the image above, you will notice that two separate goods are being manufactured by a company: computers and printers. Any point on the line is known as a **point of efficiency**, which means the company is producing at maximum capacity, expending all of their resources to the fullest to produce whatever goods they choose to produce. Any point beneath the line represents **underutilization**, which means the company is not using their resources to the fullest capacity. For example, they may not be using a certain piece of equipment because it is slow.

Each point on the line (A–E) represents different ways the company could allocate its resources to produce these goods. Point A in the diagram illustrates how many computers can be produced if all the resources (factors of production) are used to make computers and no resources are spent making printers. In total, it shows that if all the company's resources were used to produce computers, they would produce 17 million computers and zero printers. Point E shows the opposite: if all a company's resources were spent making printers and no resources were used to make computers, the company would produce 16 million printers and zero computers.

Each of the other points illustrates how many printers and computers can be made if some resources are allocated to make printers and some are allocated to make computers.

Now test yourself. How many computers and printers are made if a company produces at points B, C, and D?

If a company produces at point B, they will produce 15 million computers and 4 million printers. If a company produces at point C, they will produce 10 million computers and 10 million printers. If a company produces at point D, they will produce 4 million computers and 15 million printers.

Illustrations of the Production Possibilities Curve

The only way to produce beyond the PPC is by adding additional resources. This is known as **growth** and can include adding more working space to the building, hiring more employees, and buying additional equipment to aid production. By adding these resources, the company's ability to produce is increased, which would extend the curve outward. If for some reason workers were laid off or a piece of equipment was destroyed, the PPC would move inward, demonstrating a smaller capacity to produce goods or services. This is known as **contraction**.

But what happens if a piece of equipment is ignored or if employees are slow to do their jobs? In this case, the PPC would remain intact because it is showing the potential production of goods or services if they are used efficiently. This would be demonstrated by showing a point somewhere inside the PPC. This point, and any point inside the line, is underutilization. This means that a company or individual is underutilizing their resources, or using them at less than their potential. This point of underutilization is also called a **point of inefficiency**.

Shape

The specific shape of each PPC indicates certain facts about the trade-offs involved in producing one product over another. If the PPC is concaved, or shaped significantly like a semicircle, the opportunity cost for producing one good instead of another is significant. The more concaved the PPC is, the more significant the trade-off between the two goods being measured. If the PPC is shaped more like a straight line, the opportunity cost for producing one good instead of another is insignificant. The more vertical a PPC is, the less significant the trade-offs.

The graph below is the same one used in an earlier example. The concaved shape indicates there is a significant trade-off to produce one good rather than another.

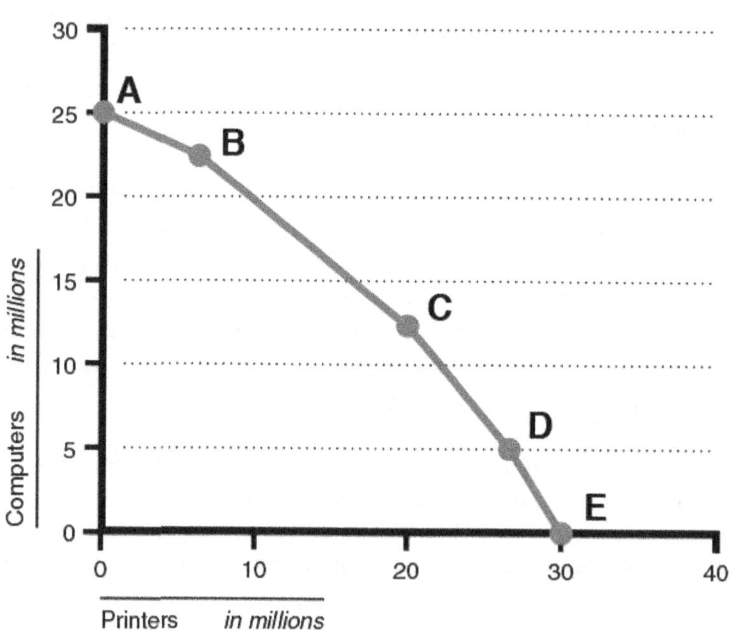

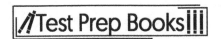

Opportunity Cost

Before we consider how to measure trade-offs on the PPC, we must define a particular type of trade-off known as an **opportunity cost**.

Let's begin on the individual level. Suppose on a Thursday afternoon one of your close friends asks you to go shopping on Friday after school. You have $50 in your wallet and know if you go with your friend, you are certain the money will be gone. As you think about your friend's offer, you begin to think of all the things you could do with the money if you don't go with your friend: put all of it in your savings account, pay your monthly car insurance, or buy your mom a gift for Mother's Day. There are a host of great options. In the end, you narrow down your choices: going with your friend to the mall or buying your mother a gift. After being pressured a little more by your friend, you decide to go shopping and wait on buying your mother's gift.

In this scenario, economists would define your second choice (buying your mom a Mother's Day gift) as the opportunity cost. The opportunity cost is the next best alternative to whichever option you chose. It is a type of trade-off.

At a macro level, the opportunity cost as well as the additional trade-offs can be illustrated and measured on a PPC. Let's consider the same PPC we used earlier in the diagram below.

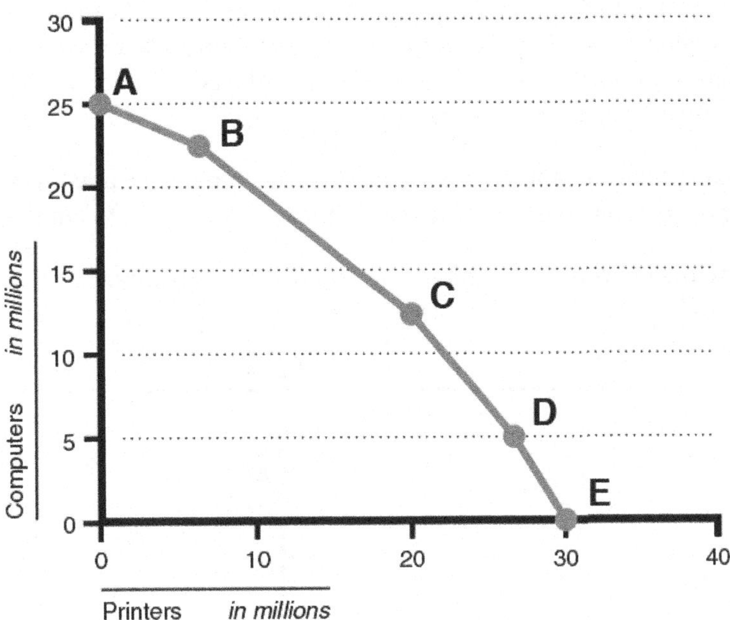

If a company has narrowed down its business decisions between producing at point A or point C but eventually selects point C, the opportunity cost for choosing point C was 20 million computers, the difference in computers between points A and C. At the same time, every other point located on the PPC, including ones you could create, are rightly called trade-offs.

For the sake of clarity, remember that you make these kinds of decisions every day. They usually sound something like this:

> "If I do my homework after school, then I won't be able to play video games." The opportunity cost of doing your homework is playing video games.
>
> "If I run track in the spring, then I won't be able to work a job and save to buy the car I want to drive." The opportunity cost of running track is working the job and getting the car.

In addition to the opportunity cost is a multitude of other options you could have chosen, and they are also labeled as trade-offs.

Comparative Advantage and Trade

Absolute Advantage and Comparative Advantage

To be most useful in any given economy, a person or business benefits from having skills that help them produce goods or services in demand. As might be expected, it is even better if the person producing these goods and services is able to do so better than others who also have that skill.

Let's take for example two people, Judson and Emmett, who both make toy cars and airplanes. In an eight-hour day, Judson is able to make twelve airplanes, whereas Emmett can only make ten. Judson's ability to make more airplanes than Emmett is known as an **absolute advantage**, or the ability by one party (individual, business, or government) to produce more of a good or service when given the same amount of time and resources as another party.

This differs from a comparative advantage. If someone has a **comparative advantage**, it means an individual has a lower opportunity cost for producing one good compared to another individual.

To better illustrate the concepts of absolute and comparative advantage, consider the PPCs and explanation below.

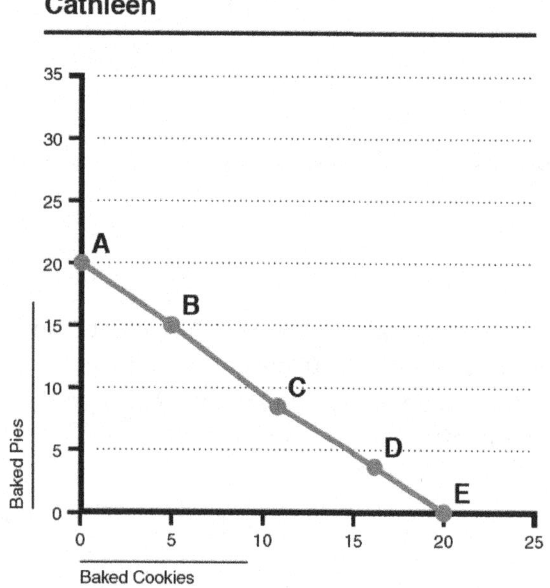

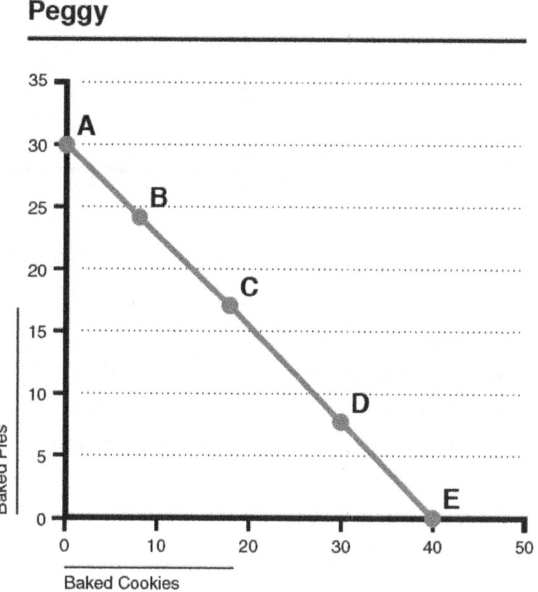

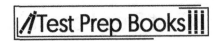

Cathleen and Peggy have decided to open a business baking pies and cookies for family reunions, birthday parties, and other celebrations. To maximize production, they create a PPC.

If you compare the two diagrams, you will notice that Peggy has an absolute advantage at baking cookies and pies. When she devotes all of her time to pies, she can produce ten more pies than Cathleen (thirty for Peggy versus only twenty for Cathleen), and if she only bakes cookies, she can produce twenty more cookies than Cathleen (forty for Peggy versus only twenty for Cathleen).

At first glance, one might think that Peggy would be better off producing both items on her own. But a better understanding of specialization, trade, and comparative advantage will reveal Peggy and Cathleen can maximize their production if they work together.

Specialization

Specialization is when someone devotes all of their energy and resources to a task they are particularly good at performing. In the modern era, that is how market economies tend to work. Most people in a market economy specialize in providing a particular good or service because they know the more they focus on this task, the better they are able to hone the skills needed to produce these goods or services effectively and efficiently.

The concept of specialization is best understood by using the example of an assembly line. Assembly lines were made famous in the automobile industry in the early twentieth century when Henry Ford arranged his factory in a way that required one person to perform the same task repetitiously while building an automobile. As each person would complete their task, they would move the automobile down the line so the next person could complete a different task. Because each worker was performing the task over and over, he or she developed certain distinct skills that were necessary to perform the task quickly. This specializing enabled each individual to speed up their individual operation, and the result was an increase in the number of vehicles the factory was able to produce.

Calculate Mutually Beneficial Terms of Trade

The goods or services gained through specialization are then able to help the economy provide a higher standard of living because the additional items can be traded and more people can enjoy them. The additional items also provide an opportunity for trade. **Trade** is when people produce a good or service they specialize in and exchange it for a good or service they want from other people.

The major benefits of trade become evident when associated with the concept of comparative advantage. In the scenario with Cathleen and Peggy, it seems like Peggy has no need to trade with Cathleen because she is superior at producing both cookies and pies. But a closer look at the situation will reveal that it is in Peggy's and Cathleen's best interests to trade with one another.

As previously mentioned, an absolute advantage is when someone can produce more of a good or service than someone else with the same amount of resources. A comparative advantage is when an individual can produce something with a lower opportunity cost than someone else. To better understand comparative advantage, let's review the PPCs involving Cathleen and Peggy from earlier.

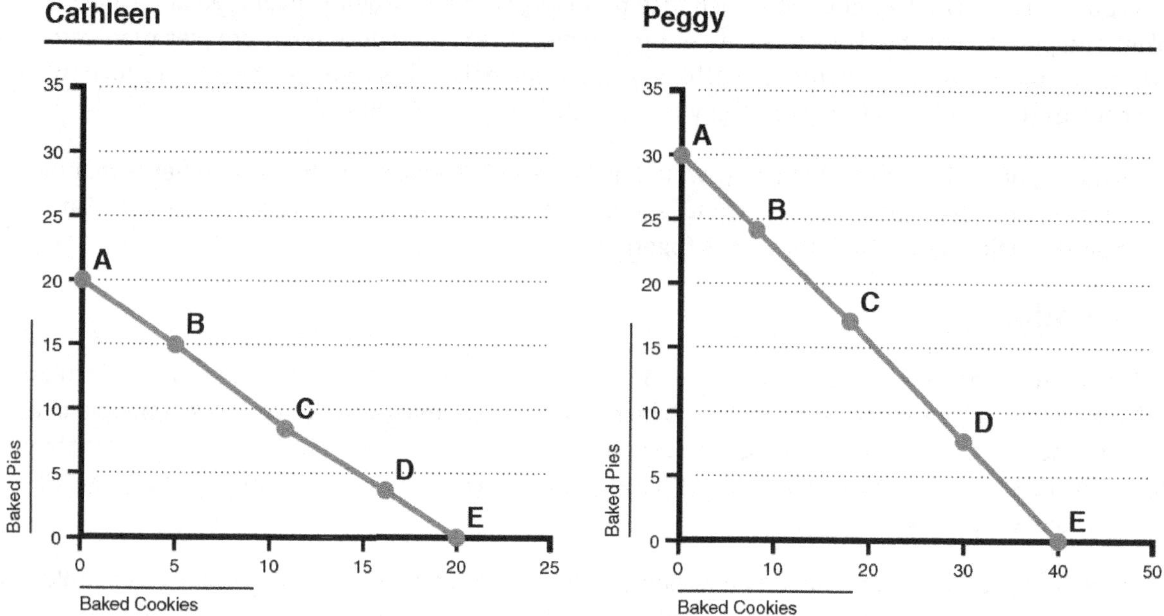

In this scenario, Peggy has an absolute advantage over Cathleen in producing both pies and cookies. But Cathleen actually has a comparative advantage over Peggy in producing pies because the opportunity cost is less for Cathleen than Peggy. On the other hand, Peggy has a comparative advantage over Cathleen when making cookies because the opportunity cost is lower if Peggy makes cookies. The chart below illustrates the comparative advantages in the situation.

	Peggy's Opportunity Cost	Cathleen's Opportunity Cost
1 pie	1 1/3 cookies	1 cookie
1 cookie	¾ pie	1 pie

To describe it more simply, each time Cathleen bakes a pie, it only requires her to lose one cookie she could have baked if she hadn't baked that pie. Because it costs Peggy more than that, $1\frac{1}{3}$ cookies, Cathleen has a comparative advantage over Peggy. In contrast, each time Peggy bakes a cookie, it requires her to sacrifice baking $\frac{2}{3}$ of a pie, but it costs Cathleen 1 pie. This means Peggy has a comparative advantage when baking pies. Because Cathleen and Peggy both have a comparative advantage over one another in making one of these baked goods, they can both end up better off if they specialize and then trade. The table below illustrates these benefits from trade.

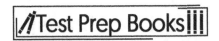

		Without Trade		With Trade		Gains from Trade
		Production	**Consumption**	**Production**	**Consumption**	
Cathleen	**Cookies**	10	10	0	12	+2
	Pies	10	10	20	10	0
Peggy	**Cookies**	28	28	40	30	+2
	Pies	9	9	0	10	+1

When Cathleen and Peggy trade with one another, they both benefit. Cathleen ends up with two additional cookies, and Peggy ends up with one additional pie and two additional cookies. But this will only be the case if they both agree to develop **mutually beneficial terms of trade**, or rates at which one good can be traded for another. Therefore, when Cathleen and Peggy decide to trade with one another, they must both put a proper value on their baked goods so their trade is mutually beneficial. To be mutually beneficial, they must set the value of their goods between the producer's opportunity cost and the buyer's opportunity cost. If they fall outside of those terms, it is not a beneficial trade for at least one of the parties.

Cost-Benefit Analysis

Opportunity Cost and the Metric Utility

Opportunity cost is the next best alternative to the choice you make. It is a type of trade-off and can be measured on a micro level (involving small personal decisions) or macro level (involving the production of various goods and services by a nation). It also includes financial and nonfinancial benefits that are forfeited in order to make a different choice. Therefore, when a person is making a decision, they must be aware of all the benefits they are receiving and all the benefits they are forgoing to make this decision.

Take, for example, a person who decides to go on vacation but cannot decide between Disney World and a weeklong cruise. When they calculate all of the expenses for their trip to Disney World, it equals approximately $5,000. When they calculate the expenses for a cruise, it is approximately $4,000. On the surface it seems as though the opportunity cost for going to Disney World instead of the cruise is $1,000. But in reality, people rarely make decisions based only on costs. They usually take into consideration the totality of the experience (both financial and nonfinancial) before making the decision.

In economics, the measurement of satisfaction that can be understood in behavior but not in explicit practice is known as **utility**. The utility is measured by hypothetical units known as **utils**. Inherent in this measurement is the assumption that people try to maximize their personal satisfaction from their consumption of goods and services.

Opportunity Costs Associated with Choices

In addition to the financial costs, a person calculating the opportunity cost must also calculate the nonfinancial costs of making this decision: they will not enjoy the unlimited buffet of a cruise, they won't experience the culture of the islands, they won't be able to relax on the beach, etc. They must also consider the things they could have done with the additional $1,000 in their pocket by going on the cruise rather than to Disney World. For example, perhaps they could pay down credit card debt, update the washing machine that has been on the fritz, or donated to a child's school. By considering all of these financial and nonfinancial costs, a person is accurately calculating the opportunity cost.

But how can a person calculate nonfinancial costs and benefits? If a person loves to ride specific roller coasters at Disney World but also loves the sandy beaches they would experience on a cruise, how can these subjective pleasures be measured?

Because it is difficult to measure the intangible satisfaction one may gain from participating in an activity, economists use the concepts of utils to measure the amount of pleasure or utility derived or lost from participating in an activity. The opportunity cost to making a certain decision can be measured quantitatively (through a specific amount of money or time) and also qualitatively (through the loss of intangibles, such as experience and feelings).

Calculate Opportunity Costs Associated with Choices

If we calculate the decision between going on the cruise or to Disney World, we can attempt to measure the opportunity cost in the situation. If the vacationer decides to go to Disney World rather than on the cruise, one part of the opportunity cost is the $1,000 they must pay above the cost of the cruise. This is the quantitative measure that is measured in dollars. In addition to the tangible costs, they may also list the pleasures of the unlimited buffet, seeing the beauty of the ocean, various excursions, and the big waterslide they could ride on the cruise. For each activity, they can assign an amount of utils they would derive from partaking in the activity. Below is a possible example:

- Unlimited buffet: 30 utils
- Beauty of the ocean: 10 utils
- Excursions: 50 utils
- Waterslide: 25 utils

The total opportunity cost for choosing Disney World over the cruise is $1,000 and 115 utils. Evidently, the anticipated amount of utils the vacationer thought they would experience at Disney World was more than the utils they would experience by going on the cruise. Furthermore, the amount of utils was significant enough that they were willing to pay an additional $1,000 in order to experience them.

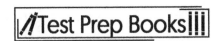

Comparing Total Benefits and Total Costs

The moment an additional unit of consumption begins to diminish their total satisfaction is the moment a person ceases to consume the good or service. Let's consider the chart below to help explain.

Quantity of Slices of Pie	Utils	Marginal Utility per Wing
0	0	0
1	10	10
2	25	15
3	38	13
4	44	6
5	43	−1

The **total utility** is a summation of the amount of total pleasure derived from consuming a given product or service. If Monte eats one slice of pie, the total utility of eating the pie increases from zero to 10 utils. As he adds more slices of pie, the total utility and marginal utility both increase when moving from one slice to two slices. **Marginal utility** is the change in total utility caused by consuming one additional unit of that good. But notice that as Monte moves from two to three slices of pie, his total utils increase from 25 to 38, but his marginal utility decreases from 15 to 13 utils. This is known as **diminishing marginal utility**. It increases the total utility, but the marginal utility diminished when an additional unit was added. In simpler terms, Monte enjoyed his second and third slice of pie but enjoyed his second slice (15-util increase) more than his third slice (13-util increase).

This pattern of diminished utils continues until his fifth slice of pie, where he actually sees a **negative marginal utility**. When an additional unit is added, the total utility is actually lowered, and the marginal utility sees a negative rate. This means Monte should have stopped eating pie after the fourth slice.

Calculate Total Benefits and Total Costs

The final aspect of a decision-making process includes the calculation of the total benefits and total costs of a decision. The **total benefit** refers to the total satisfaction one gains from consuming a specified number of goods or services. The **total cost** is the cost incurred from consuming a product or participating in an activity. These two concepts are important to consider when determining whether a rational consumer should make a certain decision or not.

For example, if a man is trying to decide how many ice cream cones to buy, he finds himself willing to pay $6 for the first scoop. But the cost is only $3. The man is willing to pay $4 for the second scoop. But the cost is only $3. The man is only willing to pay $1 for the third scoop, but the additional scoop is also $3. This means the total cost of a three-scoop cone is a total of $9, and the total benefit of buying three scoops to this particular man is $13. Therefore, he has a net benefit of $4 if he decides to buy all three scoops.

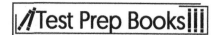

Marginal Analysis and Consumer Choice

Consumer Choice Theory

The **consumer choice theory** is the study of how consumers get the optimum amount of desirability by choosing between the various combinations of goods and services they are looking to produce. This theory is predicated on five distinct assumptions made by economists that include the following:

- **Consumers are knowledgeable**. This means consumers can effectively rank their preferences ordinally rather than cardinally. **Ordinal utility** means consumers select which goods or services bring them optimum satisfaction based on quality, not quantity. In other words, you cannot use a form of measurement to describe the level of satisfaction one feels from a good or service. This differs from **cardinal utility**, which can be quantitatively measured. For example, a producer can measure the amount of profit they receive and thus measure the overall benefit.

- **Consumers are rational**. This means consumers are not indifferent toward combinations which give them more or less utility, but prefer those combinations of goods and services which maximize their utility.

- **Consumers maximize utility**. This means consumers will select the combination of goods and services that brings them the highest level of satisfaction.

- **More is preferred to less.** This assumption means it is better to have more of, not less than, the good or service being preferred.

- **The law of diminishing marginal rates of substitution (LDMRS) applies**. This means that when one desired good is taken from a consumer, they will need more of a substitute good to maintain the maximum level of utility. In other words, if one of these preferred goods is taken, the level of satisfaction will decrease, and more of another good will be needed to increase to maintain the level of satisfaction.

Use of Marginal Benefits and Marginal Costs

When a person is making a decision about consumption, they are often using the economic concepts of marginal benefits and marginal costs without realizing it. The **marginal benefit** is what a consumer is willing to pay in order to add one more unit of a particular good or service. As the amount of units increases, the marginal benefit tends to decrease because of the diminishing marginal utility. Conversely, the **marginal cost** is the additional cost that will be incurred by adding an additional unit.

Consumers use marginal benefits by considering how much more pleasure or utility one additional unit of a good or service will bring. If the marginal cost is greater than the marginal benefit, consumers are unlikely to add one more unit of a good or service. If the marginal benefit is greater than the marginal cost, they are likely to add one more unit. When a person is making decisions, their final decision usually comes down to the margin. This means they decide the specific number to consume or produce close to the point at which the marginal cost and marginal benefit meet. If the marginal cost and marginal benefit are equal, economists usually encourage producers or consumers to add the additional unit.

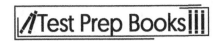

Calculate Use of Marginal Benefits and Marginal Costs

If a group of friends are eating at a Mexican restaurant, it is likely that a woman is willing to pay quite a bit for her first taco because she is eating with friends, and all of them are eating tacos as well. As she orders more tacos, the marginal benefit decreases because her satisfaction with each additional taco lessens. As she orders each additional taco, the marginal cost is the cost of each one. Eventually, her total cost will surpass the total benefit. At that point, the woman will quit eating tacos because if she continues to eat, her overall utils will decrease because she is so full. The chart below shows this concept.

Total Tacos	Marginal Cost	Marginal Benefit	Utils	Total Cost	Total Benefit
0	$0	$0	0	$0	$0
1	$3	$8	15	$3	$8
2	$3	$6	27	$6	$14
3	$3	$3	30	$9	$17
4	$3	$1	28	$12	$18

Notice that the amount of satisfaction the woman gains from adding an additional taco begins to decrease when she goes from three tacos to four. It is also at that point that the marginal benefit to the woman is lower than the marginal cost.

Marginal Analysis and Related Terms

Sunk Costs

An additional variable consumers must consider are sunk costs. A **sunk cost** is a cost that is unrecoverable. This is often found in the form of membership fees or "All-You-Can" ride or eat activities. If Justin goes to a buffet that offers unlimited food, the money is nonrefundable. No matter what he does, he cannot get the money back. The idea that he needs to "keep eating" because he wants to "get his money's worth" is a fallacy. The best thing for Justin to do is eat until the point that he has experienced the maximum utils because eating another bite of food would actually lower his overall enjoyment of the meal.

Optimum Quantity

The moment he has reached his optimal level of satisfaction is known as **optimum quantity**. At this point, he should stop consuming food.

Marginal Analysis

The **marginal analysis** is the study of the costs and benefits of doing a little bit more of an activity instead of a little less. This can be measured from the producer's side (how many units should be produced at a given price to maximize profit) and from the consumer's side (how many more units of a good or service should be added to increase satisfaction).

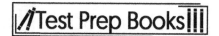

Decision Using Marginal Analysis

Total Tacos	Marginal Cost	Marginal Benefit	Utils	Total Cost	Total Benefit
0	$0	$0	0	$0	$0
1	$3	$8	15	$3	$8
2	$3	$6	27	$6	$14
3	$3	$3	30	$9	$17
4	$3	$1	28	$12	$18

Using the chart above, the woman is willing to pay a substantial amount of money for her first taco because all of her friends are eating, she is hungry, and the marginal cost is less than the marginal benefit. As she continues eating tacos, her desire for them decreases because she is slowly getting full (her utils decrease), and the marginal benefit reaches a point below the marginal cost. As a result, she eats three tacos because if she added the fourth taco, her marginal cost is higher than her marginal benefit, and her total utils would decrease.

Macroeconomics: Economic Indicators and the Business Cycle

Circular Flow and GDP

GDP is a Measure of Final Output of the Economy

Gross domestic product (GDP) is the total value of everything an economy produces within its borders in any given year. Only final goods and services are included in the GDP data. GDP provides a picture of the economic activity that takes place within a nation. To put it in simple terms, a country with a high GDP has a lot of recorded transactions taking place. In a country with a relatively low GDP, there is not much economic activity to report.

Consumer goods, investment goods, government purchases of goods and services, and exports are all included in GDP. Imports are subtracted from an economy's total output. Only final goods are included in the calculations for GDP. **Intermediate goods**, or goods that are made as part of the production of final goods, are not included as part of overall GDP. Otherwise, double-counting would occur and overstate the level of production. For example, the engine that is produced as part of a new car would not be included as part of the GDP.

Purchases of used goods are not included as part of GDP. When a car is resold with help from a site such as Craigslist or OfferUp, the dollar amount that changes hands is not included in GDP figures. However, if the sale is made through eBay Motors, the commission that eBay makes from the sale of the used vehicle is included in GDP. Stock and bond purchases are not included as part of the GDP because an exchange of financial assets does not represent production of any new good or service.

Circular Flow Diagram

The **circular flow diagram** is a simplified representation of the income and expenditures within an economy. On one side of the diagram are households who own the factors of production. On the other side of the diagram are business firms who are the resource processors in the **factor market**, which represents all the purchases of resources in the economy.

There are a total of four **factors of production**: land, labor, capital, and entrepreneurship. **Land** includes any preexisting natural resource, **labor** represents paid work, **capital** embodies both physical capital (buildings, tools) and human capital (skills, knowledge), and **entrepreneurship** describes innovative individuals who combine land, labor, and capital to form businesses. Payments to entrepreneurs come in the form of profit.

The **product market** encompasses all the goods and services produced within an economy. Businesses are the ones who take the factors of production (land, labor, capital), process them, and then sell the resulting output to households. Whereas firms are the buyers and households are the sellers in the factor market, the reverse is true in the product market.

The physical flow of goods and services represents one aspect of the circular flow diagram. When households provide land, labor, and capital, this is the portion of the factor market that represents the **physical flow** of resources within the economy from the household to the business firm. When firms deliver final goods and services to households, the other half of the physical flow manifests itself. The

monetary flow tracks the dollar amount that changes hands from the business to the household and the household to the business in the factor market and product market, respectively.

The basic thesis of the circular flow diagram is that when money changes hands, income and expense transactions simultaneously occur, depending on one's point of view. For example, if Chidi Anagonye purchases a book on moral philosophy and ethics from Barnes & Noble, the transaction would qualify as both an expense and a source of income. For Mr. Anagonye, this is a purchase in the product market and gets counted on the expenditure portion of the circular flow. However, Eleanor Shellstrop, the worker who helps the indecisive Mr. Anagonye choose the right book, is being paid income in the factor market for her services. The circular flow diagram is not a perfect representation of the goings-on in an economy by any means. It's merely a rough sketch of how an economy functions, not unlike how an architect might initially lay out a design for a building.

Money that leaves the economy is referred to as **leakage** and serves to decrease the size of economic activity. There are three basic types of leakage: savings, imports, and taxes. When individuals take income they make in the factor market and do not spend the entirety of their income (savings), this is one form of leakage. When consumers make purchases from foreign producers (imports), money leaks out of the economy. Taxes the government charges its people is the final form of leakage.

Injections within the circular flow function are the opposite of leakage. The three basic types of injection are investment, exports, and government spending. Cumulatively, these actions will lead to expanded total economic output. **Investment** represents capital spending by firms on items such as new technology. **Exports**, unlike imports, take money from foreign countries and "inject" the newfound cash into the country. **Government spending** has the opposite impact of taxes by adding to the GDP rather than taking away from economic output.

Three Ways of Measuring GDP

The **expenditures approach** to GDP totals up the purchase of all goods and services within a country's borders in a given year. It is represented by the famous Keynesisan macroeconomics equation:

$$Y = C + I + G + NX$$

$\boldsymbol{C}$ represents consumer expenditures, which makes up the majority of GDP in the United States. $\boldsymbol{I}$ is short for business investment and encompasses the total amount of expenditures on capital goods. $\boldsymbol{G}$ stands for government expenditures on items such as national defense or education. $\boldsymbol{NX}$ denotes net exports, or exports minus imports.

The expenditure approach is not unlike an individual meticulously keeping track of all of his or her expenses and sorting the items appropriately in each category. However, instead of just one person doing this, imagine that the entire country participates and collectively reports the total every quarter (or three months) into four different categories.

The **income approach** to GDP takes the sum total of all the income in the form of wages, interest, profit, and rent. The amount of factor income includes all money received by individuals, businesses, and government. In theory, the GDP amount using the income approach should yield the same amount using the expenditure approach. This, however, is usually not the case, and at times the discrepancy can be in the hundreds of billions of dollars. Although the income approach might be more accurate than the expenditure approach, the latter way of calculating GDP provides better data on how a country spends its hard-earned income.

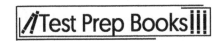

The **value-added approach** to GDP takes the contribution of each company until the total value equals the final value of goods and services. Suppose the value of all goods (final and intermediate) produced in Bobbleland is $100,000. There are only three companies in Bobbleland: Bobbles Company, Plastics Company, and Ceramics Company. Bobbles Company sells $75,000 worth of bobbleheads annually, but it also purchases $20,000 of ceramic from Ceramics Company. Of that $20,000 in ceramic sales, however, Ceramics Company purchases $5,000 from Plastics Company, so Ceramics Company adds a total value of $15,000. Bobbles Company has sales worth $75,000, but $20,000 has to be subtracted from that total.

So, how would one go about calculating GDP using the value-added approach?

The first stage of production for the bobblehead is the $5,000 added to the production process from Plastics Company. The second stage of production goes to Ceramics Company with the firm adding a value of $15,000. The third and final stage of production ends with Bobbles Company. The total sales of $75,000 is reduced by the $20,000 of purchases that went to Ceramics Company, so the value added is $55,000.

The GDP of Bobbleland is $5,000 (Plastics Company) + $15,000 (Ceramics Company) + $55,000 (Bobbles Company) = $75,000 using the value-added approach. Of the $100,000 in total sales by the three companies, intermediate good sales accounted for $25,000, or ¼ of the total amount. The total ends up being $\$100{,}000 - \$25{,}000 = \$75{,}000$, which makes sense because Bobbles Company is the only one in Bobbleland that sells final goods and services. Both Plastics Company and Ceramics Company sell intermediate goods, so their sales would not count using the expenditure approach. And, not coincidentally, the $75,000 in sales for Bobbles Company would be the GDP using the expenditure approach as well.

Limitations of GDP

The GDP is only one measure of economic production. Another measure is the **gross national product (GNP)**, which is the GDP plus the total amount of net foreign investments. Whereas GDP focuses production within a country's borders, GNP emphasizes production of a country's citizens both living within the country and abroad. GDP has become the world's preferred economic indicator; the United States abandoned using GNP as a means of economic comparison in 1991.

The GDP is not a perfect measure. The underground economy is not included in GDP totals. The **underground economy** refers to transactions that are untaxed and are often (but not always) illegal. Although the underground economy is generally associated with illicit activities such as narcotics trafficking, this does not always have to be the case. If two working parents drop off their child at Sunnyside Daycare Services, the amount of money allocated toward childcare would officially be part of GDP. However, if these same parents opt to hire their church friend's sister's daycare provider and pay cash to her in an unmarked white envelope, these individuals are taking part in the underground economy.

Another limitation of GDP is that **negative externalities** are not considered in the calculation of overall GDP numbers; for example, $20,000 worth of medical services count the same as $20,000 worth of tobacco, gambling, or fast food. If the bulk of a country's GDP comes from cigarette manufacturers that thrive on nicotine addiction, casinos that profit from the financial misery of others, and food companies that promote less than optimal eating habits, perhaps other economic measures should be considered in conjunction with the GDP.

The king of Bhutan, Jigme Singye Wangchuck, coined the termed **gross national happiness (GNH)** in the early 1970s. GNH takes into account a citizen's level of "happiness" to measure economic output, taking a more holistic approach to economic wellbeing than GDP's more conventional methodology. Although mainstream economists generally do not consider GNH as significant an economic indicator as the universally accepted GDP, GNH does lend credence to the idea that one cannot encapsulate the totality of a country's economic output into one solitary figure.

The United Nations publishes an annual happiness report (unrelated to Bhutan's GNH figures), and Finland has come out on top as the "happiest" country in the world for three straight years (2017, 2018, and 2019). In 2019, Finland's happiness score measured 7.769 out of a maximum of 10. The United States ranked nineteenth with a score of 6.892, slightly edging the Czech Republic's 6.852 but falling short of Belgium's 6.923. The worst country, of the 156 measured, was South Sudan with a happiness score of 2.853.

Unemployment

Labor Force, the Unemployment Rate, and the Labor Force Participation Rate

The **labor force** consists of all individuals aged sixteen years and older who are capable and willing to work. Individuals within the labor force who currently have a job are considered **employed**; those who do not are considered **unemployed**.

The **unemployment rate** is the number of unemployed individuals divided by the labor force (unemployed ÷ employed). Individuals who are not actively looking for employment would not be considered part of the labor force. There are a variety of individuals who do not meet the criteria of being unemployed despite not having a job. Kids under sixteen years of age, housewives and househusbands, and the retired are among the group of people who are not unemployed despite not having a job; they simply are not part of the labor force.

In March 2020, total nonfarm payroll employment decreased by 701,000 from the previous month, and the unemployment rate increased from 3.5 percent in February to 4.4 percent in March. The 0.9 percent increase indicated a massive increase in the unemployment rate in the United States. The March numbers represented the beginning of the sharp rise in unemployment as a result of the coronavirus disease 2019 (COVID-19) crisis that rocked the globe. The April 2020 numbers were far bleaker, with an astronomical spike to 14.7 percent. Unemployment skyrocketed into double digits—something the United States had not seen since the Great Recession of 2008. The COVID-19-induced unemployment in the United States might be more comparable to the massive unemployment the United States faced during the Great Depression when unemployment peaked at nearly 25 percent in 1933.

The **labor force participation rate** takes the sum total of the employed and unemployed and divides that number by the population. For example, if there were 300 million people living in the country of Trumania and 180 million people are employed and 20 million are unemployed, the unemployment rate would be 10 percent, and the labor force participation rate would be $200\ million \div 300\ million$, or 66.7 percent. The United States has seen an increase in its labor force participation rate since the 1950s when it hovered in the high 50 percent range. The height of the labor force participation rate occurred in the late 1990s and early 2000s, when it reached nearly 68 percent. In March 2020, the Bureau of Labor Statistics (BLS) reported the U.S. labor force participation rate at 62.7 percent. Although the proportion of women who have joined the working world has nearly doubled from the low 30 percent range in the 1950s to approximately 60 percent in 2020, the ratio of men seeking labor dropped from nearly 90 percent to approximately 70 percent during that same timeframe.

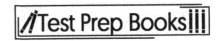

Changes in Employment and the Labor Market

The labor market is not a static entity. Depending on a variety of factors, individuals constantly enter and exit the labor force on any given day. The BLS actually adjusts the unemployment rate based on seasonal factors. For example, the labor force tends to be greater during the summer and winter months when students enter the labor market. As a rule, unemployment data that is reported automatically adjusts for seasonal fluctuations, so the unemployment numbers in June may be compared more accurately with the numbers reported in September.

Since 1977, the Federal Reserve System (the Fed) has operated under the **dual mandate** of maintaining maximum employment and a low rate of inflation. When the national unemployment rate dips to an unacceptably high level, the Fed will typically lower interest rates in an attempt to lower the unemployment rate. However, the labor force participation rate is also a key employment measure that is used in conjunction with the unemployment rate in determining the health of the economy. A relatively low labor force participation rate can hint at structural weakness in the labor market.

Calculate the Unemployment Rate and the Labor Force Participation Rate

Let's look at the population numbers for the fictitious country of Tomlinville to determine the unemployment rate and labor force participation rate.

Labor Market Data in Tomlinville (2020)	
Population	1,000,000
Employed	400,000
Unemployed	100,000
Not in the labor force	500,000

First, let's calculate the unemployment rate in Tomlinville. It would be incorrect to take the number of unemployed and divide by the population. A rookie economist's mistake would be to simply take 100,000 and divide by 1,000,000 to naively assume that 10 percent of the population is unemployed. Although the ratio of the unemployed to the population may be 10 percent, the unemployment rate is the number of unemployed divided by the labor force, which is found by adding the employed and unemployed. Hence, the correct unemployment rate is $100{,}000 \div 500{,}000$ (400,000 employed + 100,000 unemployed), or 20 percent.

The labor force participation rate is found by dividing the labor force by the entire population. The labor force, as determined previously, is 500,000 individuals who are either working or actively looking for labor. Hence, this cohort of employed and unemployed persons totals 500,000. The combined total of individuals in the labor force and those not in the labor force equals the population, so the labor force participation rate is $500{,}000 \div 1{,}000{,}000$, or 50 percent.

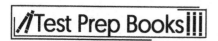

Now, let's imagine that there is a wave of senior citizens who return to work in Tomlinville the following year. How would the employment figures change given the numbers below?

Labor Market Data in Tomlinville (2021)	
Population	1,000,000
Employed	425,000
Unemployed	125,000
Not in the labor force	450,000

In this scenario, although the population has remained constant, both the unemployment rate and labor force participation rate have changed. There are now 425,000 employed individuals in Tomlinville, but the number of unemployed persons has increased by the same number of 25,000, for a total of 125,000 jobless Tomlinville residents who are actively seeking employment. The unemployment rate increased from 20 percent in 2020 to $125{,}000 \div 550{,}000$, or 22.73 percent, in 2021.

Although the surface numbers admittedly do not look good, a deeper look into the data shows at least some room for optimism. The number of individuals who are in the labor force increased by 10 percent, or from 500,000 to 550,000. The increase in the unemployment rate is attributed to the fact that only half of the 50,000 individuals who entered the labor force were able to procure employment. One plausible explanation for senior citizens being unable to find jobs might be that the skills they have do not match the skills employers demand of their employees. Individuals who have not been in the labor market for an extended period of time tend to have difficulty acquiring the necessary skills employers desire.

Limitations of the Unemployment Rate

A **discouraged worker** is an individual who is discouraged by the inability to get a job and therefore drops out of the labor force. At times, the unemployment rate will *decrease* as a result of turning unemployed workers into discouraged workers. With this in mind, a low unemployment rate is not the be-all and end-all of economic health.

Another limitation of unemployment lies in the fact that full-time workers are treated in exactly the same manner as part-time workers for the purposes of measuring the unemployment rate. A worker who logs fifty hours is counted as employed; a worker who logs ten hours is also counted as employed. There is no way to distinguish how many hours an individual has worked when determining the unemployment rate. As long as a worker has worked one hour in the past week, he or she is considered to be employed.

An **underemployed** worker is a person who is qualified for a job that requires a much lower level of human capital than he or she possesses. Another type of underemployed worker is a person who works less than the amount he or she actually wants to work. For example, Walmart might employ a group of workers who only work twenty-five hours and are classified as part-time workers even though they might prefer to work a full forty-hour week. The combination of underemployed workers and discouraged workers serves to underestimate the actual level of unemployment in an economy.

Types of Unemployment

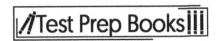

There are three distinct types of unemployment: cyclical, frictional, and structural. The **natural rate of unemployment** is the sustainable rate of unemployment in the long run and is represented by the equation:

$$Natural\ rate\ of\ unemployment = Frictional\ unemployment + Structural\ unemployment$$

The **actual rate of unemployment** = $Natural\ rate\ of\ unemployment + Cyclical\ unemployment.$

Cyclical unemployment is the type of unemployment that results from a recession. When individuals are laid off from jobs due to a decrease in **aggregate demand (AD)** (total demand for goods and services) stemming from a decrease in consumer expenditures, the resultant unemployment is cyclical. During the Great Recession of 2008, the unemployment spike in the real estate sector was primarily cyclical in nature. During good economic times, cyclical unemployment is relatively low. During poor economic times, cyclical unemployment is relatively high, and the government implements fiscal and monetary policies designed to reduce unemployment.

Frictional unemployment is the type of unemployment that occurs as a natural process of individuals who are looking to either start their careers or switch to different ones. For example, Donya, a recent college graduate from Claremont McKenna College who is mulling over two job offers between Boston Consulting Group and Bank of America, would be considered frictionally unemployed because she has entered the labor force but does not meet the definition of being employed. Donya has not worked the requisite one hour in the past week, so she is categorized as being frictionally unemployed.

Structural unemployment results from changes in job skills required in the marketplace, usually related to technology. For example, let's say that Johnny grew up wanting to be a milkman his entire life. He interviews other successful milkmen to find out what skills are required to procure employment in the industry. But Johnny will have to face the harsh reality that the invention of the refrigerator has obviated the need to have individuals delivering milk on a daily basis.

Full employment means there is no cyclical unemployment in the economy—just frictional and structural unemployment.

Consumer Price Index (CPI)

The **consumer price index (CPI)** is a popular inflation measure that takes the weighted average of prices of a basket of goods and services for a "typical" urban consumer. There are other price indices, including the **producer price index (PPI)**, an index that measures prices from the seller's point of view, and the **GDP deflator**, which measures price changes by dividing the nominal GDP by the real GDP and multiplying by 100. However, the CPI is the most frequently used measure to determine aggregate price level (PL) increases, and it is the most recognizable inflation measure by the general public.

Inflation is a decrease in the purchasing power of money. For example, because of inflation, $100 today does not buy what $100 bought ten years ago. The prices of goods and services tend to increase over the years because the cost of inputs and wages go up. This is known as **cost-push inflation**. When minimum wage goes up, companies will respond in kind to the higher costs of doing business by raising the prices of their products.

Another reason why prices go up is because consumers vie for scarce items and thus drive prices upward through **demand-pull inflation**. Demand for goods and services increases, and therefore shortages would occur if prices remained the same despite the change in demand. For example, let's say that the economy is enjoying an economic boom, and the government lowers the income tax rate and the Fed increases the money supply by reducing interest rates. This confluence of good economic events leads to more consumers wanting to buy more Teslas or iPhones than suppliers can produce at existing prices. So, what happens? Prices increase because demand has "pulled" up prices.

The combination of cost-push inflation and demand-pull inflation leads to a **wage-price spiral** with prices rising slowly but surely over periods of months, years, and decades until the price of taking a family of four to a movie somehow exceeds $100.

Deflation occurs when prices decrease over time. The natural inertia is for prices to increase over time. However, there may be periods of time when overall prices decrease in value. Deflation is closely associated with periods of recession because when AD decreases, the PL decreases. Most economists agree that sustained levels of deflation are not good for the economy. Lower PLs generally mean reduced business investment and higher unemployment rates.

The most salient example of deflation occurred during the Great Depression. Prices of goods and services dropped dramatically from 1930 to 1933 by nearly 10 percent a year. The price drop was accompanied by a drop in real output, indicating that AD decreased because rising unemployment and tough economic times meant consumers simply weren't making the big purchases they were capable of making a decade before.

Disinflation, not to be confused with deflation, happens when the rate of inflation slows. Whereas deflation might occur when the PL decreases by 5 percent, disinflation occurs when the rate of inflation slows from 5 percent to 3 percent. Deflation is a negative number and usually precedes a recession; disinflation implies a positive inflation rate in an economy that is slowing down but not to the point of prices going negative. Left unchecked, inflation can be ruinous for an economy. **Chronic inflation** refers to a perpetually high rate of inflation month to month. Most central banks set a target for inflation that hovers around the 2 percent range on a yearly basis. Chronic inflation might be a monthly inflation rate of 5 percent or even 10 percent.

Hyperinflation is when inflation spirals out of control. The most prominent example of hyperinflation occurred in post-World War I Germany under the Weimar Republic. The Treaty of Versailles that ended the Great War placed the blame of global conflict squarely on the shoulders of Germany to the tune of 112 billion marks ($26.3 billion). The German strategy of printing currency to cover its debt obligations turned a bad inflation situation into an economically ruinous one. A loaf of bread that sold for 160 marks in Germany's capital city in 1922 cost 200 billion marks a year later.

Price Indices and Inflation

Tracking the CPI

The BLS tracks the CPI on a monthly basis. The BLS first reported inflation numbers in 1913. The index average is based on the index average from 1982 through 1984. So, in the very unlikely scenario that CPI goes back to 100 in the year 2183, it would mean that the aggregate PL would have reverted to where it was two hundred years later! In March 2004, the CPI was 188, meaning that inflation increased 88 percent during a twenty-year time span. The March 2020 CPI reading came in at 258, which meant inflation increased 158 percent since the base period.

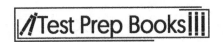

Other price indices, such as the PPI, can be used to track inflation and compare nominal values over time periods. The PPI tracks inflation from the producer viewpoint by tracking cost increases from a seller's perspective. For example, the most heavily weighted item in CPI is owners' rent, but a similar component is not found in the PPI. Also, CPI includes imports, whereas PPI does not because, by definition, imports are not domestically produced items. CPI is the most commonly accepted inflation measure used by the government.

Calculate the CPI, the Inflation Rate, and Changes in Real Variables

The numbers below are the PLs for the economy of Starkville, which produces only two goods: iron and steel.

Time	Price of Iron	Quantity of Iron	Price of Steel	Quantity of Steel
Year 1	\$2	25	\$5	10
Year 2	\$3	25	\$6	10

The weighted market basket has not changed from year 1 to year 2. In both years, 25 units of iron and 10 units of steel are produced. In order to accurately compare PLs, a constant market basket must be used to identify the increases in PL rather than measuring increases in total output.

In year 1, the CPI is $(\$2 \times 25) + (\$5 \times 10) = 50 + 50 = 100$.

In year 2, the CPI is $(\$3 \times 25) + (\$6 \times 10) = 75 + 60 = 135$.

In order to find the inflation rate, one would subtract the previous CPI from the current CPI, divide by the previous CPI, multiply by 100, and then tack on a percentage.

Hence, the inflation rate from year 1 to year 2 is $(135 - 100) \div 100 \times 100 = 35 \div 100 \times 100 = 35\%$.

The neighboring country of Hulkland produces two goods: microscopes and barbells. Hulkland's leader, Bruce Banner, who has a scientific background, was able to compile three years' worth of data in his country.

Time	Price of Microscopes	Quantity of Microscopes	Price of Barbells	Quantity of Barbells
Year 1	\$4	10	\$3	20
Year 2	\$3	10	\$2	20
Year 3	\$5	10	\$6	20

In year 1, the CPI is $(\$4 \times 10) + (\$3 \times 20) = 40 + 60 = 100$.

In year 2, the CPI decreases to $(\$3 \times 10) + (\$2 \times 20) = 30 + 40 = 70$.

In year 3, the CPI increases to $(\$5 \times 10) + (\$6 \times 20) = 50 + 120 = 170$.

Between year 1 and year 2, Hulkland experiences deflation. The CPI decreases from 100 to 70, so the inflation rate is negative, or:

$$(70 - 100) \div 100 \times 100$$

$$-30 \div 100 \times 100$$

$$-30\%$$

Between year 2 and year 3, Hulkland experiences inflation. The CPI increases from 70 to 170, so the inflation rate more than doubles, or:

$$(170 - 70) \div 70$$

$$100 \div 70 \times 100$$

$$142.9\%$$

Inflation affects the real amount of money. A dollar today simply isn't worth a dollar next year. Let's say that Mookie gets a 6 percent increase in salary as a teacher from year 1 to year 2, but inflation also increases by 4 percent. His real income is less than his nominal income. The formula is as follows:

$$Real\ wage = Nominal\ wage - Inflation\ rate$$

Therefore, the real wage is $6\% - 4\%$, or 2%. Even though Mookie did get a well-deserved increase in salary, the actual (real) amount was far less than the nominal amount by 33 percent.

Inflation tends to benefit borrowers, whereas deflation helps lenders. Imagine that Harry Homeowner takes a loan from a Bank of America with a nominal interest rate of 7 percent with an expected inflation of 3 percent. The expected real interest rate is 4 percent ($7\% - 3\% = 4\%$). So, if the actual inflation rate is 5 percent instead of 3 percent, who "wins" from the transaction: Harry Homeowner (the borrower) or Bank of America (the lender)?

Because the actual inflation is higher than the expected inflation by 2 percent, the real interest rate on the home loan turns out to be 2 percent ($7\% - 5\% = 2\%$). Harry Homeowner "wins" in this transaction because the money he pays back to Bank of America will be worth "less" than what both parties believed it would be due to the expected inflation rate of 3 percent.

Shortcomings of the CPI

There are two major shortcomings of CPI. One is the **substitution bias**, which means that the CPI overstates the true impact of inflation because consumers can simply substitute higher-priced items with lower-priced items. Imagine that an economy sells only two items: bananas and strawberries. A pound of bananas and a pound of strawberries both sell for $5. If the price of bananas doubles and the price of strawberries stays constant, CPI will increase by 50 percent. But has inflation actually increased by 50 percent? According to CPI, yes. However, a rational consumer could simply decide to purchase fewer bananas and more strawberries in order to maintain an equivalent standard of living.

Another shortfall of the CPI is its inability to take into account the increase in quality over the years. A car priced at $10,000 in 1980 might have doubled to $20,000 in 2020, but there's no way to take into account the increase in quality of the car. Did the quality of 1980 cars to 2020 cars double? Did it triple?

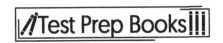

Or did it quadruple? Although the answer to these questions are subjective, we do know that any increase in the quality serves to overstate inflation's impact on the economy.

Costs of Inflation

Unexpected inflation (or deflation) imposes real costs on society. Inflation's unpredictability and volatility make it difficult for both consumers and businesses to accurately gauge what's actually going on in the marketplace. People can mistake economic growth for an increase in the PL and obfuscate what is truly transpiring in the economy.

Inflation also arbitrarily redistributes wealth by transferring wealth from savers to borrowers. If there is an unexpected spike in inflation, the real amount of money that borrowers pay back to lenders will be less than what was originally intended. Savers will be hurt because inflation will eat away at real returns over the years.

Real Vs. Nominal GDP

Nominal GDP and Real GDP

Nominal GDP takes the final value of goods and services that are made within a nation's borders in a given year using current prices. **Real GDP** uses constant prices to determine the value of the nation's economic activity. When nominal GDP increases, it is impossible to know whether output is going up or prices are increasing. Real GDP solves this problem by using the base prices to calculate the output for every single year. If the real GDP increases by $20 million, the change is because output increased, not because prices have increased. Nevertheless, the nominal GDP provides a good starting point to track an economy's total output. It's just that real GDP does a better job than nominal GDP in "keeping things real."

The GDP deflator tracks inflation by dividing the nominal GDP by the real GDP and multiplying by 100. If, for example, the GDP deflator is 100 in year 1 and then increases to 105 in year 2, the inflation rate is 5 percent. The major difference between CPI and the GDP deflator is that CPI uses a fixed basket of goods and services to measure the PL, whereas the GDP deflator's "basket" is all the goods and services that people consume from year to year. It is possible that this basket changes from year to year based on the spending patterns of an economy.

Let's look at the table below to calculate the nominal GDP, real GDP, and GDP deflator of the country of Asgard in which only two products exist: hammers and umbrellas.

Time	Price of Hammers	Quantity of Hammers	Price of Umbrellas	Quantity of Umbrellas
2020	$10	7	$5	6
2021	$15	8	$10	10
2022	$20	14	$10	12

The nominal GDP in 2020 is $(\$10 \times 7) + (\$5 \times 6) = \$70 + \$30 = \$100.$

The nominal GDP in 2021 is $(\$15 \times 8) + (\$10 \times 10) = \$120 + \$100 = \$220.$

The nominal GDP in 2022 is $(\$20 \times 14) + (\$20 \times 12) = \$280 + \$120 = \$400.$

If nominal GDP is used to measure economic growth, the economy from 2020 to 2022 would have quadrupled. But because nominal GDP tracks increases in prices as well as output, real GDP is the better measure to track economic growth. Real GDP uses constant prices every year rather than current prices. Assume the base year is 2020.

The real GDP in 2020 is $(\$10 \times 7) + (\$5 \times 6) = \$70 + \$30 = \$100.$

The real GDP in 2021 is $(\$10 \times 8) + (\$5 \times 10) = \$80 + \$50 = \$130.$

The real GDP in 2022 is $(\$10 \times 14) + (\$5 \times 12) = \$140 + 60 = \$200.$

The GDP deflator in 2020 is $\$100 \div \$100 \times 100 = 1 \times 100 = 100.$

The GDP deflator in 2021 is $\$220 \div \$130 \times 100 = 1.69 \times 100 = 169.$

The GDP deflator in 2022 is $\$400 \div \$200 \times 100 = 2 \times 100 = 200.$

The economy in Asgard did grow from 2020 to 2022, but because the GDP increased from \$100 to \$200, economic growth doubled and did not actually quadruple like nominal GDP data might suggest. Real GDP measures the actual output growth by keeping the price constant at the base year, and the GDP deflator does exactly as the term suggests by "deflating" the nominal GDP to its "true" value.

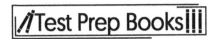

Business Cycles

Turning Points and Phases of the Business Cycle

The business cycle model shows four distinct phases in which the real GDP increases and decreases over the short run while simultaneously increasing in the long run. The four phases in the business cycle are expansion, peak, contraction, and trough. The **expansion** phase is when real GDP is increasing and unemployment is decreasing. The **peak** represents the height of the business cycle. If the **contraction** phase (when the economy at large is in a decline) lasts for an extended chunk of time, a **recession** takes place, a period in which real GDP declines for at least two consecutive quarters (six months). Once the recession hits the **trough**, or the bottom point of the recession, the business cycle starts all over again with the expansion phase.

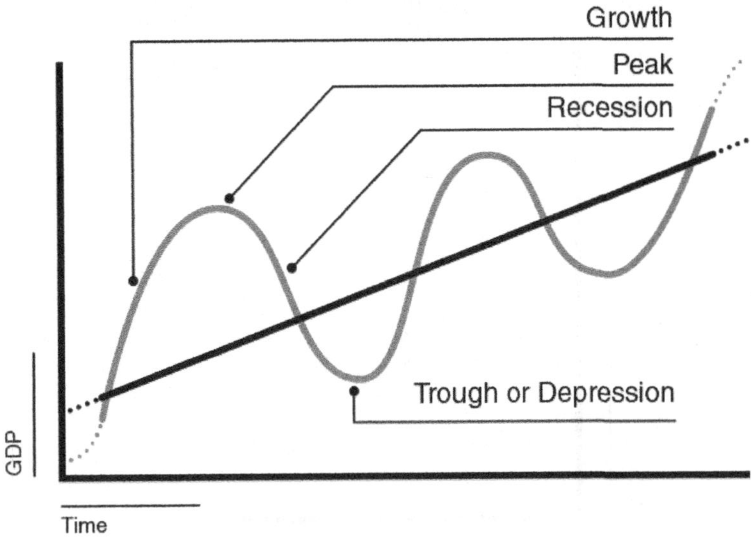

The Business Cycle

On September 20, 2010, the National Bureau of Economic Research (NBER) officially announced that the trough of the Great Recession of 2008 took place in June 2009. The official start of the Great Recession was in December of 2007, meaning that the economic downturn lasted a total of eighteen months, which was the longest recorded recession since World War II. The two previous recessions occurred between 1973 and 1975 during the presidencies of Richard Nixon and Gerald Ford and from 1981 to 1982 during Jimmy Carter's presidency. Both recessions lasted sixteen months.

In the fourth quarter of 2019, U.S. real GDP increased 2.1 percent, marking the peak of an extremely long expansionary phase of the business cycle that began in June 2009 when the Great Recession officially hit its trough. Real GDP in the first three months of 2020 decreased by an astounding 4.8 percent. The last part of the first quarter data coincided with the beginning of the COVID-19 crisis and the subsequent shelter-in-place orders that effectively shuttered a huge swath of economic activity in the United States.

Macroeconomics: National Income and Price Determination

Aggregate Demand

Aggregate Demand (AD) Curve

The aggregate demand (AD) is the collective quantity of all goods and services demanded by the economy at all price levels (PLs). This is not to be confused with the demand found on a supply and demand graph. Whereas demand deals with an individual good or service, AD encompasses the entirety of goods and services within an economy. When graphing an AD curve, real gross domestic product (rGDP) is found on the *x* axis, and PL is found on the *y* axis.

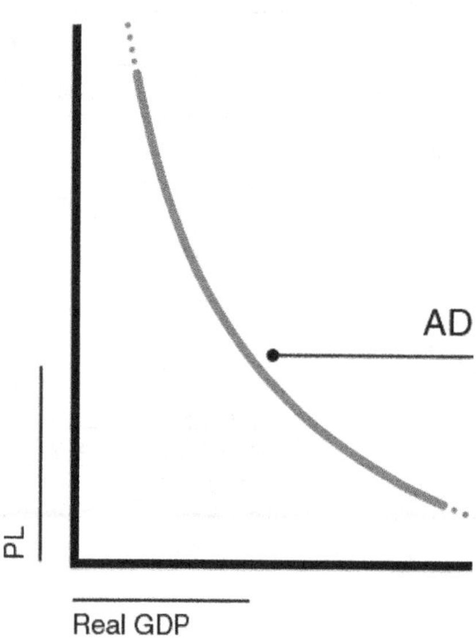

Aggregate Demand Curve

Slope of the AD Curve and its Determinants

The AD curve is downward sloping because of three different types of effect: the wealth effect, the interest rate effect, and the exchange rate effect.

The **wealth effect** refers to the fact that consumers have more real income when the PL decreases. People receive income and pay for goods and services with nominal amounts of money. However, the nominal wage or the nominal price of a good or service does not accurately depict the level of a consumer's wealth. The real PL is a more accurate indicator of true wealth. If the PL drops from $10 to $5, an individual is wealthier and able to consume more goods and services. Similarly, if the PL increases from $10 to $15, individuals are relatively worse off because they are not able to purchase as many goods and services with the same, fixed nominal level of income.

The **interest rate effect** is also known as the **Keynes interest rate effect**. As the PL decreases, the quantity demanded for cash will also decrease because less money will be required to make purchases. Individuals will therefore increase the amount of loanable funds because there will be lower levels of cash demanded, which will in turn decrease the real interest rate of money. The relatively lower interest rate will increase interest-sensitive consumption and investment and therefore induce the AD to slope downward.

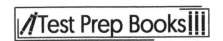

The third and final reason the AD curve slopes downward is the **exchange rate effect**. Recall that as the PL decreases, the interest rate will decrease as well. In the domestic country where the interest rate has decreased, investments will flow out and flow into countries with higher interest rates. This will cause an appreciation of currency for the country with the relatively higher interest rate and depreciation of currency for the country with the lower interest rate. In the nation with the depreciated currency, net exports will increase. And because net exports are a component of AD, AD will be higher at a lower PL.

Let's imagine that the interest rate in the United States drops from 5 percent to 3 percent and South Korea maintains its 5 percent interest rate. In South Korea, investment opportunities are relatively more attractive now that there is a 2 percent higher return in the "Land of the Morning Calm." The higher interest rate will draw American investors to send their money across the Pacific, which will appreciate the Korean won and depreciate the U.S. dollar. The reduced value of the U.S. dollar will cause an increase in U.S. GDP because American-made goods will be relatively cheaper on the world market. The increase in net exports will be a boon to AD.

The wealth, interest rate, and exchange rate effects are why the AD curve slopes downward. But what shifts the AD curve? Why does the AD increase or decrease? The macroeconomic equation at play here is:

$$Y = C + I + G + NX$$

C represents consumption, **I** represents investment, **G** stands for government, and **NX** is net exports, or exports minus imports.

Consumption is the total expenditure of individuals in the economy. If there is an increase in consumption, the AD curve shifts to the right. If there is a decrease in consumption, the AD curve shifts to the left. For example, if the Conference Board, which produces monthly data on consumer confidence, releases a favorable report showing an unexpected surge in consumer confidence, AD would increase. On the other hand, if the U.S. government announces an increase in personal tax rates, there will be a decrease in AD because disposable income would decrease as Uncle Sam takes a bigger share of people's paychecks.

In the United States, consumer expenditure represents approximately 70 percent of GDP. The U.S. economy is largely driven by personal consumption. The percentage, however, has fluctuated over time. During the Great Depression, the ratio exceeded 80 percent when investment spending dropped precipitously because businesses did not see many opportunities for profit and stopped expanding. During World War II, the government stepped in and took a greater role in economic output than it did during times of relative peace when consumption represented only 50 percent of overall GDP.

Investment increases when profit-maximizing businesses see viable opportunities for expansion. If expected profitability increases or general business sentiment becomes more optimistic, investment increases and AD will subsequently increase and shift to the right. Interest rates also play a factor in increasing or decreasing investment. When interest rates decrease, businesses are more likely to expand business operations. The converse is true as well. When interest rates increase, businesses are less likely to open up a new factory, and therefore investment decreases and AD shifts to the left.

John Maynard Keynes believed that **government spending** was necessary in times of economic decline as a means of stimulating growth. The classical approach maintained that, in the long run, everything would eventually return to its long-run equilibrium. Keynes famously quipped that "in the long run, we're all dead." Hence, he believed it was the government's job to fill any gaps in economic output. If the government increases spending, AD increases and the short-run output and PL both increase. During a recession, most economists agree that an increase in spending to return the economy back to long-run equilibrium might be the prudent approach. During times of inflation, decreasing government spending is considered the responsible thing to do.

Net exports (NX) are the imports of a country subtracted from its exports. When a country increases its exports or decreases its imports, AD increases. When a nation does the opposite by decreasing exports or increasing imports, AD decreases. China is the world's leading exporter, and the United States ranks first in world imports. A country with an increase in inflation will see its exports decline as its products become relatively more expensive on the world market. A nation with a reduced PL will see a boost in net exports.

Multipliers

The **expenditure (or spending) multiplier** is the amount by which a change in spending changes the total output. If the government increases spending by $100 million, there will be an increase in GDP that is greater than $100 million. As the name suggests, the increase in spending is multiplied as the initial round of spending begets more and more spending.

The **tax multiplier** works exactly like the spending multiplier with one notable exception. When individuals receive a tax cut, the entirety of the money they receive will not go back into the economy. People will simply hold onto a certain amount of money in the form of savings. This saved money will not circulate back into the economy.

The **marginal propensity to consume (MPC)** is the percentage of money that consumers will spend out of any additional amount of income. For example, if Donald receives a tax rebate of $1,200 and his MPC is 0.75, he will spend $900 of the $1,200, or 75 percent. If society receives a collective tax rebate of $12 million with an MPC of 0.75, $9 million of that money will be spent. The **marginal propensity to save (MPS)** is the percentage of money that consumers will save from additional income. Taken together, the $MPC + MPS = 1$. So, if the MPC is 0.75, the MPS is 0.25. People can do only one of two things: spend or save.

The equation for the spending multiplier is the amount of increased (or decreased) spending $\times 1 \div (1 - MPC)$ or $1 \div MPS =$ increased (or decreased) GDP. The equation for the tax multiplier is the decrease (or increase) in taxes $\times$ $MPC \div (1 - MPC)$, or $MPC \div MPS$. An alternative way to find the tax multiplier is through the simple equation:

$$Tax\ multiplier = Spending\ multiplier - 1$$

Changes in Spending and Taxes

Let's assume the MPC is 0.8, and the government wants to close a recessionary gap of $500 million. How much spending is necessary to "fill the gap"? Because the MPC is 0.8, the spending multiplier is $1 \div (1 - MPC)$, or $1 \div (1 - 0.8) = 1 \div 0.2 = 5$.

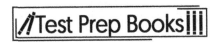

And because the amount of spending times the multiplier equals the change in output, the equation is as follows:

$$G \times 5 = \$500\ million\ (Government\ spending)$$

$$G = \$100\ million$$

The government would need to increase its spending by $100 million in order to generate a $500 million increase in GDP.

If the government chose to decrease taxes to boost economic output, what would the equivalent tax cut have to be in order to generate $500 million of additional real output? Would the tax cut be greater than, equal to, or less than the $100 million increase in government spending? In order to answer that question, we have to first figure out the tax multiplier. Remember that the tax multiplier is $MPC \div (1 - MPC)$, or $MPC \div MPS$. Because the MPC is 0.8 and the MPS is 0.2, the tax multiplier is $0.8 \div 0.2 = 4$. Recall that another way of figuring out the tax multiplier is by subtracting 1 from the spending multiplier. And because the spending multiplier is 5, perhaps the simpler way of figuring out the tax multiplier is $5 - 1 = 4$.

In order to close the recessionary gap through a tax cut, the government would have to cut taxes by more than an equivalent increase in government spending to generate $500 million in additional real output. The equation for the tax multiplier is $T \times 4 = \$500\ million$, or $\$125\ million$.

The government would need to decrease taxes by $125 million in order to generate the same $500 million increase in GDP as a $100 million increase in spending. Government spending has a greater impact on real output than tax cuts because the spending multiplier is greater than the tax multiplier by 1.

In the country of Spendthrift, the MPC is a whopping 0.95. Residents in Spendthrift do not believe in the virtue of saving money. When citizens receive their paychecks, most of their income disappears on luxurious consumer purchases. If rampant inflation takes hold in Sprendthrift and there's an inflationary gap of $200 million, by how much must the government decrease spending in order to close the gap? Because the MPC is 0.95, the spending multiplier is:

$$1 \div (1 - 0.95) = 1 \div 0.05 = 20$$

$$G \times 20 = -\$200\ million$$

$$G = -\$10\ million$$

The government would have to decrease spending by $10 million in order to get the economy back to its long-run equilibrium.

Before Spendthrift's leader, Fred Kayak, has a chance to implement his vision of cutting government spending, an election thrusts John Maine Canes in the spotlight, and he opts to increase taxes by $10 million because of his insistence that government spending must not be decreased. Will his approach quell the rising tide of inflation? Let's take a look.

The MPC remains at 0.95, but the tax multiplier is $0.95 \div 0.05 = 19$.

$$\$10\ million \times 19 = Decrease\ in\ total\ output$$

A $10 million increase in taxes will generate a decrease in $190 million in total output, meaning that the inflationary gap will not be closed. Almost, but not quite. A reduction in government spending by the same amount would have been more potent.

If the government decides to simultaneously increase government spending by $10 million and increase taxes by $10 million, will the real output increase, decrease, or stay the same? We know the outcomes individually. When the government increases spending by $10 million, total output increases by $200 million and total output would decline by $190 million with a $10 million increase in taxes. So, the net increase in real output would be $\$200\ million - \$190\ million = \$10\ million$.

If the government decides to decrease government spending by $50 million and decrease taxes by $50 million, the impact of decreased spending would be greater than the impact of decreased taxes and total real output would decrease. Just like the previous example, the change in real output would be the same amount as the decrease in spending and decrease in taxes. In this case, real GDP would decrease by $50 million.

Short-Run Aggregate Supply (SRAS)

Short-Run Aggregate Supply (SRAS) Curve

The **short-run aggregate supply (SRAS) curve** is the total output firms will produce at a given PL. Whereas the AD curve slopes downward, the SRAS curve is upward sloping and therefore has a positive relationship between PL and real output, at least in the short run.

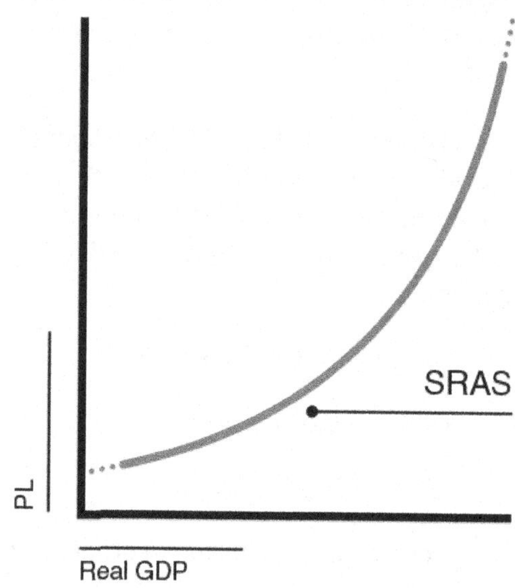

A Short-Run Aggregate Supply Curve

On a supply and demand graph, the supply curve slopes upward because as prices increase, the quantity supplied will increase and the quantity demanded will decrease. Producers have more incentive to produce a product if the price increases because there is more profit potential. Similarly, if the PL increases, real output will increase because all suppliers will be more motivated to produce at higher PLs.

Slope of the SRAS Curve and its Determinants

There are three reasons why the SRAS curve shifts to the right: decreased wages, reduced input prices, and decreased inflationary expectations. The entire curve increases outward, but the slope of the SRAS curve stays the same. If wages were to decrease as the result of a recession, employers would have to pay their workers less income because a relatively higher level of unemployment gives employers a bit more leverage than employees. Another reason for the shift is the cost of inputs such as oil decreases. And if inflationary expectations were to decrease, the SRAS curve would also shift to the right.

There are three reasons why the SRAS curve decreases to the left: increased wages, increased input prices, and increased inflationary expectations. If wages were to increase because of inflation, employers would have to pay their workers more income because a relatively lower level of unemployment gives employees some leverage over employers. Another reason for the shift is the cost of inputs such as oil increases. And, finally, if inflationary expectations were to increase, the SRAS curve would respond in kind and shift to the left.

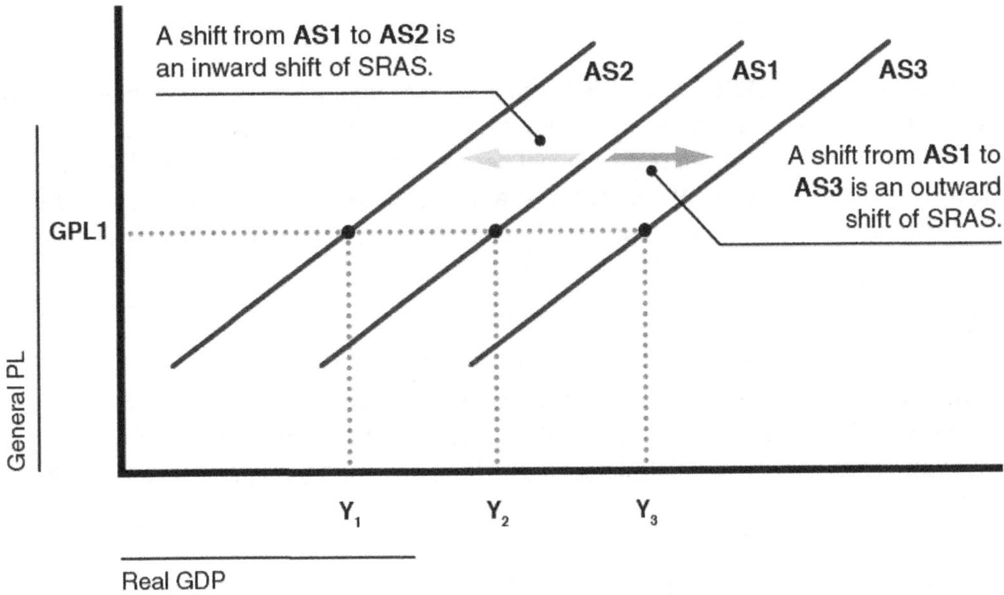

Showing Shifts in Short-Run Aggregate Supply

Movement Along the SRAS Curve

A movement upward and to the right on the SRAS curve implies an increasing PL and an increase in real GDP, which means a lower rate of unemployment. Conversely, a movement downward and to the left on the SRAS curve shows a decreasing PL and decrease in real GDP, which is correlated with a higher rate of unemployment.

During the Great Depression, there was a notable drop in national income. Millions of Americans lost their jobs as the expansionary boon of the 1920s came to a crashing halt. The United States entered into a contractionary phase of the business cycle, so there was a movement downward and to the left on the SRAS. The AD decreased during this time, but the aggregate supply (AS) (in the short run) did not change. It was a movement along the SRAS curve.

Long-Run Aggregate Supply (LRAS)

Short Run and Long Run

One factor that differentiates the SRAS and long-run aggregate supply (LRAS) is time. In the short run, the assumption is that certain inputs are fixed and cannot be changed. For example, in the short run, a new factory cannot be built. In the long run, a new factory can be built if necessary. Labor, on the other hand, can be increased or decreased in the short run. If the economy is facing a recessionary environment, employers can reduce worker salaries. Conversely, if the economy is facing an inflationary environment, workers can be compensated with higher wages. The SRAS can also be affected by short-term price fluctuations in input prices, whereas the LRAS does not respond to such changes.

The long run is not affected by short-term changes in wages or input prices. The long run refers to the stock of existing factors of production—a fully employed workforce, size of capital stock, education levels, and labor productivity. If there is an increase in the quantity of the workforce, capital stock, human capital (through higher levels of education), or technology, there would be an increase in the LRAS.

The natural inertia of history dictates that the LRAS increases as time progresses. What would it take for the LRAS to decrease? The most salient example of a country facing a decrease in the LRAS was Japan in 1945. When Harry S. Truman made the controversial decision to drop the atomic bomb on Hiroshima and Nagasaki on August 6 and August 9, respectively, a tremendous amount of capital, both human and physical, was destroyed. Japan's devastating loss of human life was accompanied by a decrease in its LRAS curve.

LRAS Curve

The **LRAS curve** is a theoretical construct whereby an economy is operating at its maximum capacity. When everything is firing on all cylinders and at full employment, the economy is at its long-run equilibrium with the LRAS curve as a vertical line. In the long run, the PL will not impact the LRAS as it would the SRAS.

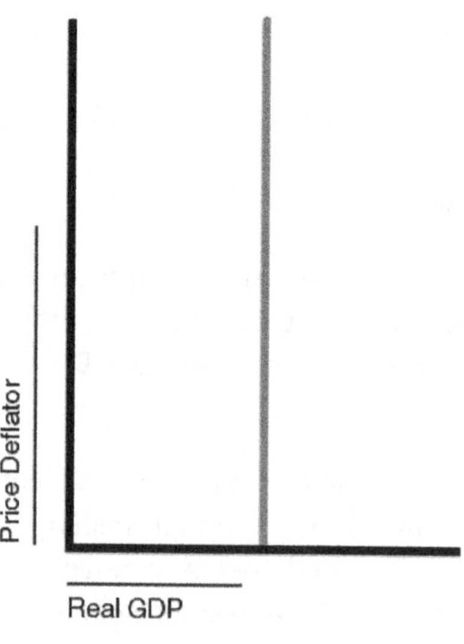

LRAS Curve

The LRAS is associated with the natural rate of unemployment. In other words, there is no cyclical unemployment when the economy is at the LRAS. The only type of unemployment that exists when the economy is at the LRAS is frictional and structural unemployment. If the economy is operating below its LRAS, the actual unemployment rate is less than the natural rate. Conversely, if the economy is beyond the LRAS, the natural unemployment rate is less than the actual rate.

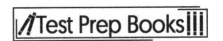

Equilibrium and Changes in the Aggregate Demand-Aggregate Supply (AD-AS) Model

Short-Run and Long-Run Equilibrium Price Level and Output Level

When the SRAS curve and the AD curve intersect, an economy has reached an equilibrium in the short run. Recall that the LRAS curve is a vertical line that represents when an economy has reached full employment. In other words, there is no cyclical unemployment at the LRAS. When the short-run equilibrium intersects with the LRAS, an economy has reached the long-run equilibrium PL and output level. When the SRAS, LRAS, and AD come together in an asterisk-like arrangement, the economy has reached its potential output.

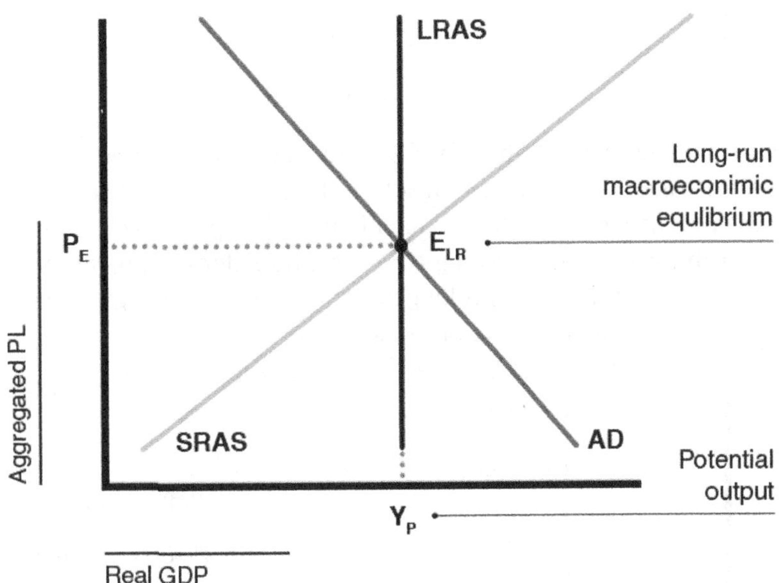

When the SRAS, LRAS, and AD come together in an asterisk-like arrangement.

Sometimes the short-run equilibrium falls short of the long-run equilibrium. When the short-run equilibrium is less than where it would be in long-run equilibrium, it is referred to as a **recessionary gap** in which the LRAS is to the right of the short-run equilibrium. If the current output is less than the potential output, there is a recessionary gap. Its existence does not automatically mean that the economy has entered into a recession, which officially occurs when there are two consecutive quarters of negative GDP growth. However, a recessionary gap will typically indicate harsh economic times in the future.

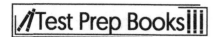

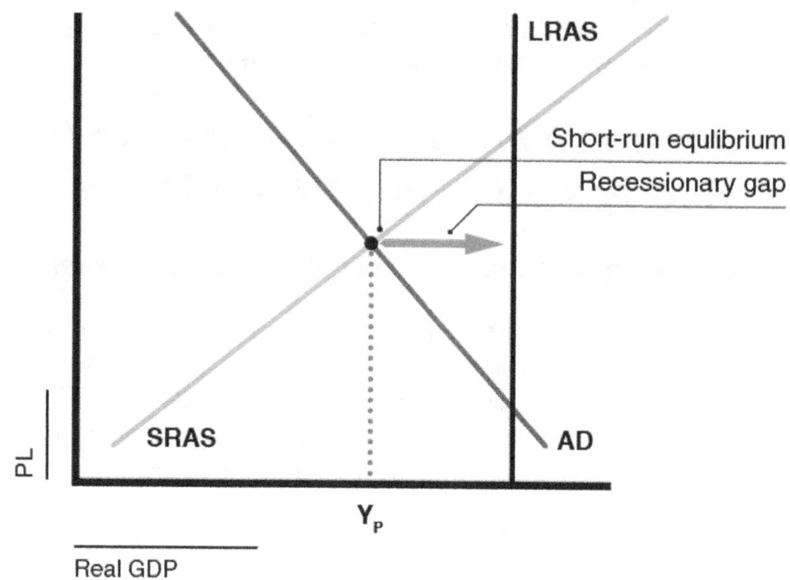

Recessionary Gap

Sometimes things might heat up too fast and there is more output than the economy can handle in the long run. In this inflationary gap, the LRAS is to the left of the short-run equilibrium. If the current output is more than the potential output, there is an inflationary gap in the economy. This situation in which the short-run equilibrium exceeds the long-run equilibrium does not mean the PL will remain sky-high for the foreseeable future. However, a prolonged period of inflation might mean government intervention is on the horizon to quell the tide of rising prices.

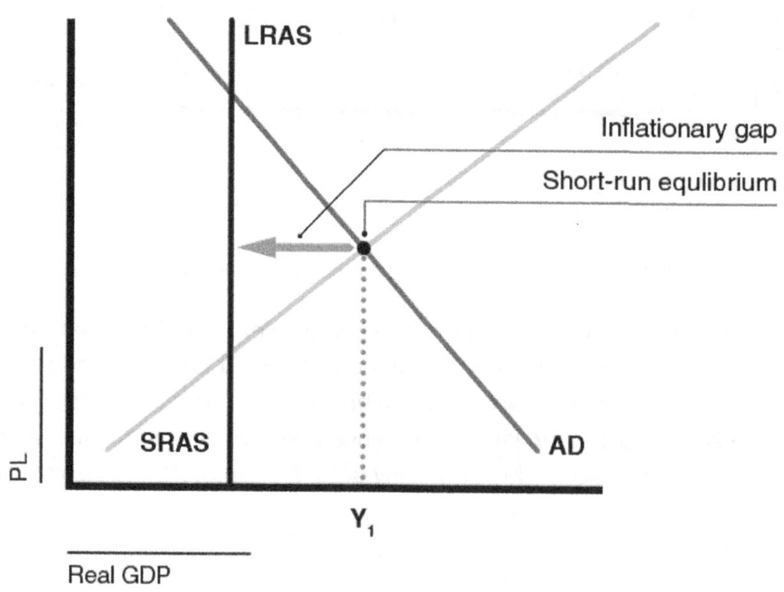

Inflationary Gap

Response of Output, Employment, and the Price Level

A **demand shock** is a sudden event that can either positively or negatively impact the AD. A **positive demand shock** would shift the AD curve to the right and cause a short-term increase in the output and PL. A **negative demand shock**, on the other hand, would shift the AD curve to the left and cause a short-term decrease in output and PL. A negative aggregate demand shock reduces real GDP and increases unemployment.

One example of a positive demand shock was in the early 2000s when President George W. Bush decreased income tax rates. Consumers increased their disposable income, which led to an increase in AD. The obvious upside of tax cuts is increased GDP levels, whereas the downside is that an increased PL means inflation. In 2008, a negative demand shock roiled the entire global economy as a combination of falling house prices and a crashing stock market, and the subprime mortgage crisis led to a significant decrease in consumer spending. The AD shifted to the left as the United States entered into the Great Recession.

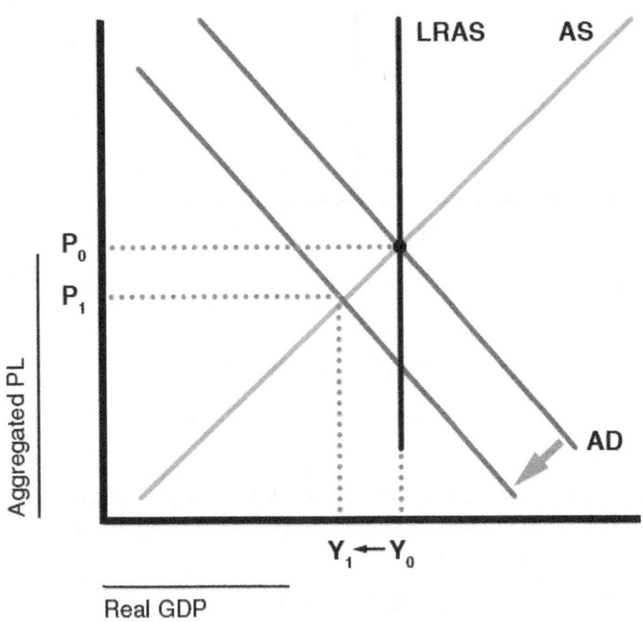

Negative Aggregate Demand Shock

A **supply shock** is a sudden event that can either positively or negatively impact the SRAS. A **positive supply shock** would shift the SRAS curve to the right and cause an increase in the output but a decrease in the PL in the short run. Conversely, a **negative supply shock** would shift the SRAS curve to the left and cause an increase in the PL and a decrease in output in the short run. In the late 1970s, the United States experienced a negative supply shock as oil prices increased drastically and decreased the SRAS curve. In the early 2000s, the rise of technology and use of the internet contributed to an increase in productivity and a subsequent shift of the SRAS curve to the right.

If there was a sudden increase in the supply of raw materials, there would be a decrease in the price of inputs, which would shift the SRAS curve to the right. Lower costs lead to lower prices, a higher real GDP, and a lower level of unemployment. However, the more common type of supply shock would be a negative supply shock. If political turmoil in the Middle East causes a sharp increase in oil prices, the

SRAS curve would be adversely impacted and shift to the left because oil is an input for a variety of industries. Not only would inflation increase due to the increase in the PL, real GDP and employment would take a hit, creating a situation that economists have coined **stagflation**, which is when the economy has stagnated with an increasing PL.

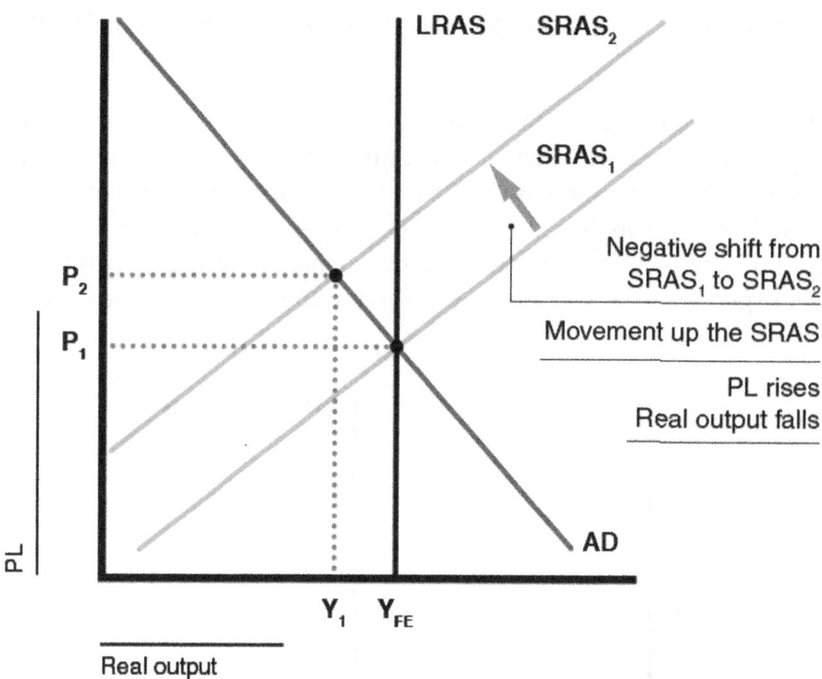

Supply Side Shock

Inflation Changes

John Maynard postulated that inflation takes place as a result of an increase in the AD curve and a decrease in the SRAS curve. When AD increases because the AD for goods and services exceeds the AS of services, this is called **demand-pull inflation**. When the PL increases as a result of an increase in wages and other inputs, this is known as **cost-push inflation**. Because the AD has stayed constant, only the SRAS curve will shift to the left, creating inflation from the supply side.

Imagine that the leaders in the land of Inchonia raise the minimum wage in an attempt to increase the earning power of its citizens. What type of impact will this have on the people of Inchonia? AD will increase, but because AS has stayed constant, there will be demand-pull inflation, as the AD curve will be greater than the SRAS curve with the new influx of consumer income. So, what will happen as a result? Suppliers will increase the prices of their goods as they see that individuals have more disposable income at hand. In addition, businesses must raise the prices of their goods and services to combat the shrinking profit levels from increases in wage levels. This combination of demand-pull inflation and cost-push inflation is known as a **wage-price spiral**.

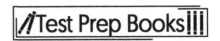

Wage-Price Spiral

This wage-price spiral usually takes place over a period of many years. When workers get the higher wages they want, there's an increase in overall demand for goods and services for consumers who are flush with cash. But for every reaction, there's an equal and opposite reaction. Companies will pass on the higher labor costs to consumers and prices will rise, causing the process to repeat until wages and prices continually get higher and higher. It is difficult to pinpoint one reason why inflation has occurred, but the cumulative impact of years and years of increases lead to workers getting paid higher nominal wages and consumers generally seeing the purchasing power of their money decrease as time goes on.

Long-Run Self-Adjustment

If a negative demand shock occurs in a country, leaders essentially have two options if the goal is to return the economy back to its full equilibrium output level. Expansionary fiscal or monetary policy could be used to attack the recession. The government can either increase the money supply, reduce interest rates, increase government spending, or decrease taxes to shift the AD curve to the right. Prior to the rise of Keynesianism in the middle of the twentieth century, however, the government generally did not intervene heavily in economic matters either from a monetary or fiscal perspective. A **laissez-faire** ideology of simply leaving businesses with the government taking a minor or nonexistent role in economic matters was the normal state of affairs. It wasn't until after the Great Depression that the American people expected its policymakers to take an active role in managing the state of the economy. In fact, many economists, including former Federal Reserve System (the Fed) Chairman Ben Bernanke, believe the Federal Reserve's use of contractionary monetary policy exacerbated the effects of the

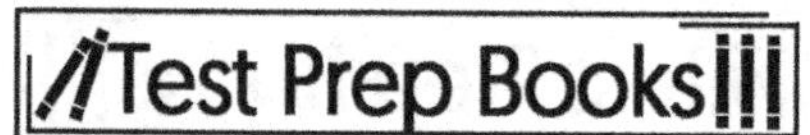

Great Depression. The Fed needed to inject money into the economy rather than contract the money supply.

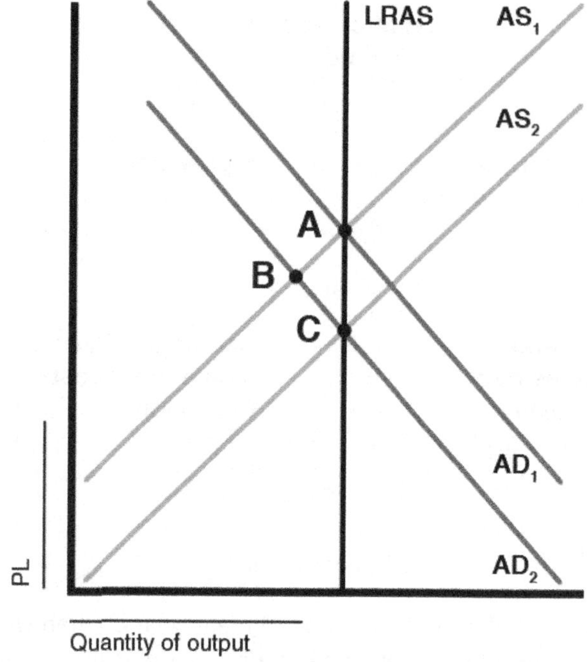

The graph above shows what happens when the government takes a hands-off approach to the economy. When the economy enters into a recession because of a negative AD shock, a laissez-faire approach would be to do absolutely nothing. If millions of people lose jobs as a result of an economic downturn, the classical approach would be to simply leave things alone and let the forces of supply and demand work in order to get the economy back to its long-run equilibrium. This type of government response would be unacceptable to most modern-day citizens who have come to expect the government to take action when the economy is faltering. Barring any government intervention, the economy would (in the long run) return to its equilibrium. During a recession, employers generally have leverage over employees because individuals as a whole would be willing to take a lower wage in order to go back to work.

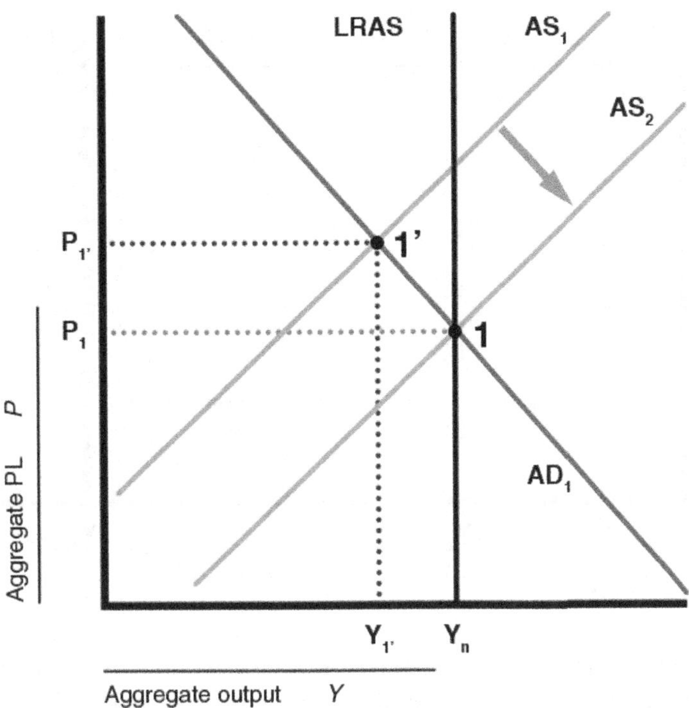

Response to a Supply Shock

A negative supply shock, like a negative demand shock, can also cause a recession because the output level will decrease and unemployment will increase. The difference between a demand shock and a supply shock, however, is that a demand shock leads to deflation and a supply shock would create **stagflation**, a situation in which the output level has decreased *and* the PL has increased. If the government wanted to intervene, it would have to choose whether to attack either inflation or unemployment.

In a situation in which the government does nothing and the economy responds to market forces, what would happen? Wages, input prices, and/or inflationary expectations will decrease, causing the SRAS to shift to the right. Similar to when a negative demand shock hits the economy, the economy will return to its long-run equilibrium. However, both output and prices will return to their original level, unlike in a situation with a negative demand shock when the economy's long-run PL has decreased.

Shifts in the Long-Run Aggregate Supply Curve

Although a shift in the SRAS is usually unanticipated, a shift in the LRAS is an expected occurrence that generally happens over the course of many years. What are some reasons why the LRAS might shift? An increased level of spending on new technology could cause an improvement in both quantity and quality of output. An increase in the labor force through immigration and population growth could increase the amount of human capital in the economy. In addition, a reduction in corporate income taxes could cause the LRAS to shift to the right because there would be an increase in capital stock that would change the level of real GDP.

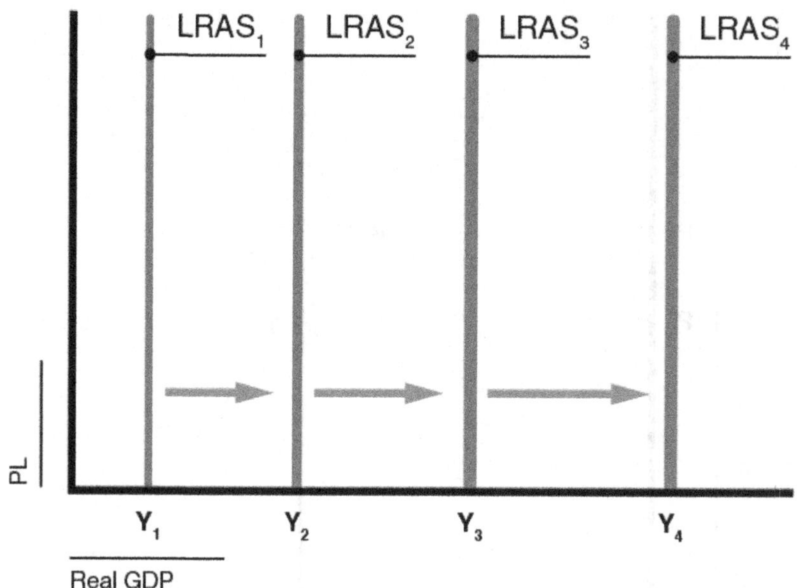

An increase in the level of capital stock will shift the vertical LRAS curve to the right. The term **capital stock** refers to the total quantity of capital used to make goods and service. Items such as tools, buildings, and machinery are different types of capital. Without capital, it would be difficult for workers to produce goods and services. An increase in business investment means there would be an expansion of capital formation, which would naturally lead to a higher level of potential GDP. There would be an increase in both the short-run SRAS and long-run SRAS when capital stock increases.

Although an increase in the LRAS is by no means an automatic process, businesses tend to increase their production above and beyond the amount of capital depreciation except in times of recession. If, however, there is a decrease in capital stock within an economy, the LRAS would shift to the left. If there is a massive emigration from a country, capital stock would decrease, and the potential level of GDP would be reduced when the LRAS curve shifts to the left.

Investment plays a dual role in shifting both the AD curve and LRAS curve. Recall that when interest rates decrease, there is an increase in interest-sensitive expenditures, and so when investment increases, AD follows and shifts to the right. However, investment also affects the capital stock and therefore the LRAS. The big difference is that investment affects the LRAS at a far slower rate than it affects the AD. The shift to the right in the LRAS curve is imperceptible in any given year, but the change becomes very apparent as time progresses.

Fiscal Policy

Fiscal Policy and Related Terms

Fiscal policy refers to the actions the government takes to influence the level of economic growth, PL, output, and unemployment. There are three basic types of fiscal policy: raising or lowering government spending, increasing or decreasing income taxes, and increasing or decreasing government transfer payments.

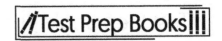

Expansionary fiscal policy comes in three forms: increasing government spending, decreasing income taxes, and increasing government transfer payments. All three methods of stimulating economic growth will shift the AD curve to the right. The government will usually employ expansionary measures when the economy is experiencing a recession. For example, in the immediate aftermath of the COVID-19 crisis, Congress and the president agreed on a fiscal stimulus package that included sending $1,200 to individuals who met the income eligibility requirement.

Contractionary fiscal policy takes place when the government is concerned about rampant inflation and opts to decrease spending, raise taxes, or decrease government transfer payments. All three of these options are politically unpopular, and therefore politicians tend to avoid these measures. Contractionary policies serve to decrease AD, and although doing so might be construed as the "responsible" thing to do, voters do not respond well to politicians who vote to increase taxes and cut Social Security payments. Modern voters do not rank fiscal discipline and national debt reduction as their primary concerns when casting their ballots.

Short-Run Effects of a Fiscal Policy Action

Imagine that the United States is stuck in a recession precipitated by a negative demand shock. What would be the most appropriate fiscal response? An increase in government spending, a decrease in taxes, or an increase in transfers would work, but the change in government spending would affect the AD directly, whereas taxes and transfers would have an indirect effect. If the United States was mired in high demand-pull inflation, the opposite approach would work: Decrease government spending, increase income taxes, or decrease government transfer payments.

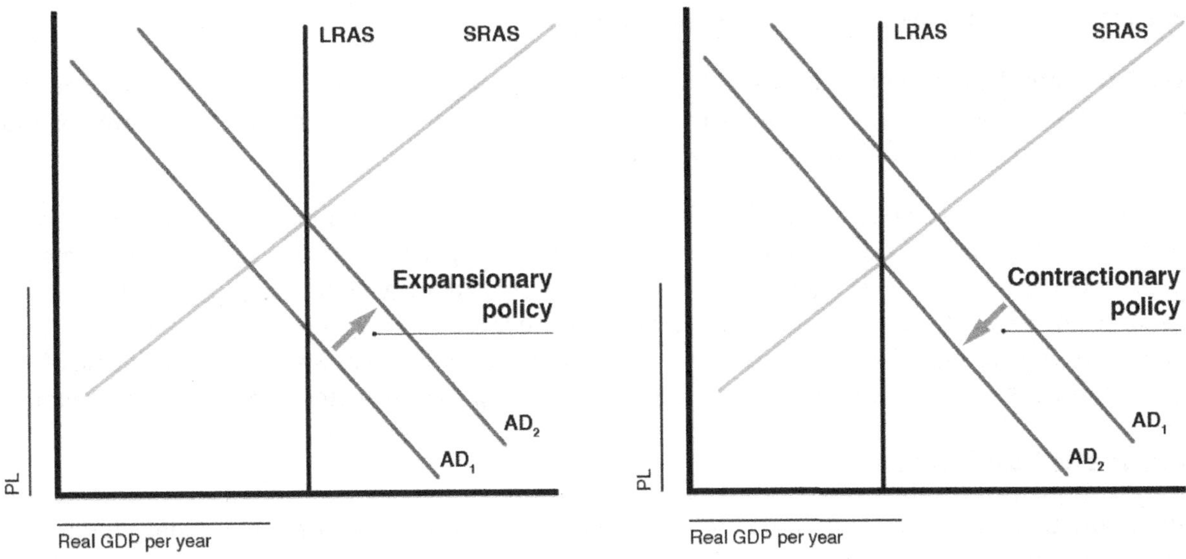

When the government employs expansionary measures and the AD increases, the PL and output both increase to their original level. When the government decides to use contractionary measures to reduce AD, the PL and output both decrease to their original level. Expansionary fiscal policies close recessionary gaps; contractionary fiscal policies close inflationary gaps.

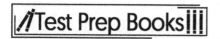

Recall that the spending multiplier is defined as $1 \div MPC$ and the tax multiplier is $MPC \div (1 - MPC)$. An increase in government spending of $10 million will not have the same impact as an income tax cut of $10 million. If the MPC is 0.8, the multiplier is:

$$1 \div (1.0 - 0.8) = 1 \div 0.2 = 5$$

The $10 million increase in spending will boost real GDP by $\$10 \times 5 = \$50\ million.$

If the government, instead, employs a $10 million tax cut, the $MPC \div (1 - MPC)$ equation would be used and $0.8 \div 0.2 = 4$. The $10 million decrease in taxes would not have quite the same effect as the increase in government spending:

$$\$10\ million \times 4 = \$40\ million$$

Why is this the case? Is government spending somehow superior to decreasing income taxes? Not exactly. The problem with closing an output gap by changing the income tax rate is that individuals do not simply spend the entirety of their tax cuts. They hold onto some of that money, which makes tax cuts and government transfer payments an indirect means by which the government stimulates the economy.

Lags to Discretionary Fiscal Policy

The president and Congress do not always agree on policy matters, especially when there is a Republican president and Democrat Congress, or vice versa. A new president may be able to use the bully pulpit to advance his or her agenda, but the honeymoon period between the president and the people usually does not last a long time. President Bush's tax cuts and President Obama's proposed changes in government spending under Obamacare both occurred early in their respective presidential administrations. Had either president waited to enact their fiscal policy agendas, they may have experienced more pushback to their proposals and may not have achieved their desired goals.

Even if the president and Congress agreed on all fiscal policy matters, there would still be lags because there is a natural time delay, known as an **inside lag**, between when an economic problem develops and when the government actually recognizes the problem.

Then there are the **outside lags**, which represent the time it takes for government policies to have an impact on the economy. If the government provides a grant to a particular business, it will take some time before the full effect of the government subsidy will circulate throughout the economy. The increased government spending causes the business to hire more workers, but the impact is not immediate. The increased income workers receive from the business will be spent over the course of many days, weeks, and months before the full impact of fiscal policy circulates throughout the economy.

Automatic Stabilizers

Automatic stabilizers are features within modern economies that help stabilize the economy during recessions because the government provides relatively higher amounts of welfare benefits to those who are unemployed, whereas the amount of money that is doled out to the population naturally declines during relatively more prosperous times as unemployment claims decrease and the population begins to enjoy more economic prosperity.

In addition, household tax burdens are lower when incomes are lower. For example, if Bernie Businessman makes $200,000 as a result of a booming economy, he might owe $50,000 in federal income taxes for the year. In the following year, however, if Bernie Businessman sees a reduction in his earnings and a profit decrease of 50 percent to $100,000, he might only have to pay $20,000 to the Internal Revenue Service (IRS). Making more money is obviously preferable to making less money, but the $30,000 decrease in Bernie's tax bill helps make up for his reduction in income.

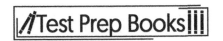

How Automatic Stabilizers Moderate Business Cycles and How Tax Revenues Affect Them

Government budget deficits tend to increase during contractions because the government plays a more prominent role in providing income to the population by providing transfer payments. National income increases without any direct government action. As a result, the recession's severity is reduced because the government has helped prop up AD. Conversely, budget deficits will decrease during expansionary periods because tax revenues will see a spike when businesses report higher incomes.

Most U.S. state constitutions adhere to balanced budget provisions, which makes it difficult for states' expenses to exceed their revenues in any given year. The U.S. federal government does not face such restrictions and essentially ensures that the government will be handing out more money than it takes in during recessions and (theoretically) taking in more money than it spends during expansions.

Some fiscal hawks, typically Republicans, have advocated for a balanced budget amendment to be added to the U.S. Constitution. Most economists, particularly Keynesians, claim that requiring Congress and the president to adhere to a balanced budget would do more harm than good. A balanced budget amendment would possibly serve to worsen things by limiting the federal government's ability to inject a stimulus into the economy.

When the economy slows, federal tax revenues will naturally decline, which is when automatic stabilizers would automatically kick in. For example, when the unemployment rate shot up from 4.4 percent in March 2020 to 14.7 percent in April 2020, there was a monumental increase in the amount of unemployment benefits that were given to the American people. If policymakers were required to balance the budget even during the COVID-19 crisis, the federal government would be in an unenviable position of having to slash more government programs or raise taxes, which would serve to make a bad economic situation even worse. And even the goal of reducing the budget deficit might backfire because the contractionary fiscal policies enacted to close the budget gap would ultimately weaken the economy and actually increase the budget deficit.

Social Service Programs

Prior to the Great Depression, social programs revolved around individual, family, and church efforts. However, the severity and prolonged nature of the Depression made Americans rethink the federal government's role in providing a safety net for the people. In 1935, President Franklin Delano Roosevelt (FDR) passed the Social Security Act, which essentially created a nationally funded retirement program. In addition, the federal government began taking a more active role in providing welfare benefits for its citizens, which collectively acted as automatic stabilizers in the budget process.

President Lyndon Baines Johnson (LBJ) expanded the federal government's role in his War on Poverty by creating Medicare and Medicaid, passing the Economic Opportunity Act in 1964, and generally expanding both the scale and scope of FDR's New Deal. Although Ronald Reagan cut social spending in the early 1980s, many of the social programs created under FDR and LBJ have remained in place.

In 1996, Democrat President Bill Clinton and a Republican Congress passed the Welfare Reform Act. The law was a pivotal portion of the Republican party's Contract With America, which advocated for a decrease in government spending and reduction in government transfer payments. It wasn't the Republicans alone who pushed for welfare reform. Clinton supported a reduction in federal handouts and said that the Personal Responsibility and Work Opportunity Reconciliation Act (PRWORA) of 1996 would "end welfare as we know it."

PRWORA essentially ended welfare as an entitlement program. The Temporary Assistance to Needy Families (TANF) program replaced the more generous Aid to Families With Dependent Children (AFDC) program with more control of the welfare process given to the states in the form of a block grant. Reviews have been mixed on PRWORA. Proponents claim that welfare and poverty rates declined during the 1990s while giving states more autonomy in how they direct their programs. Critics have attacked the bill because of the implication that poverty results primarily from individual failure and irresponsibility. Others point to the bill's bias against single-mother households and claim that "welfare reform" essentially forced people off of welfare rolls and into homeless shelters.

The debate about the role of the federal government in providing a safety net and the extent of its involvement in fiscal matters still exists today. However, very few question whether the government should actually intervene in the economy. It's a matter of *how much* intervention is acceptable.

Macroeconomics: Financial Sector

Financial Assets

Liquidity, Rate of Return, and Risk

Liquidity is the rate at which a financial asset can be immediately sold without any major changes in its price. The financial asset with the most liquidity is cash because it does not easily lose value and can be instantly spent. A demand deposit also has high liquidity because it can be withdrawn and used for purchasing quickly and easily. Other financial assets like stocks and bonds do not have as much liquidity as cash, but still can be converted to cash in case of immediate financial need. Most financial assets have more liquidity than other types of assets because they can be directly sold or purchased without being converted into other forms.

Rate of return is the amount gained or lost on an investment. A return is a profit on your investment, and the rate of return is the amount you have profited over time. The rate of return is usually expressed as a percentage of the initial investment amount. To find the rate of return, the current value of a held investment should be subtracted from the original value; this amount should then be divided by the original value, then multiplied by 100 in order to get the rate of return percentage. The formula is:

$$((Current\ value - Original\ value) \div Original\ value) \times 100$$

This percentage is the amount of return, or profit, you have earned compared to the amount initially invested.

Risk is the amount of uncertainty one faces when making an investment. If an investment has high risk, it means there is more of a chance that the investor will lose money. However, higher risk investments often carry higher chances of a larger rate of return. Lower risk investments are usually safer, but do not have the higher return rates of a high-risk investment. Financial assets like stocks and bonds carry a certain amount of risk because their value fluctuates over time. Cash has less risk and does not increase or decrease in value as quickly.

Relationship Between the Price of Previously Issued Bonds and Interest Rates

Bonds and interest rates have an inverse relationship, which means that when one increases, the other decreases. If the interest rate rises, bond prices will go down, and when interest rates are going down, bond prices will increase. This is because a bond will generally pay a fixed interest rate to its holder, which will correspond to the interest rate at the time of purchase. If interest rates were to fall in the market after the bond was purchased, the fixed rate of the bond would pay out more than other bonds that correspond to the falling interest rate. If the interest rate increases, the bond will not be as valuable, because it will have a fixed rate that is now below the general interest rate. For example, if someone purchased a bond at a 5 percent interest rate, and then interest rates dropped to 3 percent, the bond would be worth more to investors because it gives a return of 2 percent greater than what one could buy a bond at after the decrease of interest rates. Likewise, if the interest rates were to rise to 7 percent, the bond would not be as valuable, as it still carries its fixed rate of 5 percent, and its price would have to drop for the bond to be able to be sold.

A bond's market price is initially determined by the national interest rate of the moment. New bonds that have just been issued will generally be around this national interest rate or higher. What one can sell a bond at on the market depends on how much return an investor will receive on the bond. The price of a bond will decrease if an investor can find a better rate of return from the current market; therefore, the bond must be sold at a lower price. If the return rate is less than the current interest rate, the value will have to decrease, because the bond will not return as much as others at the same time. Because of interest rates, the value of a bond will fluctuate a lot more than liquid cash; therefore, the financial asset cash carries the opportunity cost of the potential interest earned from a bond.

Nominal Vs. Real Interest Rates

The **nominal interest rate** is the general amount of interest paid on a loan, without considering any other factors such as inflation. When advertising a bond or loan, the nominal interest rate will usually be what is advertised because it does not include the interest that could compound or any associated fees on the loan. It is simple and to the point, and can be easily calculated to determine interest to be paid. The nominal interest is a direct reflection of the current market at the time of the loan, and will not take into effect how that market will change over time. Therefore, the nominal rate will often not be the actual rate that one will pay or receive on a loan; it is more of a general idea of the loan's current value.

The **real interest rate** is the amount of interest paid on a loan adjusted for inflation. This rate is a more accurate description of what the rate will be to pay off the loan because it removes the effects of inflation. The value of money will change over time, and real interest rates reflect this change by considering how such changes will affect a loan.

Changes in Nominal Interest Rates, Expected Inflation, and Real Interest Rates

Nominal interest rates are based on what the market is expected to do, instead of how it will actually fluctuate. A nominal interest rate can be determined by adding the expected real interest rate to the expected inflation. The real interest rate is the actual amount won or lost by a lender, while the nominal rate reflects the amount the loan was purchased for. An investor can determine whether they gained or lost money on a loan by comparing the nominal rate they paid with the real interest rate. If inflation is higher than the nominal rate on the loan is, then the investor will have lost money on the investment, resulting in a negative real interest rate.

Calculate the Nominal and Real Interest Rate

The equation for nominal interest is:

$$Nominal\ interest\ rate = Real\ Interest\ rate + Inflation\ rate$$

For example, if a loan has a real interest rate 10 percent and the loan servicer estimates an inflation rate of 3 percent, the nominal interest rate will be 13 percent.

The formula for calculating the real interest rate is:

$$Real\ Interest\ rate = Nominal\ interest\ rate - Inflation\ rate$$

If a loan has a nominal interest rate of 8 percent, and the current inflation rate is actually 4 percent, the real interest rate will be 4 percent.

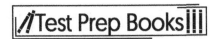

Definition, Measurement, and Functions of Money

Money and its Functions

Money is any asset that can be used as a form of payment in the buying and selling of goods and services. Money can be any amount that is accepted on a large scale for the financial transactions between parties. Money is usually thought of as physical coins and banknotes, but it can take on many different forms, such as the form of a commodity. In economics there are three major functions of money: a medium of exchange, a unit of account, and a store of value.

Money is used as a **medium of exchange** for financial transactions. Money was created as the ultimate bartering tool, involving the trading of one form of good or service for another. Society has made it so money is accepted in almost all transactions, eliminating the difficulty of bartering between people who may not possess something the other wants for trading. It can instead be used as a universal medium of exchange. Money is also a **unit of account** because it can measure the value of goods and services. The worth of a certain good or service can be determined by the amount of money it costs to purchase the good or service. Both the seller and purchaser can come to an agreement over the purchase by determining what amount of money should be exchanged, eliminating the complications of bartering with other forms of assets.

Money in turn also is a **store of value**. The value of money does not fluctuate as quickly or frequently as other assets might, and it has more liquidity than other forms of assets. It can be immediately used for purchasing when collected because it loses fairly little value upon exchange. Inflation over time may change the value of money, making other assets better at storing value, but money is the most immediate and simplest way to quickly convert into other forms of assets. It is also easy to handle and transport, making it useful for all types of purchasing transactions. Because money has become so widely accepted throughout the world, it has become the main form of financial exchanges.

Calculate Measures of Money

There are many different assets that can be classified as money. To determine the amount of money supplied in the economy at one time, or measure of money, all money types need to be accounted for. In economics, the money supply is measured using monetary aggregates that have different scopes depending on what type of money is measured. Two such aggerates used to calculate the measure of money are designated in economics as M1 and M2, in addition to the base monetary base or M0/MB. This data is usually reported by a country's central bank and dictate the flow of money circulated into the economy.

M1 calculations include the most liquid forms of assets, including all cash/currency, travelers' checks, and demand deposits held by the public, not including the federal government or national reserve. The money counted in M1 can be seen as money that is intended to be part of financial exchanges, like deposits into bank accounts that are intended to be spent quickly. M1 is the narrowest reflection of the money supply because it considers only the money that is currently circulating through the economy. **M2** is a measure of money that is calculated by taking everything added in M1, but also including fewer liquid assets such as savings deposits, time deposits, money market accounts for short-term investments, and term repurchase agreements. It is broader in scope than M1 because it includes money that is not in direct economic circulation, but money that is being saved for use in the economy at a later date. To calculate M2, the total of M1 must be added to the additional assets mentioned. Another measure of money is the **monetary base**, labeled **M0** or **MB**. This includes only the currency in circulation and bank reserves. The money supply is counted using the most liquid assets at the base, then increased to include fewer liquid assets for the additional measures of money.

Banking and the Expansion of the Money Supply

Key Terms Related to the Banking System and the Expansion of the Money Supply

Depository institutions are financial institutions that accept money deposits from customers. These include commercial banks, credit unions, and various savings institutions. Establishments that are legally allowed to only lend money are not considered depository institutions. Depository institutions give security to those who utilize them by keeping their money safe, but at the same time, easy to be liquidated if desired.

Balance sheets are statements that list the financial balances of a person or organization. They include assets, liabilities, and shareholder's equity to indicate monetary worth at a specific moment in time. The balance sheet is divided into two sections: assets and liabilities/shareholders' equity. The balance sheet is a financial statement used in accounting to organize and determine the overall financial position of an organization or individual.

Fractional reserve banking is the amount of money a bank keeps on reserve related to the amount it loans out. A bank keeps only a fraction of the total amount deposited in order to make loans to other borrowers. The amount of actual cash available to be withdrawn from the bank is much lower than what is actually deposited overall. Fractional reserve banking is the most used form of banking by commercial locations. They set a reserve ratio based on their total deposits, and the rest is used for the bank's own financial transactions.

Required reserves are the minimum amounts of cash reserves that a bank must have in relation to the amount of deposits it receives. The federal reserve uses this amount to regulate the growth of the money supply in the economy. The lower the required reserve, the more liquid the money in the bank becomes, because more of it is available for immediate use without banks having to hold on to the money for longer periods of time in order to back up deposits. Banks with deposits of more than $124.2 million are required to reserve at least 10 percent of deposits.

Excess reserves are the amounts of money reserved by a bank over the required reserve amount. All bank reserves are divided into required and excess reserves, with the excess reserves being determined by subtracting the required reserves from the total amount of reserved money. A bank might hold excess reserves for safety insurance of anticipated upcoming transactions or large numbers of withdrawals.

The **money multiplier** is how many dollars' worth of deposits are created with each additional dollar of reserve. It is the amount of money that a bank can turn deposits into after loaning them back out. The more money a bank has in reserve, the lower its money multiplier will be, because it cannot turn that money into additional profit. The money multiplier is expressed as a ratio of deposits to reserves. The higher the ratio, the smaller the amount of money that will be available for lending, because the bank will be using this money to in turn make more. The max value of the money multiplier can be determined by the reciprocal of the required reserve ratio. Often, the money multiplier might be overstated because banks will often keep excess reserves; the public may also hold more currency at the given time, with less deposits coming to banks.

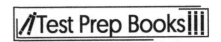

The **reserve ratio** is the percentage amount of deposits a bank must keep as cash. The lower the ratio, the more money banks can use to give loans to make money back. It expresses the ratio of reserves to deposits, and is used by the Federal Reserve in the United States to regulate the money supply in the economy.

How the Banking System Creates and Expands the Money Supply

The banking system controls the money supply through a process called **monetary policy**. In the United States, the Federal Reserve Bank is the central bank that regulates the money supply and creates monetary policy. The most straightforward way to expand the money supply is to print new money to increase the amount available in the market; however, this method is not commonly used because it could quickly lead to a decreased value of money and inflation.

A more popular way to expand the money supply is to modify the reserve requirements for banks. When the reserve requirement is lowered, banks can loan out more money to increase the total amount circulating in the economy. If the reserve requirement is increased, the money supply will consequently decrease as well, because less will be available for immediate loans. A bank can also use its excess reserves to increase the money supply by loaning more money out. This creates money for circulation in the economy by making money more liquid and available for use, rather than stored. The money multiplier is used to predict change in the money supply because it shows the amount of money a bank will make on loans made from excess reserves. If a bank has a lot of excess reserves, they can easily increase the amount of money in the market through loaning out these reserves.

The central bank can also change the money supply by modifying interest rates in the short term. Low interest rates increase spending as well as the amount of money being loaned out in the market. Lower interest rates mean a larger demand for debt, incentivizing more people to demand loans from banks. If the interest rate is too high, people will not want loans and the bank will have a larger amount of excess reserves—money that is not circulating in the economy.

The central bank can also purchase government securities in the form of government bonds to change the money supply. This is called conducting **open market operations**. If the central bank buys more government bonds, it gives bond sellers additional cash to use in the economy, increasing the money supply. If the central bank decides to sell its own bonds, the cash that it receives for these bonds would be taken out of circulation in the economy, leading to a decrease in the money supply.

Calculate Effects of Changes in the Banking System

When a bank first opens, it has no deposits to make loans with, which means it has an empty balance sheet; it has no assets or liabilities. When someone makes a deposit into the bank, the bank has to record the amount of the deposit as both an asset, because this money can be loaned out for profit, and a liability, because the bank is obligated to return the money to the depositor if asked. For example, if someone deposits $20 into the bank, the balance sheet will have recorded $20 on both the assets and liabilities sides. For a bank to increase its assets and bring in profit, it needs to loan some of the money it has taken in as deposits to receive interest.

The central bank regulates the required reserves a bank must keep, depending on the amount of deposits a bank receives. If the required reserve for is 10 percent of deposits, a bank with $20 is required to hold at least $2 in its reserves. The remaining $18 would be considered excess reserves, which can be circulated back into the economy. This would be shown on the balance sheet as two separate assets, the required reserve asset of $2 and the excess reserve amount of $18. If the bank then lends out $10 of its $18, a separate asset is created, the loan asset of $10. When a bank lends out money from its excess reserves, it is increasing the money supply in the overall economy. The money measure M1 also changes when a bank makes loans from its excess reserves. Because $M1 = cash\ available\ in\ the\ economy + Deposits$, the new available cash in circulation will be added to the initial amount of deposits, i.e., $M1 = \$10 + \$20 = \$30$. If the central bank decides to decrease the required reserve, more money can be circulated back into the economy to increase the money supply, and vice versa.

The Money Market, Money Demand, and Money Supply

The **money market** is a model that identifies the supply and demand of money in a country's economy. The amount of money in circulation as well as current interest rates both influence the money market. The more money there is in the money market, the less demand for money there will be. Also, if there are high interest rates, the demand for money will decrease as well. This can be expressed on a graph with the *x*-axis, or independent variable, labeled with the quantity of money in the market, and the *y*-axis, or the dependent variable, labeled with the nominal interest rate.

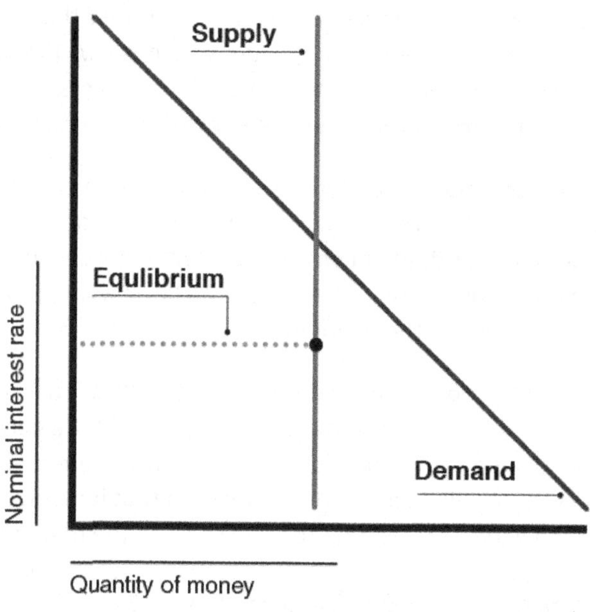

Graph 1

Money demand is a measure of the value of money at a certain interest rate. It represents the amount of money people want to hold on to. The demand for money is represented as an inverse relationship between the nominal interest rate and the quantity of money. When interest rates are high, people do not want as much money, instead opting for bonds or other investments that hold these higher interest rates. Therefore, a negative demand curve is used on the graph to represent the relationship between the interest rate and the money supply. When there is an increase in money demand, the demand curve will move up, creating an increase in interest rates.

Money supply represents the amount of money put into the economy for circulation at a certain interest rate to meet demand. The money supply is regulated by the central bank, which provides its monetary base. The nominal interest rate is independent of the money supply. When represented on the money market graph, the money supply curve is fixed; therefore, it is represented by a vertical line. Equilibrium occurs in the money market when the supply matches the demand for money.

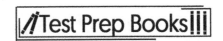

Relationship Between the Nominal Interest Rate and the Quantity of Money Demanded

The money supply and the nominal interest in a country are inversely related. When the money supply decreases, the nominal interest rate will increase, making borrowing money more expensive. When the money supply increases, interest rates will decrease, making it less expensive to borrow and take out loans. This is represented on the money market graph by placing the nominal interest rate on the *y*-axis and the quantity of money on the *x*-axis (see Graph 1). When there is more money available, interest rates will be lower. Because the nominal interest determines the amount of return one receives when saving money, the money supply and the money demanded influence the nominal interest rate.

Placing the negatively sloped demand curve on the money market graph visually shows how the nominal interest rate and the quantity of money demanded are related. Looking at a graph, if the quantity of money moved positively to the right, the corresponding point on the demand curve will represent a decreasing nominal interest rate. Going back to the left, or decreasing the quantity of money, will represent a higher value of interest. A higher point on the demand curve will represent a higher interest rate with a lower quantity of money.

Equilibrium in the Money Market

Equilibrium is the point at which the money supply matches the money demand. Because the supply of money is determined by a country's central bank, the central bank will adjust this amount to meet equilibrium in the market. The central bank buys and sells government bonds in order to increase or decrease the money supply to meet this equilibrium. Surpluses in the money supply make prices lower, while shortages of money make prices increase. The central bank meets this equilibrium when all the money that the central bank puts into the market is demanded for, and people hold only that amount of cash available without wanting to hold more.

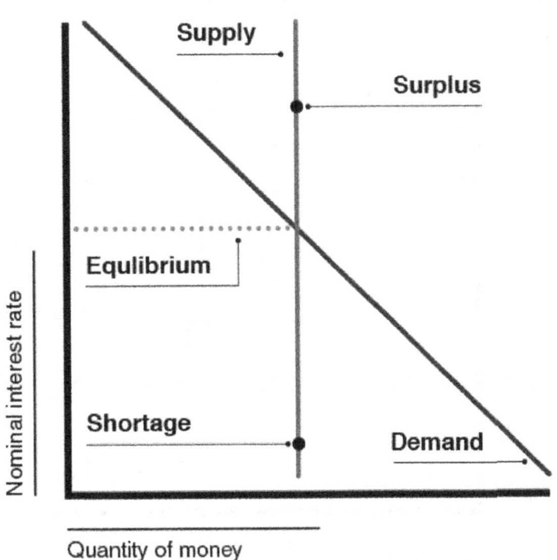

Graph 2

On Graph 1, the point where the negatively sloped demand curve meets the vertical supply curve is the point of equilibrium. This is how the nominal interest rate for a specific quantity of money is found. When a point on the supply curve corresponds to a point above the demand curve, there is a surplus of money in the market. If the point on the supply curve is below the demand curve, there will be a shortage of money, and more will need to be circulated into the economy to match demand. Because the demand for money cannot be controlled directly, the central bank increases interest rates by moving the supply curve. The supply curve can be moved to the left, decreasing the quantity of money, or it can be moved to the right to increase the quantity of money. This ability is represented on the graph by movement of the vertical supply curve. Where the supply curve touches the demand curve is where the new equilibrium will be after a shift in either curve.

How Nominal Interest Rates Adjust to Restore Equilibrium in the Money Market

The nominal interest rate will adjust based on how much money a country's central bank decides to supply. To meet an equilibrium, where the demand for money equals what is supplied by the central bank, the supply for money must match the demand; therefore, when the central bank increases the supply of money, the interest has to go down in order to meet equilibrium. Conversely, if the supply of money is decreased by the central bank, the interest rate will need to be raised to match the higher demand for the shorter supply of money. For example, if the central bank supplies too much money, interest rates will need to decrease to incentivize more demand for a return to equilibrium.

At the highest point seen on Graph 2 of the demand curve, the *x*-axis, labeled as the quantity of money, is at its lowest point, while the *y*-axis, representing the interest rate, is at its highest. At the point where the quantity of money is the highest, the interest rate is the lowest. By creating the vertical supply curve perpendicular to the *x*-axis, equilibrium can be determined by identifying where the supply curve intersects the sloping demand curve. If the supply curve is placed at the very right-hand side of the graph, where the quantity of money is the lowest, the point of intersection with the demand curve will represent a very low interest rate. As the supply curve is moved to the left, the point if intersection is higher on the graph, representing a higher interest rate. Moving the supply curve left and right shows how the interest rate is affected at the intersection with the demand curve (see Graph 3). The central bank is the one that moves this curve in relation to demand in order to find the equilibrium level and even out the demand and supply of money in the market.

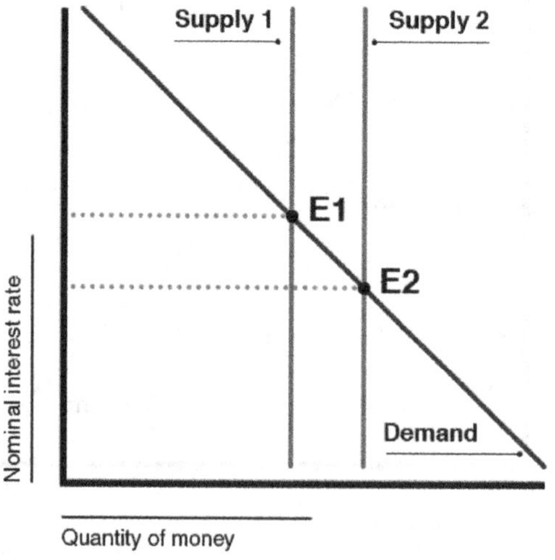

Graph 3

Disequilibrium Nominal Interest Rates

When the equilibrium is not met in an economy, there is disequilibrium, and there will ultimately be shortages and surpluses. Disequilibrium can lead to market crashes and inflation. To avoid disequilibrium, the central bank needs to regulate the supply of money in the market. However, market forces can also drive the nominal interest rate toward equilibrium without the aid of the central bank. When there is a surplus of money in the market, sellers are more likely to create lower prices in order to sell more and compete when there is a lower demand for money. Prices will increase if there is a shortage in the market because money will be scarcer and have a higher value. For example, a soda producer makes 500 cans of soda to sell at $3 each. However, if only 400 people want soda, there will be a surplus of 100 cans. The seller will then have to decrease the price on the unsold cans of soda to get buyers to purchase the remaining surplus. The market will then adjust itself to the equilibrium because of the decrease in price creating an increase in the demand so that the supply of soda cans matches the amount sold. The money market works the same way, with money increasing or decreasing in value to match demand and obtain equilibrium.

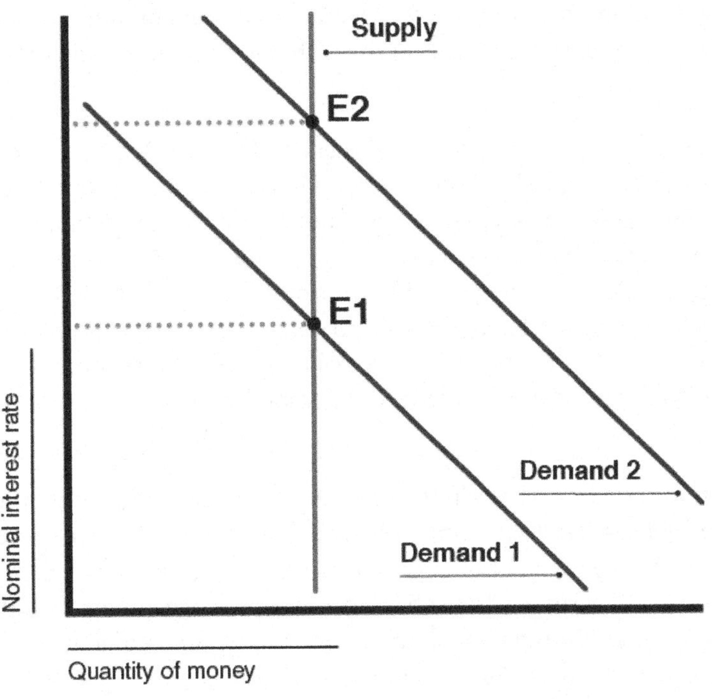

Graph 4

On Graph 4, a surplus is represented by a point on the supply curve above where the demand curve intersects (see Graph 2). For equilibrium to be reached, the demand curve needs to be raised until it meets the supply curve point. When the price for an item or the price of money decreases, it creates more demand. When there is more demand, the demand curve moves up to intersect at the supply curve point (see Graph 4). The demand will have been increased because of the higher value of holding money, and the demand curve will move upward without having to decrease supply. Sellers and loaners always want to meet equilibrium to avoid surplus, but they also do not want to have too low a supply not to meet demand. When there is a shortage of money, the value of money will increase. To equalize a market with a money shortage, the value of holding money will be decreased in order to lower demand. Because the most optimal efficiency comes when the supply meets demand, the money market will correct itself so that banks avoid surpluses and shortages.

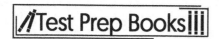

Determinants of Demand and Supply in the Money Market

The opportunity cost of holding money as opposed to another asset at a given time determines the demand for money in the market. If the value of money is high, there will be more demand, because it will be a profitable asset. If the value is low, people will want to invest in other forms of assets. A determiner of this change in value includes people who will hold more money if they intend to purchase goods and services at a later date. This determinate of the demand for money depends on the quality and quantity of goods that can be purchased with it. Holding more money in a wallet or in a savings account to be used at a later date for a future purchase means that money is no longer in circulation in the market at that moment, decreasing the overall quantity of money. This in turn raises the demand for money because the decrease in its availability gives money more value, making it more desirable to hold onto. On the graph this change is represented by a point on the supply curve. When people hold money, the supply and circulation of the money in the market decreases, marking a point on the supply curve below the demand curve. In order for the market to get back to equilibrium, the value of money will be increased to incentivize a raise in the demand curve, so that it intersects again with the supply curve for equilibrium.

Another determinant in the demand for money is the price of bonds. Because bond prices fluctuate so frequently, it can be advantageous to hold on to bonds in favor of holding on to money, decreasing the demand for money in the market. When people sell bonds, they are converting these bonds into money, increasing the supply of money and thus also decreasing its demand. On the graph, when more people hold bonds over money, the money supply reaches a surplus, shown by a point above the demand curve. To balance out the money market and return to equilibrium, the value of money will increase in order to remove the surplus, and the demand curve will move upward to meet the supply point. Also, when people expect prices on bonds to decrease, the demand for money may increase due to the speculations of value.

Household income is another determinant in the demand for money. The higher the household income for a family, the higher their demand for money will be because they will have more money to save, taking that portion of what they earn out of circulation, decreasing the money supply. When a country's gross domestic product (GDP) increases, household incomes increase as well, and the demand for money will also increase. When exemplified on the graph, the larger income will initially be given out to its earners in the form of money being supplied to the economy, increasing supply. However, when this money is saved instead of spent, the money supply will no longer be at equilibrium, and the value of money will have to increase in order for the demand curve to meet this point.

The price of goods and services can be another determinant in the demand for money. The higher the prices in the market, the higher the demand for money will be in order to meet these increased prices. The demand curve as represented on the graph will move upward, and the quantity of money will need to be increased in order to get back to the intersection of the supply and demand curve.

Costs associated with transferring between money and other assets also play a role in determining the money demand. Fewer transfers will take place if there is a high associated fee. In turn, the demand for money will increase because the cost of converting this money to other forms of assets will be too high to be advantageous.

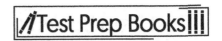

Simple preference can also dictate the demand for money. The preferability of cash over other assets depends on the individual. Some may simply prefer cash to other forms because of its liquidity, while others may not. This preference makes a difference in the overall demand for money, depending on how many people may prefer it to another form such as bonds, at a given time.

The major determinate of the money supply curve is a country's central bank. The central bank controls the amount of money to be supplied in the economy at a given time through open market operations. The central bank will often increase or decrease the supply of money to meet the equilibrium between quantity and the nominal interest rate.

Changes in Demand and Supply in the Money Market

The demand for money changes depending on how valuable money is related to the nominal interest rate. When there is a high demand, there must be an equally high supply to get equilibrium in the market, lowering the nominal interest. When there is low demand, the supply must be decreased, raising the nominal interest and thus the return on holding money. The demand for money can be shifted in this way by controlling its supply. On the money market graph, the supply curve is moved to the left to decrease the quantity of money in the market, and moved to the right to increase the quantity. The farther to the left the supply curve is, the higher the nominal interest rate will be to meet equilibrium because the demand curve slopes down as the quantity of money increases. Therefore, the more the supply curve moves right, it intersects the demand curve at an increasingly lower point, dropping along with it the nominal interest rate at the equilibrium level. The central bank can place this supply curve anywhere along the *x*-axis, but the equilibrium point must always correspond to where the two curves intersect.

Monetary Policy

Monetary Policy and Related Terms

Monetary policy is the procedure a country's central bank uses to regulate short-term loans and the money supply. Monetary policy is used to stabilize the money market and prevent major fluctuations in prices and interest rates. The central bank is using monetary policy when it changes the money supply by taking actions like modifying interest rates or the amount of required reserves a bank needs to keep. The objective of a country's monetary policy is to achieve equilibrium in the money market and prevent inflation by reacting to changes in the value of money in the economy. Tools used for conducting monetary policy include open-market operations, modifying the required reserve ratio, or modifying the discount rate. Of these tools, open-market operations are the most frequently used.

In macroeconomics, the central bank uses monetary policies to achieve goals it has discussed and agreed upon, such as stabilizing prices, maximizing employment rates, and controlling long-term interest rates. Prices are stabilized by monitoring and regulating the amount of money in the market and supplying just enough to meet demand while avoiding inflation. When inflation occurs, the value of money decreases significantly, causing prices to jump. Monetary policy creates procedures to maintain a stable ratio of money to supply to meet demand. When the inflation rate is stable in a country, prices stay consistent, leading to higher employment rates because businesses are more willing to expand and hire more employees. When businesses are not worrying about fluctuating prices, they are also more likely to make loans that last for longer amounts of time, controlling and stabilizing long-term interest rates as well.

Tools of Monetary Policy

Open-market operations are what occur when a country's central bank buys or sells government securities, such as bonds, to control the money supply. The **open market** refers to the competition between businesses to supply the central bank with these securities. The central bank uses this competition to determine a target rate for interest rates on loans made between banks. These inter-bank loans are what banks use to meet reserve requirements. A bank's money supply is likely to frequently fluctuate throughout a day of business, so the amount of money available often needs to be adjusted at the end of the day to meet reserve requirements. A bank will then make loans on an overnight basis to make sure that another bank always has enough reserves to meet the central bank's requirement. If the interest rate on these loans is increased, the rates on other types of loans, like home loans and car loans, increase as well, having an impact on the economy as a whole. When the central bank sells securities, it reduces the money supply by increasing the reserves, and when it buys securities, the money base is increased, lowering reserves. Buying securities from banks gives banks more excess reserves that they can in turn loan back out to make profit.

The required reserve ratio is an expression of the required reserves as it relates to the total amount of deposits a bank receives. This ratio is regulated by the central bank as well, with a higher ratio meaning a higher amount of reserves a bank must keep. When banks make loans to other banks or individuals, they must not give out more than this ratio allows.

To keep the required reserve ratio, banks will often borrow from each other. However, banks can also buy these loans from the central bank, at what is called the **discount rate**. This is often seen as the last option for a bank when it can no longer borrow from other banks due to their unavailability. The discount rate is often higher than what an institution could find when receiving loans from other banks, so its percentage is used to regulate the interest rates of loans made between banks, leading to a decrease or increase in the money supply depending on the rate. A bank will likely raise its own interest rate when lending to another bank if it knows the discount rate is high, so as to make more profit from these short-term loans.

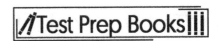

Short-Run Effects of a Monetary Policy Action

In the short term, monetary policy controls the nominal interest rate. The lower the rate, the more likely people are to buy loans and take on debt. Monetary policy controls this demand by regulating the immediate supply of money through the policies of the central bank. Such policies include increasing or decreasing discount rates. When the central bank increases the discount rate at which banks can purchase loans from it, it is decreasing the amount of money available in the market because less money will be borrowed. The nominal interest rate will then increase as well because of the increase in the discount rate. This is how the central bank can push interest rates in a certain direction through monetary policy.

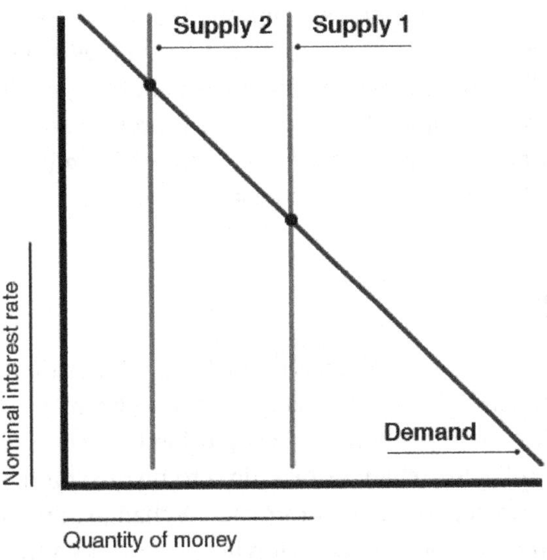

Graph 5

On Graph 5, when the central bank increases the discount rate, other interest rates will follow because banks will in turn have to make loans at a higher rate to cover the difference at which they purchase securities from the central bank. This moves the supply curve to the left, decreasing the quantity of money in the market and increasing the nominal interest rate. The opposite happens if the discount rate is decreased; more money will be circulated in the economy, and with more money the equilibrium of demand and supply will intersect at a lower interest rate.

Expansionary and Contractionary Monetary Policies

Expansionary policy is the policy the central bank uses when they want to increase the money supply and lower interest rates, decreasing the demand for money. This policy decreases the value of money in the market because of the increase in its supply. When the central bank buys securities in the open market, it is practicing expansionary policy.

Contractionary policy is the opposite of expansionary policy. In contractionary policy, the central bank is decreasing the money supply and raising interest rates. This creates an increase in the demand for money because it has a higher value. When the central bank sells securities to banks, it is practicing contractionary policy by requiring banks to purchase loans at higher rates when they need to meet the reserve ratio.

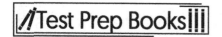

Calculate the Effects of a Monetary Policy Action

Monetary policy action determines the supply of money and the nominal interest rate in the short run. The money market model shows this change by reflecting how it effects the supply and demand of money at a given time. On the money market model graph, the demand curve represents the given demand for money at the corresponding interest rate. Using this demand, the central bank can increase or decrease the money supply—using monetary policy—to reach the equilibrium between supply and demand in order to avoid any major fluctuations in prices and rates. On the classical money market model graph, the supply curve is vertical at all times, signifying that it is not influenced by interest rates.

In the AD-AS model, the short-term effects of monetary policy are represented by changes to the supply and demand of money in relation to the price level and the real GDP of a country. The amount of output is measured against the price level it takes to produce such output. When expansionary policy is used, the real GDP will increase, and during contractionary monetary policy, it will decrease. This is because monetary policy affects the money supply, changing interest rates and inflation, in turn affecting employment rates and the output of goods and services in the economy. On the graph, when aggregate demand increases, the real GDP and output will increase because businesses will be more inclined to expand and hire.

Lags to Monetary Policy

Fiscal policy may lag because of the nature of decision making; it takes time to implement policies and for these policies to be reflected in the market. This creates a lag between when the policies take effect depending on when the policies are implemented. **Recognition lag** occurs when a problem in the money market is identified late. Data reflecting changes take time to be observed, making some changes go undetected until they have already caused a major impact. A change in the market can happen faster than the data can be interpreted or collected. **Decision lag** occurs when the central bank has identified a problem but takes time to reach and implement a decision on how to reverse the problem. Debates between the best actions to take may result in missing the opportunity to implement the change at the right time, or having too little information to make an informed decision may delay decisions as well. After implementation has occurred, **implementation lag** may occur, meaning the time it takes for the policy to take affect may also lag too long to have a positive impact, and the move may need to be changed. These types of lags usually last a few months before they can be corrected. Changes in the monetary policy are not instant, the way changes in the market may be.

Loanable Funds Market

The **loanable funds market** is a description of the behaviors of savers and borrowers in an economy. It is an analysis of interest rates compared to the quantity of loanable funds. **Loanable funds** in this case are savings that can be loaned out for profits from interest. The quantity of loanable funds represents the amount of money that has been saved and can consequently be loaned out. The real interest rate represents the cost of borrowing these loans and the amount of return on savings. On the graph, the independent variable, or *x*-axis, is labeled Quantity of loanable funds, and the dependent variable, or *y*-axis, is labeled Real interest rate (see Graph 6). By determining the demand for loans in the market, the real interest rate can be identified by matching its position to the corresponding point on the graph at a given quantity.

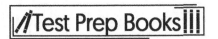

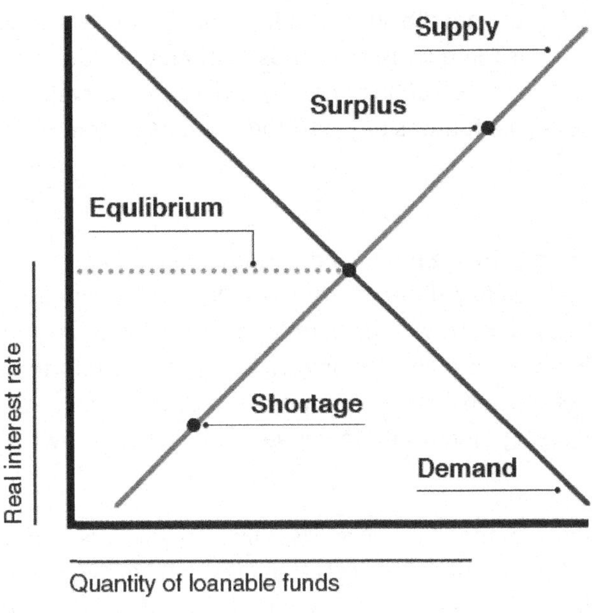

Graph 6

The **demand for loanable funds** is a measure of the amount of loans desired at a specific interest rate. The demand for loanable funds is a representation of the inverse relationship between real interest rates and the quantity of loanable funds. The higher the interest rate is on a loan, the more it will cost to borrow money, leading to less demand. The lower the interest rate, the less it will cost, leading to an increased demand for loans. On the loanable funds market graph, this gives the demand curve a negative slope, much like the graph of other markets. Equilibrium occurs in the loanable funds market when the demand for loanable funds matches what is supplied in the market.

The **supply for loanable funds** is a measure of the positive relationship between real interest rates and the quantity of loanable funds. It represents the amount of money that has been saved in the market. When people save more, there are more funds available for loans, and the higher interest rates will be. This means that on the loanable fund market graph, the supply curve is represented by a positive slope; as the supply increases, real interest rates also increase. Equilibrium is the point where the supply curve intersects the demand curve.

Relationship Between the Real Interest Rate and the Quantity of Loanable Funds Demanded

People are more likely to borrow money when interest rates are low, raising the demand for loans. When more loans are demanded, the supply of available loans in the market will decrease. This leads to an inverse relationship between the real interest rate and the quantity of loans demanded in the market. When interest rates are high, the quantity of loans demanded will decrease, and if interest rates are low, the quantity of loans demanded will increase. The price of borrowing loans and the return on loans made out is the real interest rate.

On the graph, the negative sloping demand curve represents the quantity of loans available at a certain interest rate (see Graph 6). When the demand curve is at its highest point, interest rates are also at their highest, and the quantity of loans is at its lowest. When the supply curve is added, it will intersect the demand curve at the point called the **equilibrium**. The loanable funds market is at equilibrium when the quantity of funds demanded meets the quantity of funds demanded in the market. From this equilibrium point the interest rate can be determined by the *y*-axis interval. The real interest rate will change until the quantity of loanable funds is equal to the amount of demand for loans in the market.

National Savings

In an open economy, a country is allowing money and goods to flow in and out of its own economy to other countries in the world, influencing different markets. National savings in this case would change depending on whether a country is borrowing from or lending money to another country. If it is borrowing, the amount of savings in its own economy would increase with the extra money that can be used for loans in its own market. When it is lending money to other countries, its national savings would in turn decrease because it is taking money and loanable funds out of its own market to be used in another country.

In a closed economy, the amount of money and goods is limited and is not circulating to the markets in other countries. This confines the amount of national savings to what the country itself can produce through borrowing and lending. All the savings in circulation will have a direct impact only within the country's own economy. The government is not lending or borrowing from anyone outside of its own borders in a closed economy.

Equilibrium in the Loanable Funds Market

Equilibrium in the loanable savings market occurs when the quantity of loans demanded equals the quantity of loans supplied. The real interest at this point will adjust based on the supply and demand in order to equalize the market and make them balanced. If more people are saving instead of spending, then there will be a surplus of loanable funds in the market. The real interest rate reacts to this surplus by decreasing because of the low demand. However, when the interest rate starts to decrease, the demand for loans in the market will react with an increase, because there will be a higher return on their investments, the higher the interest rate rises. The interest rate will continue to change to match a change in demand as well as supply. When more people save, the interest rate will move down in order for the demand to catch up and meet a new equilibrium. The supply is then equal to the amount of loans demanded at the corresponding interest rate.

On the graph, equilibrium can be found where the supply and demand curves for the loanable funds market intersect. If the intersection occurs at a low number of the quantity of funds variable found on the x-axis, then the point will reflect a higher interest rate. When the intersection point is at a lower interest rate, there will be a larger quantity of loans in the market. This is because the demand curve represents the inverse relationship between these two variables. The real interest rate will stabilize itself to reach equilibrium depending on how many loans are supplied in the market at the given time. If there is a surplus in loans, demand will increase to reach equilibrium, and if there is a shortage of loans, demand will need to decrease. This demand is dependent on the interest rate and the amount of loans supplied. The interest rate at the supply and demand for loanable funds is equal is the equilibrium, which the market is constantly striving for in order to be the most efficient and avoid drastic fluctuations that would jeopardize the economy.

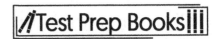

How Real Interest Rates Adjust to Restore Equilibrium in the Loanable Funds Market

When there is disequilibrium, real interest rates are used to correct surpluses and shortages in the loanable funds market. Market forces drive real interest rates toward equilibrium. The government can influence this change in real interest rates by borrowing or selling securities so as to influence the demand of loanable funds in the market. When the government sells more loans, it is increasing the quantity in the market, making the demand decrease because of the change of value that results in a market with too many loans; they will not gain as much return on their investment. The interest rate will then adjust to increase the demand for loans and get rid of the surplus in the market. This is how the interest rate adjusts based on the current supply and demand for loans in the market, which in turn is also based on how many loans the central bank is providing. Equilibrium in the market occurs when interest rates adjust just enough to equalize the supply and demand of loanable funds. When one inevitably starts to change, interest rates must also change to keep equilibrium no matter how the demand and supply may fluctuate.

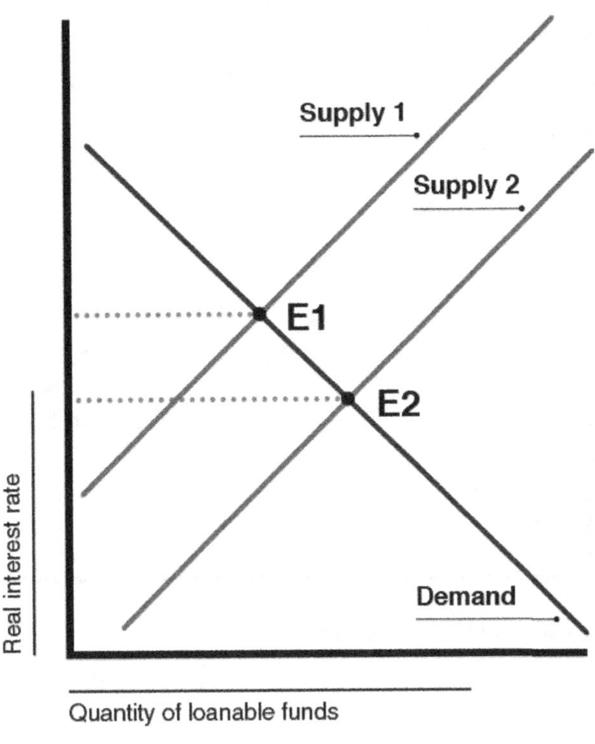

Graph 7

The loanable funds market, depicted in Graph 7, shows how the interest rate may adjust according to changes in supply or demand of loanable funds. When the supply curve is moved up or down, the equilibrium point at which it intersects the demand curve will reflect changes in the interest rate. If the point on the supply curve lies outside that of where it intersects the demand curve, the interest will change in order to shift the demand curve back toward equilibrium. A surplus, represented by a point on the supply curve above the demand curve, will need a positive adjustment of interest rates, in order to raise demand to equilibrium. A shortage, represented by a point on the supply curve that is below the demand curve, will need a negative adjustment of interest rates, in order to lower demand and move to equilibrium in the market. This interest rate, when at equilibrium, can always be measured by tracing the point of intersection on the graph to its corresponding point on the *y*-axis, labeled Real Interest Rate.

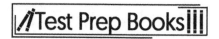

Determinants of Demand and Supply in the Loanable Funds Market

The demand and supply of loans in the loanable funds market can be determined by factors that incentivize people to borrow money. The demand for loanable funds is influenced by what people expect to earn when they save their money. People will save more when they get a higher return, which is directly related to what the current interest rate is. Changes in the interest rate will result in changes in the demand for loans in the market. When interest rates are high, more people will want to save money to earn more from their investment; when the interest rate is low, people will feel it is not worth saving and will demand more loans. On Graph 8, the negative slope of the demand curve shows that a high point on the *y*-axis corresponds to a high interest rate and leads to a higher point on the demand curve.

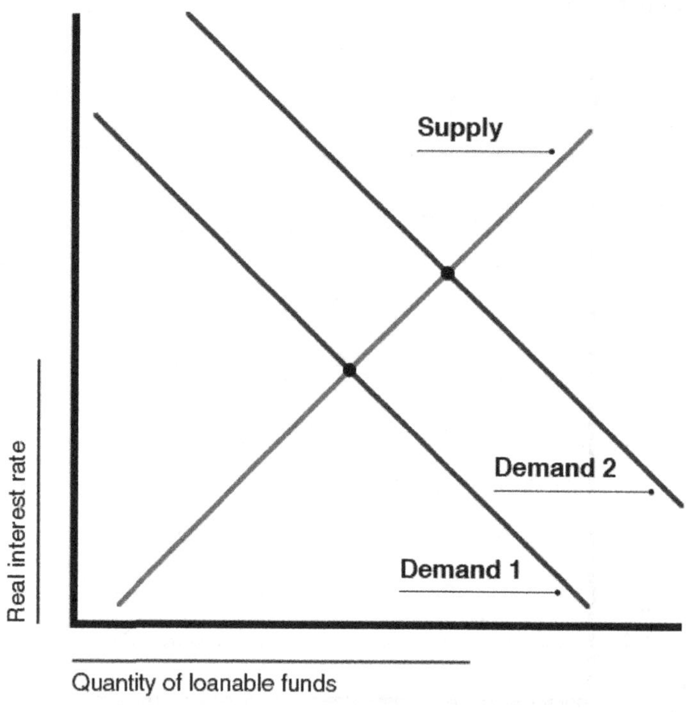

Graph 8

The supply of loanable funds is determined by savings and foreign investment. The amount that people and organizations are saving determines the amount of loanable funds available. The more savings are in the market, the more banks can make loans. There are a lot of reasons why people may want to save more at a certain time. If there are changes to an individual's income, their savings may increase or decrease. People who earn more will have more savings. Anticipation of market changes or anticipation of future purchases may also cause people to want to save more money, thereby increasing the supply of loanable funds in the market. Foreign investment in a country is also a determinate of the supply of loanable funds in its market. Money coming into a market that is outside a country's own increases the amount of funds that can be loaned out. A country can use foreign investment capital to make loans in its own market and increase supply. Likewise, making a foreign investment in a country that is outside of its own will decrease the supply of loanable funds. To determine the amount of loanable funds in a single country, the amount of savings is added to or subtracted from the amount of foreign investment.

When the government is spending money, it is giving out more money in the form of loans. When the amount of loans in the market increases, the interest rate will also decrease, leading to a decrease in their demand as well. Government spending directly affects the amount of loans available in the market. Government taxes also impact the loanable funds market by increasing the supply of loanable funds. Taxes decrease the amount of money people can spend in the market, leading to more money available for the government to lend out in the form of loans. When taxes are cut, the government will have less money available to make loans, and the supply will decrease, leading to an increase in interest rates. When the government is borrowing more money, it is also increasing the quantity of loanable funds in the market, increasing the interest rate. When a government is borrowing less than it is loaning out, the supply of loanable funds is decreasing. On the graph, the amount of government spending and borrowing leads to a corresponding shift in the supply curve. More spending shifts the supply curve to the right, and a decrease means a shift to the left, both resulting in a change in equilibrium in the market where the demand curve intersects the supply curve.

Changes in Demand and Supply

The equilibrium amount for the interest rate and the quantity of funds in the loanable funds market changes when shifts in supply and demand for loanable funds occur. When there is more demand for loans in the market, it means that investors are getting higher interest rates when they save their money. In this case, the quantity of loans in the market will also have to increase to meet this high demand. An equilibrium will be reached when the supply of loanable funds meets its demand. This means the exact amount of loans demanded will be equal to the exact amount of loanable funds available in the market. The interest rate will have also shifted to meet the equilibrium amount. The graph of the loanable funds market shows equilibrium as the point of intersection between the demand curve and the supply curve. This point shows the real interest rate where the quantity of loanable funds meets the demand for loanable funds. If investors feel that the interest rate is too low to save money, then the demand for loanable funds will decrease, leading to an opposite change in supply in order to match demand.

A change in the supply of loanable funds in the market will also cause the equilibrium point to change depending on a shortage or a surplus in the market. When there is a surplus of loans in the market, it means that the amount of loans demanded is less than the amount of loans available. The interest rate will change in order to increase demand and provide a higher equilibrium point. If there is a shortage, the supply of loans will increase in order to meet the demand. Unlike the demand for loanable funds, the supply can be directly influenced by the government either spending or borrowing more money. This supply control is used to manipulate the interest rate to meet demand and provide the right amount of loans in order to meet equilibrium. On the graph, a positive change to the right from the supply curve will result in a lower interest rate on the *y*-axis and a higher quantity of loans on the x-axis. A left shift, or a negative shift, makes the equilibrium point at a higher interest rate. It is important for the government to maintain the correct balance of loan supply to meet demand and reach equilibrium.

Macroeconomics: Long-Run Consequences of Stabilization Policies

Fiscal and Monetary Policy Actions in the Short Run

Effects of Combined Fiscal and Monetary Policy Actions

Monetary and fiscal policies affect people's choices. If the economy is either in a contractionary period or an inflationary period, the government can implement measures through **monetary policy**, which is the raising or lowering of interest rates and changing of the nation's money supply. **Fiscal policy**, on the other hand, is the raising or lowering of taxes and increasing or decreasing of government spending. The Chairman of the Federal Reserve, through the **Federal Open Market Committee (FOMC)**, a committee within the Federal Reserve System, is in charge of guiding the nation's monetary policy. The president and Congress jointly determine fiscal policy. While fiscal and monetary policies have the same effect on the direction of aggregate demand, their impact on interest rates is opposite.

When the Economy is in a Negative or Positive Output Gap

During a recession, the FOMC can use one of three **expansionary monetary policy** tools to stimulate the economy. The most oft-used way the Fed increases the money supply is through the buying of government securities (or bonds). When the Fed buys government securities, the money supply increases, meaning that there is an influx of money in circulation through the banks. In other words, buying bonds "bloats" the money supply. The way that the Fed actually achieves this is by lowering the **target federal funds rate**, which is the interest rate at which banks borrow from other banks. To lower the federal funds rate and keep it within a certain target range, the Fed will buy government securities.

The second way the Fed increases the money supply is by lowering the **required reserve ratio (RRR)**, which is the required percentage of money that banks must hold onto from their deposits. For example, if the current RRR is 10 percent and a bank has $1 million in deposits, then the bank is permitted to lend $900,000 but must keep $100,000 in reserve. Let's imagine that the current Required Reserve Ratio is an absurdly high 100 percent. That would mean banks would not have the ability to lend out any money at all. The current **fractional reserve banking system** that we have in place, in which banks lend out the majority of individual deposits and keep only a fraction of cash on hand, would cease to exist. Banks would be unable to loan money to individuals seeking a mortgage. There would be no means by which banks could lend out money to customers. In fact, the incentive for banks to hold onto customer money would be drastically reduced. Banks would be reduced to merely being a holding depository. If the Fed were to *lower* the RRR from an oppressive 100 percent to a still-high but not as egregiously high 90 percent, then there would be an increase in aggregate demand and therefore an increase in real **gross domestic product (GDP)**.

The third way the Fed can increase the money supply is by lowering the **discount rate**, which is the rate at which banks borrow directly from the Federal Reserve. In times of financial crises, banks may be forced to borrow directly from the Fed rather than borrow money from other banks in order to maintain the minimum amount of money on hand required by the Federal Reserve. The discount rate will be higher than the federal funds rate because of the Fed's preference for banks to borrow from one another rather than from the Fed. Hence, the Fed is commonly referred to as the "**lender of last resort**."

There are two basic ways that the president and Congress can implement **expansionary fiscal policy**. They can either increase government spending or decrease taxes. As a rule of thumb, Democrats emphasize increasing government spending as a way to stimulate the economy, whereas Republicans generally talk about the benefits lowering taxes have in spurring economic growth. It would be a gross oversimplification to state that Democrats *only* love government spending and Republicans *only* love lowering taxes. However, one of Democrat President Barack Obama's principal accomplishments in office was the implementation of "Obamacare," which was an expansion of government spending in the realm of healthcare. Obama's predecessor, Republican George W. Bush, on the other hand, spent a large amount of his political capital during the first year of his presidency pushing for federal income tax cuts. Bush had enough support in the Republican Congress to end up passing what has since been coined the "Bush tax cuts."

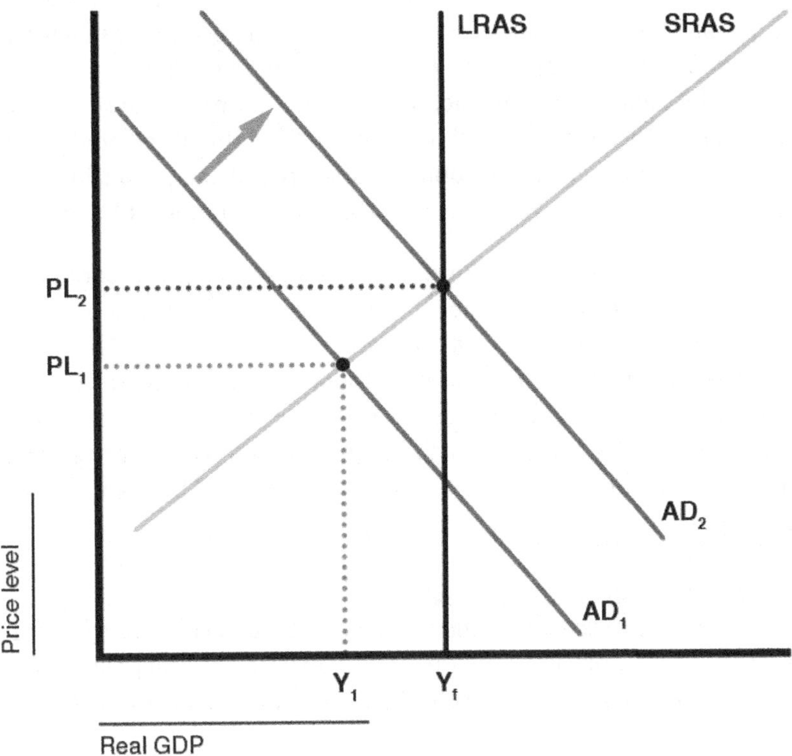

Let's imagine a global financial crisis rocks the equity markets and causes a worldwide recession. What could the Federal Reserve or the president and Congress do to counteract the effects of such a severe economic downturn? Well, the Fed could either lower the target federal funds rate (if it isn't already at zero percent), lower the required reserve ratio, or lower the discount rate. That would be the way to attack the problem through monetary policy. The president and Congress can either increase government spending or lower taxes, which would be using fiscal policy to address the country's financial woes.

Expansionary fiscal or monetary policy will shift the aggregate demand (AD) curve (as depicted in the graph above). The goal of lowering taxes or raising government spending (or increasing government transfers) is to shift the AD curve to the right so as to increase the real GDP. If the Federal Reserve lowers the target federal funds rate, lowers the required reserve ratio, or lowers the discount rate, the AD curve would also shift to the right. The goal of expansionary fiscal or monetary policy in the case of a recessionary gap is to return the economy back to its long-run equilibrium. It is worthwhile to keep in mind that the goal is to return to the original equilibrium; it does not necessarily mean the economy will *actually* get there. Expansionary policy (fiscal or monetary) increases the real GDP (moves it to the right) while increasing the price level. We just cannot necessarily predict the exact level of success in any individual policy measure. We do know that expansionary policies increase the level of real GDP and the rate of inflation.

Failure to implement the appropriate fiscal and/or monetary policy measures can exacerbate economic downturns. After the Stock Market Crash of 1929, the United States fell into a Great Depression. There is no specific definition as to what constitutes a depression, but we do know that at the height of this particularly severe economic downturn, the unemployment rate was at 25 percent in 1933.

While some of President Franklin Roosevelt's economic policies may have helped stave off the effects of the Great Depression initially, the United States was still mired in an economic malaise throughout the 1930s. And, in 1937, the Roosevelt Recession occurred. According to Keynesian belief, the insistence of maintaining a balanced budget and use of **contractionary monetary policy**, or raising of interest rates, served to worsen the effects of the Depression. Keynesians believe that if the government spent more money or if the Federal Reserve utilized **expansionary monetary policy** by reducing interest rates, it is quite plausible that the Great Depression might have ended earlier or at least been reduced in severity.

Former Federal Reserve Chairman Ben Shalom Bernanke was a tenured professor at Princeton University and devoted a good chunk of his academic career toward studying the Great Depression. In 2004, Bernanke compiled a series of essays into a book entitled *Essays on the Great Depression.* When Bernanke was the Fed Chair during the 2008 Great Recession, he was able to ensure that the Fed would use expansionary monetary policies in his power as the Fed Chair. Bernanke was convinced that the Great Recession actually *surpassed* the Great Depression in its economic severity and was determined not to make the same mistakes that he perceived the Fed made in 1937 by prematurely implementing contractionary monetary policy.

Combination of Fiscal and Monetary Policies

Expansionary fiscal and monetary policies shift the aggregate demand curve to the right and increase both the level of real GDP and the price level. However, monetary and fiscal policies have opposite impacts in terms of the direction of the interest rate. Fiscal policy affects the demand for loanable funds on the loanable funds graph, whereas monetary policy affects the money supply on the money market graph.

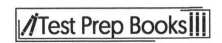

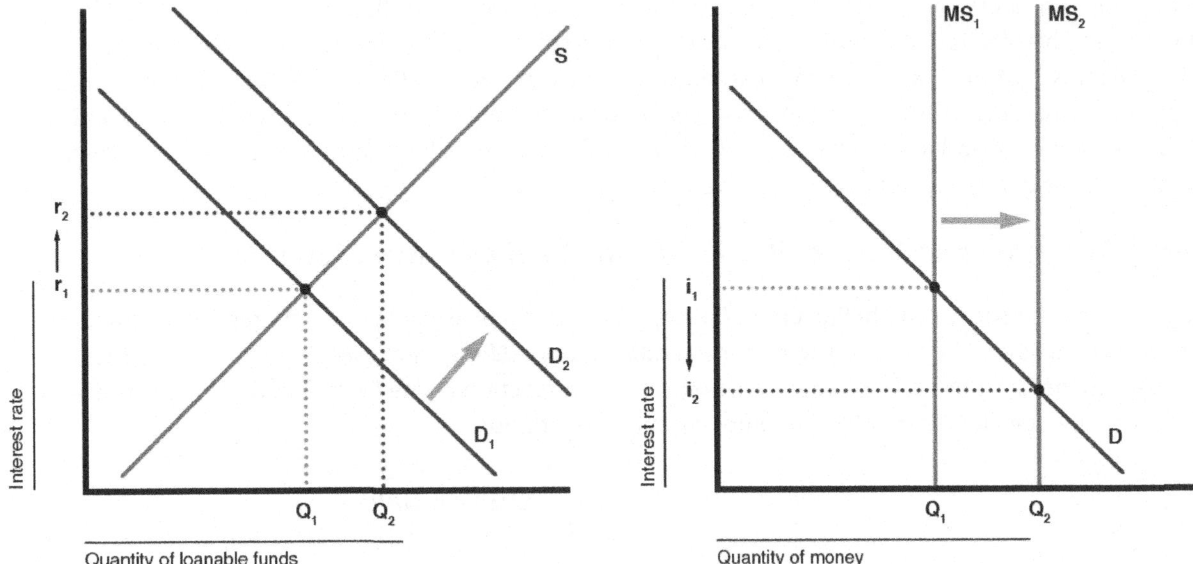

Imagine that a severe economic downturn has rocked the country of Swengland. Unemployment is skyrocketing to record levels and the real GDP at the short-run equilibrium is far below the real GDP at the long-run equilibrium. If the government (and central bank) of Swengland implemented expansionary fiscal and monetary policy measures to combat the recession, how would interest rates be impacted? As shown in the graph above, expansionary fiscal policy will shift the demand for loanable funds to the right and *increase* real interest rates. However, expansionary monetary policy will shift the supply of money to the right and *decrease* nominal interest rates. The combined effect, therefore, of *both* expansionary fiscal and monetary policies on the interest rate is indeterminate.

Let's look at the opposite situation. Imagine that a crisis of high inflation has hit the country of Venezbabwe. Prices are heating up and the real GDP at the short-run equilibrium exceeds the real GDP at the long-run equilibrium. If the government (and central bank) of Venezbabwe implemented contractionary fiscal and monetary policy measures to combat inflation, how would interest rates be impacted? As shown in the graph above, contractionary fiscal policy will shift the demand for loanable funds to the left and *decrease* real interest rates. However, contractionary monetary policy will shift the supply of money to the left and *increase* nominal interest rates. The combined effect, therefore, of *both* contractionary fiscal and monetary policies on the interest rate is indeterminate.

The Phillips Curve

Short-Run Phillips Curve and Long-Run Phillips Curve

The **Phillips Curve** is a model that attempts to describe the relationship between unemployment and inflation. In the short-run, there is a tradeoff between the amount of inflation and unemployment in the economy. For example, if the unemployment rate is 10 percent and inflation is 2 percent, expansionary fiscal and monetary policies might lower the unemployment rate to 6 percent but might increase inflation to 6 percent. Conversely, if the unemployment rate is 4 percent and inflation is 6 percent, contractionary fiscal and monetary policies might reduce inflation to a more manageable 3 percent but also increase unemployment to 7 percent. Keep in mind that the inverse relationship between unemployment and inflation occurs only in the short-run Phillips Curve model.

In the long run, there is no relationship between unemployment and inflation. The long-run Phillips curve is simply reflected as a vertical line, or the **non-accelerating inflation rate of employment (NAIRU)**. This "natural" rate of unemployment does not correlate at all with the rate of inflation in the economy. According to NAIRU, expansionary policies will temporarily decrease unemployment and increase the rate of inflation, but eventually there will be only be a long-term increase in the level of inflation while unemployment stays at a fixed level.

Short-Run and Long-Run Equilibrium in the Phillips Curve Model

Any point on the **short-run Phillips Curve (SRPC)** represents a possible level of unemployment and corresponding level of inflation. The **long-run Phillips Curve (LRPC)**, however, is a vertical line that represents the "natural" rate of unemployment. The intersection of the SRPC and the LRPC represents the economy at its long-run rate of unemployment and inflation.

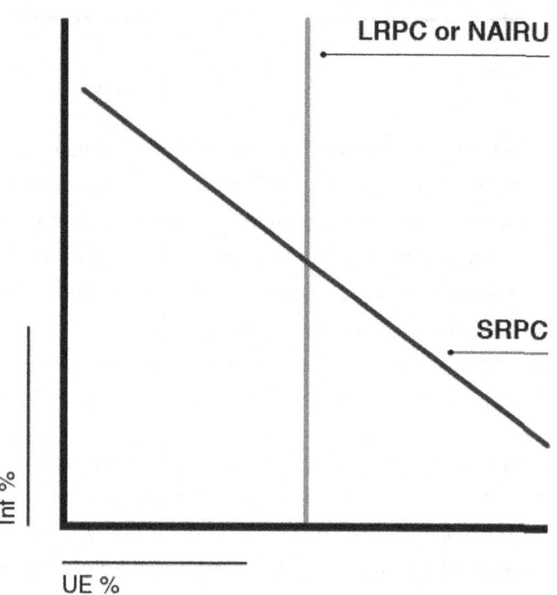

Unemployment and Inflation in the Short Run and in the Long Run

In the long run, there is a fixed level of unemployment, and there exists no correlation between unemployment and inflation. However, this is not true in the short run. High levels of unemployment correlate to low levels or inflation, and vice versa.

Demand Shocks

A **demand shock** is an event that temporarily increases or decreases the aggregate demand for particular goods or services. When a positive demand shock occurs, the **aggregate demand (AD curve)** shifts to the right. Conversely, when a negative demand shock occurs, the AD curve shifts to the left. If the FOMC makes an unexpected decision to reduce the federal funds rate, there would be a positive demand shock, shifting the AD curve to the right, increasing the price level and real GDP. How would that look on the Phillips Curve?

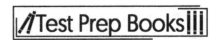

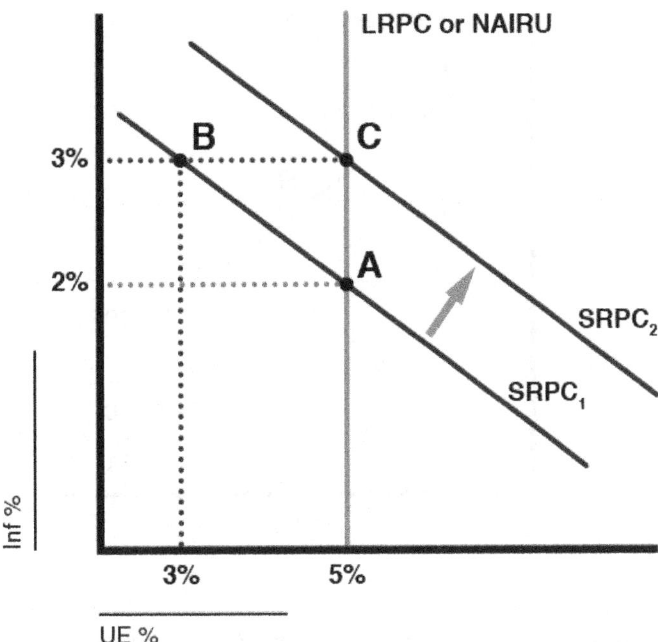

If the natural rate of unemployment is at 5 percent with a 2 percent level of inflation, then a positive demand shock would decrease the unemployment rate while increasing the inflation rate. Note that the SRPC curve itself does not shift initially; the point starts at A and then moves along the SRPC to the left to point B if there is a positive demand shock. The unemployment rate would now be 3 percent with inflation also at 3 percent at point B. However, the 3 percent level of unemployment is not sustainable, so the economy would adjust with the SRAS shifting to the left. The corresponding shift on the Phillips Curve graph would be the SRPC curve shifting to the right, with unemployment reverting back to the NAIRU and a higher rate of inflation, as reflected by point C.

Suppose that the Federal Reserve unexpectedly increases the federal funds rate, which causes a negative demand shock. How would that look on the Phillips Curve?

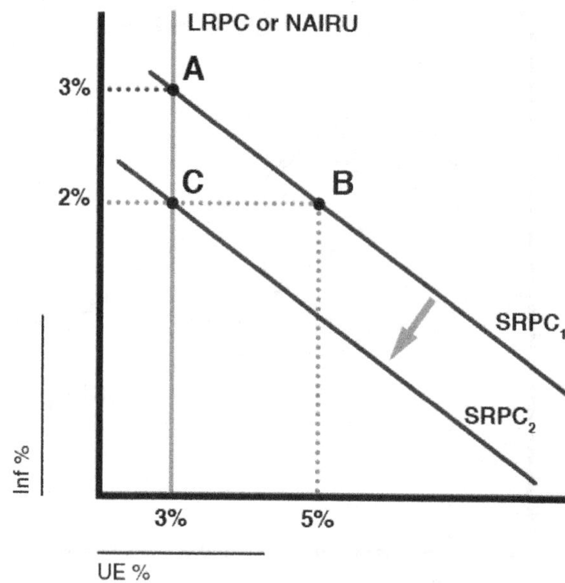

If the natural rate of unemployment is at 3 percent with a 3 percent level of inflation, then a negative demand shock would increase the unemployment rate while decreasing the inflation rate. Note that the SRPC curve itself does not shift initially; the point starts at A and then moves along the SRPC to the right to point B if there is a negative demand shock. The unemployment rate would now be 5 percent with inflation at a lower 2 percent at point B. However, the 5 percent level of unemployment is only temporary as the economy will eventually adjust in the long run with the SRAS shifting to the right as wages decrease in this recessionary climate. The corresponding shift on the Phillips Curve graph would be the SRPC curve shifting to the left with unemployment reverting back to the NAIRU at 3 percent and a lower rate of inflation as reflected by point C.

Supply Shocks

A **supply shock** occurs when there is either an increase or decrease of the price of an input and can result in either an increase or decrease of the **short-run aggregate supply (SRAS)** curve. If the price of a commodity, such as oil, suddenly increases, the SRAS curve would shift to the left, increasing the price level and reducing the GDP. Prolonged periods of high inflation and a stagnant economy are referred to as **stagflation**. Policymakers have a difficult time attacking stagflation because expansionary policies serve to increase employment but also increase inflation, whereas contractionary policies will halt inflation but also increase unemployment.

A positive supply shock takes place if there is a boost in technology that makes the production process more efficient. The SRAS curve would shift to the right, increasing the level of real GDP while also lowering the price level. Another way that the SRAS would shift to the right is if there is a steep decline in the price of oil.

Recall that the "natural" rate of unemployment is frictional unemployment plus structural unemployment. Let's assume that the NAIRU is at 5 percent. If employment sites become much more efficient at matching employers and employees, then the NAIRU can shift to the left and settle in at a lower 4 percent mark. Conversely, if there's an increase in the amount of structural employment because artificial intelligence takes over jobs previously occupied by humans, then the NAIRU might increase to 6 percent.

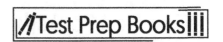

Money Growth and Inflation

How Inflation is a Monetary Phenomenon

Keynesians attribute inflation to increased demand for certain items and believe that inflation is best measured statistically by increases in price indices. **Monetarists**, on the other hand, believe that inflation is a function of money supply and occurs when there is too much money that floods the economy.

Quantity Theory of Money

The **quantity theory of money** postulates that the increase in the price level is directly attributable to the amount of money in the economy. For example, if the money supply doubles, then it stands to reason that the price level will also double. The **Fisher Equation** is $MV = PT$, where **M** represents the money supply, **V** represents velocity, which means the amount of times a dollar circulates in a year, **P** represents price, and **T** represents transactions. However, because of the difficulty in measuring the precise number of transactions in the economy, T is often substituted for Y, so that $MV = PY$. **Y** represents the amount of real output.

Monetarists believe that velocity is either fixed or at least very close to being fixed. In addition, Y is fixed in the long run. While GDP in the short run changes, the long-run GDP number does not change. Because V (left side of the equation) and Y (right side of the equation) are both constant, then an increase in the money supply (M) would necessarily lead to an increase in price level (P).

Calculate Using the Quantity Theory of Money

Let's assume that the initial money supply is $10,000, the velocity is 3, and the level of real output is $3,000. **Velocity** is the ratio of nominal GDP to the money supply and measures the number of times the average dollar is spent in a given year. Given these numbers, you would simply plug the three known variables into the equation MV = PY in order to solve for the unknown variable. When you rearrange the variables, $P = MV \div Y$, so $P = (\$10{,}000 \times 3) \div 3{,}000$, which means $P = \$30{,}000 \div 3{,}000$ or $10. If the money supply doubles to $20,000, with velocity and real output staying constant at 3 and 3,000, respectively, the price level would double. $P = (\$20{,}000 \times 3) \div 3{,}000 = \ \$20$. A doubling of the money supply leads to a doubling of the price level, or inflation. Monetarists, therefore, would argue that carefully regulating the money supply would be the best prescription for handling the economy.

Government Deficits and the National Debt

Government Budget Surplus and National Debt

A **balanced budget** is when the government spends exactly the same amount of money that it receives in tax revenue with the fiscal year. A **budget surplus** is when the government receives more in tax revenue than it spends in a fiscal year. A **budget deficit** is when the opposite is true and the government spends more than it receives in tax revenue from October 1 of the year to September 30, which marks the end of the fiscal year.

The United States **national debt** is the accumulation of all the budget surpluses and deficits over the entirety of the nation's history. Whereas the government budget surplus or deficit covers only one fiscal year, the national debt is the totality of government money that is owed to various parties. Since the first year of President Bush's presidency in 2001, the United States has produced a budget deficit. During the Bush years, a combination of increased Medicare spending, increased defense spending, and lowered tax rates ballooned the national debt from slightly under $6 trillion to nearly $12 trillion when Bush left office in January of 2009. President Barack Obama inherited a financial crisis when he took office. Under Obama's presidency, the budget deficit regularly exceeded $1 trillion annually, and by the time Obama left office in January of 2017, the national debt exploded to over $20 trillion. By the time President Donald Trump was inaugurated in 2017, the issue of balancing the budget was no longer seen as being a priority for voters, and Trump has not made any indications that balancing the budget is a priority under his administration. As of March 2020, the U.S. national debt is in excess of $23 trillion, and there is absolutely no indication that that number is going to decrease in the immediate future, barring a monumental change in the direction of American fiscal policy.

Burden of the National Debt

Most economists would agree that examining a country's GDP to debt ratio is a better indicator of a nation's debt problem than simply looking at the nominal figure. The GDP to debt ratio provides a better context with which to examine a country's debt burden than just the debt itself. For example, if Ranklinland has a $10 trillion debt, it might not be worse off than Heldville with a smaller debt of $100 billion. If Ranklinland's GDP is $20 trillion and Heldville's GDP is $50 billion, then Ranklinland's 50 percent GDP to debt ratio now appears far more manageable than Heldville's 200 percent GDP to debt ratio.

In 2008, a documentary film entitled *I.O.U.S.A.*, directed by Patrick Creadon, focused on the issue of the U.S. national debt. The protagonist of the film, David Walker, former U.S. Comptroller-General, barnstorms through the country along with Robert Bixby of the Concord Coalition to hold town hall meetings and let people know about the dangers of a high national debt. In addition, the film examines different periods in American history when the national debt was relatively high, as measured by the GDP to debt ratio, and how America generally responded by paying down debts after times of crises necessitated the government borrowing massive amounts of money.

On January 8, 1835, President Andrew Jackson achieved his goal of getting the United States out of debt. This was the first and only time that the United States had not had any public debt. Ever since the Jackson Administration, America has held a national debt even in times of government budget surpluses. The primary difference between the national debt today and the national debt in the past is that there has been no momentum toward paying off the debt even in times of relative peace. The debt to GDP ratio ballooned after World War I, World War II, and the Vietnam War, but America was quickly able to pay down the debt in the years following. Our current debt of over $23 trillion shows no sign of decreasing. The United States has consistently topped the 100 percent debt to GDP ratio in recent years.

One controversial theory regarding the national debt is **Modern Monetary Theory (MMT)**. Advocates of MMT believe that the traditional concern of the government running up the national debt is overblown. Because the government has a monopoly of currency, those who subscribe to MMT believe that the government should use its full arsenal of expansionary fiscal policy tools to achieve full employment even if it means simply printing currency to add to the money supply. One big concern that mainstream economists point out with MMT is the impact that expansionary fiscal policy has on the direction of interest rates. With increased budget deficits, economic theory predicts higher interest rates will "crowd out" private investment.

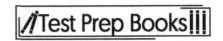

Crowding Out

Crowding Out and Long-Run Impacts

Crowding out refers to the impact that government intervention has on the economy, which serves to discourage investment in the private sector. When the government incurs a budget deficit, there is an increase in demand for loanable funds, which raises the real interest rate for all borrowers. With government competing with the private sector for a finite number of loans, crowding out refers to the quantity of private loans lost because of higher real interest rates that result from government intrusion in the loanable funds market.

Incurring budget deficits is not the principal problem, especially in the context of boosting the economy during cyclical downturns. However, if the government continues to run budget deficit after budget deficit even during economic expansions, higher interest rates will discourage businesses from investing in more equipment and machinery. There will be a decrease in capital formation in addition to the burgeoning of the national debt that will naturally result from running perpetual budget deficits.

There have been several attempts by Congress to introduce a Balanced Budget Amendment this past century. In 1995, the House of Representatives, under the leadership of House Speaker Newt Gingrich, passed a balanced budget amendment. The vote in the Senate, however, fell short by one vote of the two-thirds majority required to send the amendment for ratification to the states. Critics of the amendment pointed out that it would handcuff the ability of future Congresses to effectively deal with handling a recession or a natural disaster. In addition, many Democrats did not vote in favor of the amendment because of fear that cuts to welfare programs like Social Security or Medicare might be the casualty of a balanced budget. The last balanced budget occurred during the final year of President Bill Clinton's term in office.

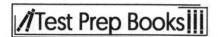

How Fiscal Policy May Cause Crowding Out

Imagine that the government incurs a $1 trillion budget deficit by increasing spending and cutting taxes. How would this scenario be depicted on the graph for loanable funds?

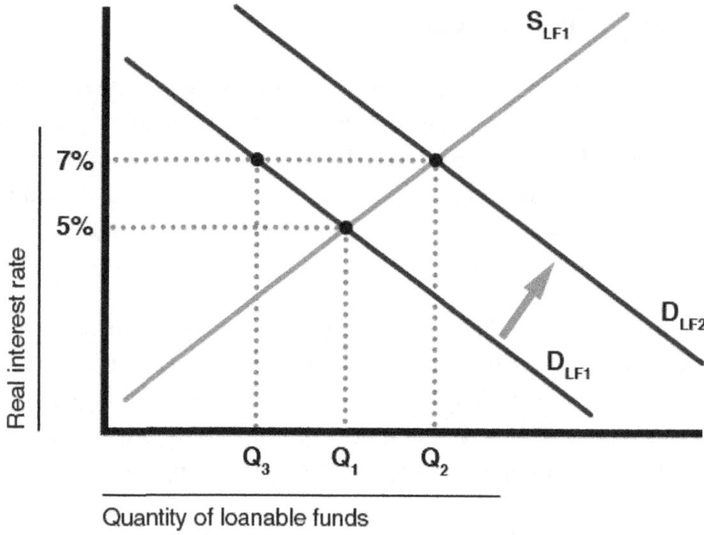

The original equilibrium is at 5 percent with quantity of Q_1 in loanable funds. With the government increasing its budget deficit, the demand for loanable funds curve will shift to the right, raising the equilibrium real interest rate to 7 percent at a quantity of Q_2. However, the quantity of private investment is at quantity Q_3. Private investment has been crowded out. $Q_2 - Q_3$ represents the amount of crowding out that has taken place as a result of the government's increase in budget deficit.

Economic Growth

Measures and Determinants of Economic Growth

There are three measures that are used to determine aggregate growth: aggregate employment, aggregate growth, and average labor productivity. Each of these three measures provides a look into the overall health of the economy. **Aggregate employment** (or **aggregate hours**) is the total amount of hours worked by employees over the course of the year. **Aggregate growth** is measured by the increase in GDP within a calendar year. An increase in aggregate employment would have the effect of increasing the GDP because more hours worked by individuals would lead to increased economic output. **Average labor productivity** refers to the change in economic output produced by an hour of labor, as measured by real GDP. Whereas employee productivity measures an individual's increased output, labor productivity refers to the amount of economic activity that increases for an entire country. An increased investment in physical capital, an increase in human capital through education, or technological progress are ways that labor productivity increases.

Determinants of Economic Growth

There are three main ways that countries achieve economic growth: increase in capital stock, increase in labor, and advancements in technology. Capital formation involves adding to the capital stock in the economy whether it is through increases in physical or human capital. Similarly, an influx in immigration or an increase in the rate of labor force participation increases the amount of labor in the economy. Labor and capital, however, can only provide so much growth. Because of diminishing marginal returns to both capital and labor, it's difficult to maintain long-run economic growth by simply increasing capital and labor. Increases in technology, however, have been responsible for the increased labor productivity and sustained long-run economic growth seen in most countries in the past few decades.

Calculate Per Capita GDP and Economic Growth

The **nominal GDP per capita** takes the nation's GDP (as measured in current dollars) and divides it by the population. The **real GDP per capita** takes the nation's GDP (as measured in constant dollars) and divides it by the population. The real GDP per capita is a better measure than the nominal GDP in measuring a country's standard of living because real GDP is adjusted for inflation, whereas nominal GDP relies on current prices.

Country	Real GDP Year 1	Real GDP Year 2	Population Year 1	Population Year 2
Mambaland	$24,000,000,000	$25,000,000,000	800,000	800,000
Kershawville	$22,000,000,000	$23,000,000,000	1,000,000	1,500,000
Kariyatown	$9,000,000,000	$9,500,000,000	100,000	200,000

Mambaland has an increase in real GDP from Year 1 to Year 2 of 4.2 percent from $24 billion to $25 billion. Kershawville experiences a similar increase in real GDP from Year 1 to Year 2 of 4.5 percent. Kariyatown experiences the most robust growth between Year 1 to Year 2 by increasing real output by 5.6 percent. Looking solely at the real GDP figures, one might conclude that Kariyatown experienced the highest amount of economic growth. This is clearly not the case, however, when you calculate the rate of real GDP per capita growth.

In Mambaland, the GDP per capita in Year 1 is $\$24\ billion \div 800{,}000$, which is $30,000. In Year 2, the GDP per capita increased to $\$25\ billion \div 800{,}000$, which is $31,250. The increase in real GDP per capita is 4.2 percent, which mirrors the percentage increase in real GDP.

In Kershawville, the GDP per capita in Year 1 is $\$22\ billion \div 1\ million$, which is $22,000. In Year 2, the GDP per capita decreased to $\$23\ billion \div 1.5\ million$, which is $15,333.33. Although the real GDP increase was comparable in Mambaland, Kershawville experienced a sizeable decline in real GDP growth of 30.3 percent.

In Kariyatown, things are even more bleak. The GDP per capita in Year 1 is $\$9\ billion \div 100{,}000 = \$90{,}000$. In Year 2, the GDP per capita dropped to $\$9.5\ billion \div 200{,}000$, which is $47,500. Kariyatown, despite having the highest real GDP growth of the three countries, dropped a disastrous 47.2 percent in real GDP per capita growth primarily because of the doubling of the population.

While this particular example uses numbers that are quite extreme, it highlights the point that per capita real GDP growth can sometimes be a better measure of economic growth within a country than simply looking at the real GDP. Although there are other ways to measure economic success and prosperity, real GDP per capita can pinpoint how much an individual citizen within the country contributes to economic production.

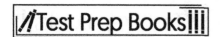

How the PPC is Related to the Long-Run Aggregate Supply (LRAS) Curve

When there is an increase in **long-run aggregate supply (LRAS)**, there is a corresponding increase in the production possibilities curve on the country's production possibilities graph. A rightward shift of the LRAS curve would occur when there is an increase in capital, labor, or technology. All points on a production possibilities frontier represent points of efficiency, so if an economy develops the ability to produce more goods than was originally possible, then the PPC will shift to the right, increasing the amount of potential goods produced in the economy.

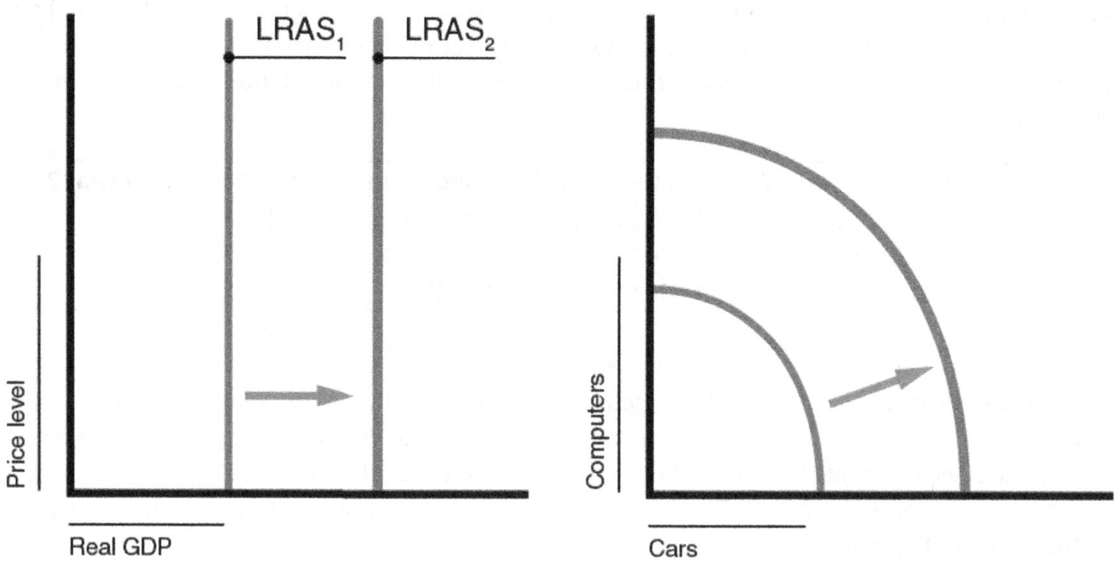

Imagine that there is an increase in technology and labor force in the country of Machineville. The only two products that are produced in Machineville are cars and computers. How would the production possibilities curve shift? Because there is an increase in available labor and technology, the PPC would increase and shift to the left, expanding the total number of cars and computers that the country is able to produce.

Public Policy and Economic Growth

Public Policies Aimed at Influencing Long-Run Economic Growth

Public policies that impact productivity and labor force participation affect real GDP per capita and economic growth. In January of 2020, the labor force participation rate in the United States increased from 63.2 percent to 63.4 percent. The government can use monetary or fiscal policy to alter individual incentives to work and save money.

If the Federal Reserve maintains low interest rates for extended periods of time, consumers might be encouraged to spend more money because of cheap credit being so readily available. However, a **liquidity trap** may occur if interest rates are lowered and consumers are still scrambling to pay off debt. During the Great Recession, the Fed lowered the target federal funds rate to a near 0–0.25 percent, creating a situation in which the central bank could no longer lower interest rates to stimulate the economy, rendering one of its policy tools (at least temporarily) ineffective.

Another criticism of using expansionary monetary policy to stimulate long-run economic growth is that lowering interest rates distorts the true value of money. In the early 2000s, the Federal Reserve maintained a consistent policy of lowering the federal funds rate, which encouraged many households to borrow cheap money. This undoubtedly helped fuel America's housing bubble that burst in 2007, leading to the Great Recession.

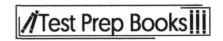

Expansionary fiscal policies are another way to increase long-run economic output from the demand side. When taxes decrease, consumers have more disposable income. When government increases spending, there is an increase in the availability of jobs in the economy. The criticism of this approach is that economic growth comes at the expense of higher interest rates if the government crowds out private investment. In addition, some economists claim that an increase in government spending permanently grows the size of the government because once money is allocated toward public purposes, it is difficult to quell the growth.

Supply-Side Fiscal Policies

During the 1980 Republican primary, Governor Ronald Reagan and George H.W. Bush battled to become the GOP's standard-bearer. Governor Reagan was the darling of the conservative movement and espoused the virtue of **supply-side economics**, which emphasizes the benefits of tax cuts in stimulating the economy from the supply side rather than the demand side of the economy. While Keynesians argue that tax cuts increase the aggregate demand curve and stimulate the economy in that manner, supply-siders argue that lowered tax rates will actually increase the amount of total revenue for the government in the form of increased employment and real economic output. In addition to calling it "voodoo" economics, critics of supply-side fiscal policies pejoratively refer to tax cuts as a means of achieving long-run economic growth as "trickle-down" economics. Despite Bush's victory in the Iowa caucus, which kicks off the presidential election process, Reagan ultimately won the nomination and chose Bush as his vice-presidential running mate despite Bush's not-so-favorable comments on Reagan's supply-side fiscal policies.

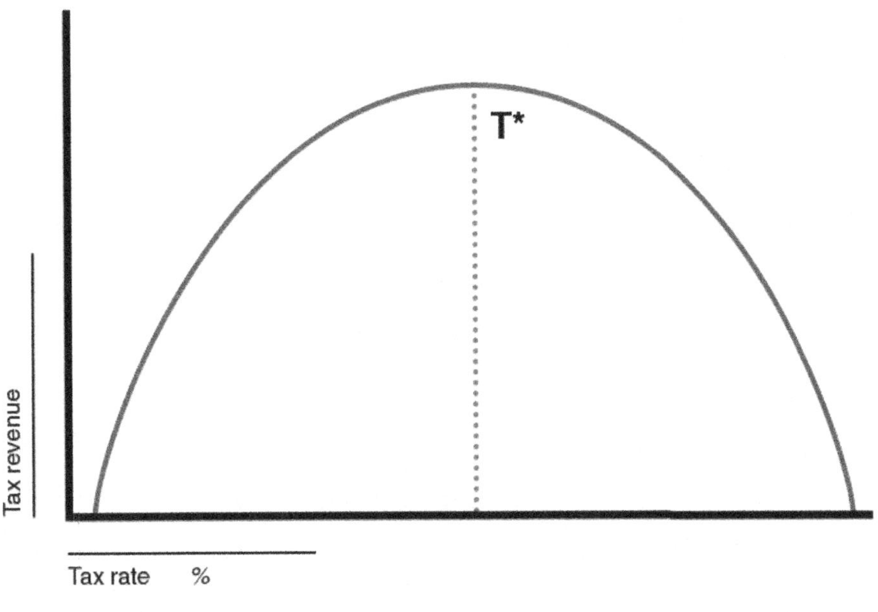

Laffer Curve

The **Laffer Curve** was coined by Jude Wanniski, a writer for the *Wall Street Journal*. Arthur Laffer (who apparently has no recollection of this encounter) allegedly drew a parabola-shaped curve on a napkin for Dick Cheney, who worked for President Gerald Ford in 1974, to argue against a proposed tax increase by the Ford administration. At both extremes of the Laffer Curve, the government would collect $0 in tax revenue. At a 0 percent tax rate, for obvious reasons, no money would be collected. At a 100 percent tax rate, the amount of money collected would also be $0 because individuals would no longer have an incentive to work, as the entirety of their earnings would go to government coffers.

Although the Laffer Curve has an optimal tax rate shown in the middle of the curve, the actual point of revenue maximization is difficult, if not impossible, to *actually* detect. Supporters of the Laffer Curve contend that the peak of the curve is to the left of whatever the current level of taxation actually is. Then, if the government lowers taxes, revenues will increase. Detractors would argue the reverse; that the peak of the curve is to the right of whatever the current level of taxation actually is. If that were the case, lowering taxes would serve to decrease government revenue and increase the budget deficit.

In the 1986 John Hughes classic, *Ferris Bueller's Day Off*, Ben Stein plays the role of perhaps the world's most famous economics teacher. In his lecture, Stein succinctly summarizes the theory of the Laffer Curve and talks about how contractionary fiscal policy (raising of tariffs under the Hawley-Smoot Tariff Act) during the Great Depression worsened the severity of the economic downturn. What's most amazing about Stein's part in this movie that launched his acting career was that Stein completely ad-libbed the scene, performing his "boring" economics lecture to perfection in one single take.

Macroeconomics: Open Economy—International Trade and Finance

Balance of Payments Accounts

Current Account (CA), the Capital and Financial Account (CFA), and the Balance of Payments (BOP)

The four components of the **current account** are a country's trade balance, net income, direct transfer payments, and asset income. **Trade balance** refers to the relative balance between exports and imports of a country. **Net income** includes the interest and dividend payments received by residents from other countries minus the interest and dividend payments sent to residents of other countries. **Direct transfer payments** include money that is sent directly from immigrants back to their home country. In addition, direct transfers include government aid to countries. Finally, **asset income** refers to increases in assets like bank deposits and real estate. If foreign ownership of U.S. assets increases, there will be a decrease in asset income. Conversely, if American ownership of foreign assets increases, there will be an increase in asset income.

The biggest part of a country's current account is its trade balance. If a country's imports exceed its exports, then the country has a **trade deficit**. If a country's exports exceed its imports, then the country has a **trade surplus**. In 2018, the world's leading importing country was the United States, with imports valued at approximately $2.6 trillion, accounting for nearly one-eighth of all world imports. In that same year, China ranked as the world's leading exporter, shipping out nearly $2 trillion worth of goods and services. Typically, countries enact policies that favor having more exports than imports, so having a trade surplus is synonymous with having a favorable balance of trade. When the opposite is true and countries have a trade deficit, this is referred to as an unfavorable balance of trade. The reality is a bit more nuanced. If a country enacts protectionist policies to generate more exports relative to imports, for example, the narrow goal of increasing exports might be achieved at the expense of an overall weaker economy.

If a country's net exports increase, there is a boost in the nation's aggregate output. Recall that the macroeconomic equation for an open economy is:

$$Y = C + I + G + NX\ (or\ X - M)$$

An increase in exports will shift the aggregate demand curve to the right, increasing the real GDP and price level. On the other hand, a decrease in exports will shift the aggregate demand curve to the left, decreasing the real GDP and price level.

The **capital and financial account (CFA)** refers to the measurement of increases or decreases in international ownership of assets and also measures financial transactions that do not affect income, production, or savings. If the CFA increases, this indicates that foreign money is flowing into the United States. Conversely, if the CFA decreases, U.S. money is entering into foreign markets.

The **balance of payments (BOP)** refers to all transactions made between entities in one country and other countries within a calendar year. The sum of all transactions recorded in the balance of payments will theoretically equal to zero. However, changes in currency values and differences in accounting practices preclude this from becoming a reality. The balance of payments equation is expressed as either of the following:

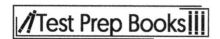

$$Current\ Account\ (CA) + Capital\ and\ Financial\ Account\ (CFA) = 0$$

$$Current\ Account\ (CA) = -Financial\ Account\ (FA)$$

When the financial account offsets the trade deficit, the country sells off its assets in order to pay for foreign goods and services. The household equivalent would be a family deciding to sell its house so as to purchase annual passes to Disneyland. Assets are "traded" for temporary consumption, which is not good for long-term economic growth.

How Changes in the Components of the CA and CFA Affect a Country's BOP

A country's balance of payment can either be a deficit or a surplus. If a country imports more goods and services than it exports, it must borrow from other countries to pay for imports. This is known as a **balance of accounts deficit**. When a country exports more than it imports, it has the ability to pay for all domestic production without borrowing from other countries. This situation is referred to as a **balance of accounts surplus**.

If a credit occurs in the current account, then a debit of the opposite amount will take place in the financial account. The reverse is also true. A debit in the current account necessitates a credit in the financial account. For example, if there is a $1 million decrease in the current account because of an increase in exports, there will be a corresponding increase of $1 million in the financial account.

Calculate the CA, the CFA, and the BOP

Imagine the country of Auturkey imports $100,000 and simultaneously exports the same amount of $100,000. The current account balance would equal zero as would the capital financial account balance. If, however, Auturkey runs up a trade deficit of $10,000 by importing $110,000 while still only exporting $100,000, the country has to borrow money to finance its trade deficit. Because Auturkey incurs a current account deficit of $10,000, there must be a corresponding financial inflow of $10,000 to bring the balance of payments balance back to zero.

If the country of Tradetopia initially imports and exports $2 million worth of goods and services, the current and capital financial accounts would equal to zero. A trade surplus of $200,000 for Tradetopia will cause the country to take in more money that it sends to other countries. This current account surplus will prompt Tradetopia to send that extra $200,000 windfall to other countries to buy assets from countries like Auturkey. Tradetopia therefore is running a financial account deficit of $200,000.

Exchange Rates

Exchange Rate, Currency Appreciation, and Currency Depreciation

The **exchange rate** is the value of one nation's currency to another nation's currency. For example, the exchange rate between American currency and European currency might be that one dollar has the equivalent value of one euro. If the dollar becomes the stronger of the two currencies—so that one dollar purchases 1.50 euros—this is **currency appreciation**. If, on the other hand, the dollar becomes the weaker of the two currencies, and now one dollar purchases only 0.75 euros, this is **currency depreciation**.

The euro was adopted in December of 1995 and is the official currency of nineteen of twenty-seven member states of the European Union. Having a common currency comes with its pros and cons. The reduction of exchange rate risk is a huge benefit in that there is more stability associated with having just one currency. Prior to the euro, trading with European countries came with a significant amount of exchange rate risk and made trade with Europe subject to sometimes random fluctuations in the value of currencies. One huge downside of a common currency was the ceding of monetary policy and inability of member countries to influence the strength (or weakness) of its currency.

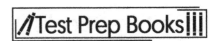

When introduced, the dollar was originally stronger than the euro. In January 2008, the dollar was at its weakest point relative to the euro, with 1 euro purchasing $1.60. Compare that to January of 2002 when 1 euro purchased only $0.90. When the currency is strong, it is extremely difficult for European businesses to export successfully, as its products have to compete with other countries' products that are produced with a relatively cheaper currency. As of March of 2020, one euro trades for $1.11, so the dollar has definitely strengthened from its weakest point in January of 2008. On the flip side, January 2008 was probably the worst time for an American traveler to visit France. American currency did not fare too strongly at that time. Today, the dollar is much stronger. What's beneficial for American business is not beneficial to the American traveler. If the trend continues with the American dollar becoming stronger relative to the euro, it might make sense for adventure-loving Americans to pack their bags and travel to Europe to take advantage of a strong currency.

Relative Value of Currencies

A **fixed currency exchange rate** exists when a government dictates the value of its currency, whereas a **floating exchange rate** is maintained by the free market through the laws of supply and demand.

Fixed currency exchange rates are mainly found in Africa and the Middle East. The central bank will peg its rate to another country's currency, most notably to the U.S. dollar. However, currency can be fixed to the euro, the yen, or a basket of various currencies. Most countries do not fix the value of their currency because of its intrusive nature into the financial markets. Fixed currency regimes are generally associated with an overly meddling government.

A floating currency exchange is one in which the value of a country's currency is determined by supply and demand. Most of the world's currencies are floating, including the U.S. dollar, the Japanese yen, the Korean won, the euro, and the Swiss franc. However, there are varying degrees of government involvement with floating currencies in that certain countries will use their central bank in an attempt to guide their currencies in one direction or another.

From the end of World War II until the early 1970s, the **Bretton Woods system** essentially established a fixed currency system in which the value of a country's currency was closely tied to the value of gold. In August 1971, however, the Bretton Woods agreement was effectively terminated when the United States no longer honored exchanges of its currency to gold; the United States dollar became a **fiat currency**. Fiat money has no intrinsic value and holds value because the government determines, by fiat, that it has value. President Richard Nixon's decision to sever the relationship between the U.S. dollar and gold allowed the United States to control its money supply, something that it would have been unable to do as effectively under a gold standard.

China does not operate under a floating currency regime. The Chinese government has actively managed the value of its yuan in order to benefit its exports. An undervalued currency helps in boosting its exports. If the Chinese yuan were allowed to float freely, it would most likely appreciate in value. To prevent its appreciation and resultant decrease in exports, the Chinese government sells its Chinese yuan, and buys U.S. dollars, keeping massive amounts of American currency in its foreign reserves.

Calculate the Value of One Currency Relative to Another

Purchasing power parity (PPP) is an economic theory postulating that exchange rates between two countries are in equilibrium when the purchasing powers of the two countries are equal, usually for a specific good or a market basket of goods. PPP depends on something known as the **Law of One Price**. While great in theory, there are several reasons why prices don't converge in different countries. First, there are various transportation costs, taxes, and tariffs that alter the price of products in a country. Second, some products like real estate, college education, and amusement parks cannot be shipped. And finally, import costs are subject to exchange rate fluctuations which, in turn, changes the price that companies charge for their products.

In 1986, *The Economist* created the Big Mac Index as a guide to measure the accuracy of the purchasing power parity theory. Because a Big Mac is quite nearly the same in all of the 121 countries that have a McDonald's, it serves as a practical proxy to test the idea that the price of all goods and services (as measured by McDonald's Big Mac) should eventually move toward the same price in every country.

Let's say that a Big Mac costs 20 yuan in China and $5.00 in the United States. The implied exchange rate is 4 yuan to 1 U.S. dollar, using "Burgernomics" to guide the value of the currency. If the actual exchange rate between the United States and China is 6 yuan to 1 U.S. dollar, the yuan is undervalued. According to the Big Mac Index, the U.S. dollar is undervalued by 33 percent compared to the Chinese yuan. Why buy a Big Mac in the United States for $5.00 when you can exchange that same $5 for 30 yuan, pay only

20 yuan for the Big Mac, and pocket the 10 yuan? Because the transaction cost of buying a "cheaper" burger in China is quite high.

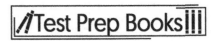

Foreign Exchange Market

Foreign Exchange Market, Demand for Currency, and Supply of Currency

The **foreign exchange market** is the market in which currency is exchanged. The equilibrium is the point at which **demand for currency** equals the **supply of currency**. The demand for currency represents individuals (or entities) who are looking to obtain a country's currency; the supply of currency represents individuals (or entities) who are looking to sell a country's currency.

Relationship Between the Exchange Rate and the Quantity of Currency Demanded

On a foreign exchange market, the *x*-axis is represented by the currency of a country. On the *y*-axis, the currency is priced in terms of another country's currency.

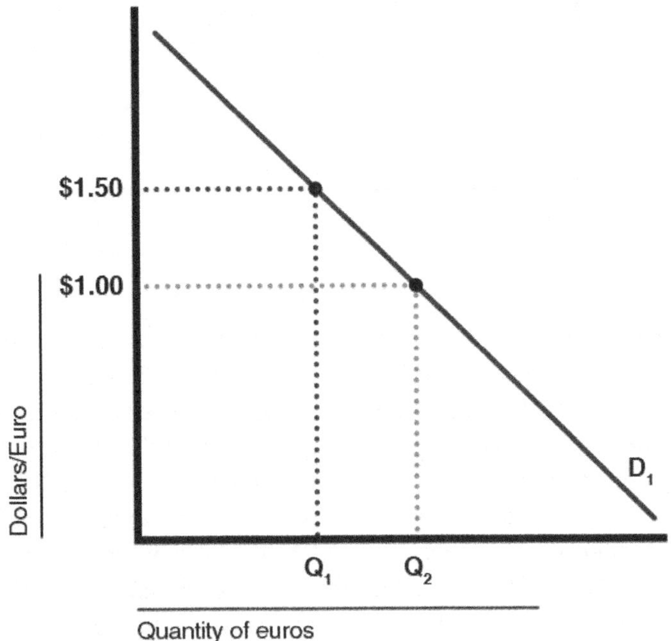

Progressing from left to right on the demand curve, there is an increase in quantity demanded for euros. As fewer dollars are required to buy euros, there is an increase in quantity demanded for euros. If it costs $1.50 to purchase 1 euro, then let's say that Q_1 (or 1 million euros) is the quantity demanded. However, if it now only costs $1 to purchase that same euro, then there is an increase in quantity demanded of euros (although the demand itself stays the same). Now, the quantity demanded is at Q_2 (or 1.5 million euros). If the reverse is true and more dollars are required to purchase euros, then there will be less quantity demanded of euros. European travelers benefit from a "strong" euro, whereas European businesses that export will prefer a "weak" euro because they will sell their products in their depreciated currency. Similarly, American travelers into Europe prefer a weak Euro, and American businesses prefer a strong Euro.

Equilibrium Exchange Rate

The **equilibrium exchange rate** follows the traditional supply and demand model in which the equilibrium point is found at the intersection of supply and demand. In the United States market, U.S. dollars would be represented on the *x*-axis. If euros are being used to purchase dollars, euro/dollars would be represented on the *y*-axis.

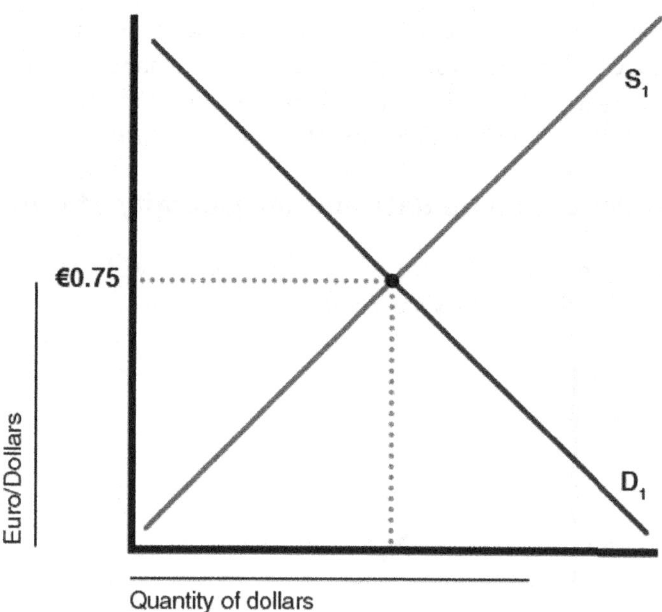

If Europeans purchase $2 million worth of U.S. dollars, let's imagine that they use that to purchase $1 million worth of goods and services and another $1 million worth of U.S. assets. A total of $2 million would have been used to purchase U.S. dollar. Now, let's say that there is a sale of $2 million of U.S. dollars to buy European goods and services, as well as assets. If $1.5 million was used to buy European goods and services, the United States would have a negative balance of –$500,000 on its current account (CA) because imports would exceed exports by that amount. Now, assume that $500,000 is used to buy European assets. Because Europeans spent $1 million to purchase U.S. assets, the financial account (FA) would be in a surplus of $500,000. Therefore, at the equilibrium exchange rate, the balance of payments on the current account plus the balance of payments on the financial account equals zero.

How Exchange Rates Adjust to Restore Equilibrium in the Foreign Exchange Market

What would happen in the foreign exchange market for U.S. dollars if interest rates in the United States increased relative to interest rates around the world? European investors would demand more of U.S. currency, shifting the demand for U.S. dollars to the right. If the existing exchange rate prevailed, then there would be a disequilibrium in the market. The dollar would have to "strengthen" in order to bring the foreign exchange market for dollars back to equilibrium.

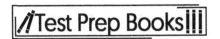

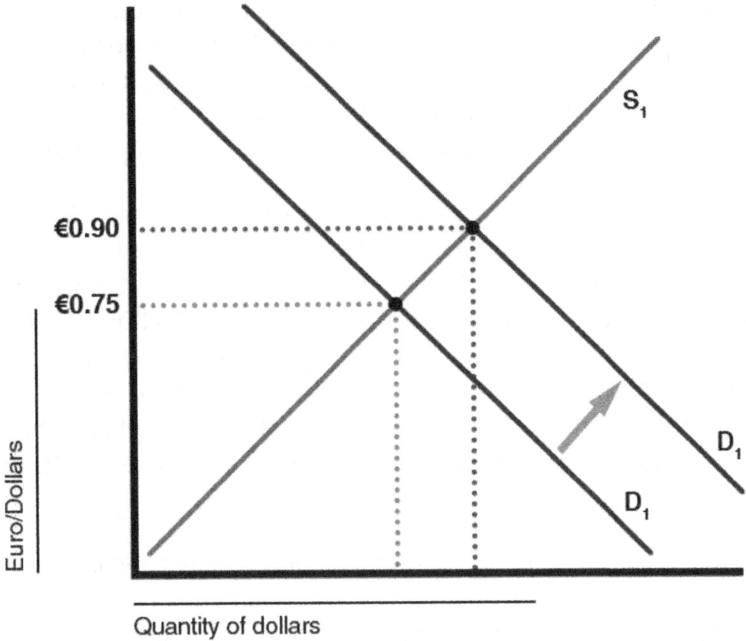

Imagine that the exchange rate for $1 equals €0.75. If interest rates increase in the United States and the dollar therefore becomes a relatively better investment than other currencies, the demand for dollars would increase and the demand curve would shift to the right. The new exchange rate would be increased such that $1 now equals €0.90. American travelers would benefit from this situation. Eric Palmer, who just got married, and is honeymooning through Europe, can now afford to buy more than he otherwise could have with his beautiful bride, Natalie. Adhering to a strict budget of $1,000 (in U.S. dollars), the Palmers can now purchase more given the more favorable exchange rate. Instead of being able to cash in that $1,000 for €750, Eric and Natalie can "buy" €150 more euros for a total of €900. With that extra money, the Palmers can now splurge on that romantic trip to the Eiffel Tower in Paris and buy that *confit de canard*, a tasty French dish of duck, instead of having to skimp on their budget and share a meager baguette.

Effect of Changes in Policies and Economic Conditions on the Foreign Exchange Market

Determinants of Currency Demand and Supply

A country's balance of trade affects the exchange rate for its currency on the foreign exchange market. When the amount of exports does not equal the amount of imports, there exists an imbalance in the supply and demand for a country's currency on the world market.

If a country has more exports than imports, the demand exceeds supply for its goods and services. The same situation, therefore, exists for the nation's currency. Hence, the currency would naturally appreciate in value. On the flip side, if a country has more imports than exports, supply exceeds demand for its goods and services. The same situation, therefore, exists for the nation's currency, and the nation's money would depreciate in value.

Let's also assume that $\$1 = 1000$ won (Korean currency). Now, let's also assume that bobbleheads are the only products sold on the open market. Imagine that South Korea's imports exceed its exports. If that is the case, Korea buys more American currency (or dollars) that it sells of its own currency (won). As a result, the value of the won might fall such that $1 will now fetch 1100 won, which is 10 percent more than before. Conversely, a Korean will now have to sell 1100 won to get that same $1.

However, the story does not stop there. Because South Korea has a depreciated currency, South Korea's bobblehead makers will have an advantage over their American counterparts because of its depreciated currency. Before the currency depreciated, a South Korean could buy a $100 American-made Elvis Presley bobblehead for 100,000 won. Now, the same "King of Rock N' Roll" bobblehead sells for $110 with a stronger dollar. An American, on the other hand, originally paid $100 for a Korean-made Elvis Presley bobblehead (or 100,000 won). But, with the currency depreciation, $91 will be enough for an Elvis bobblehead. This is good for Korean businesses who have found a market in the U.S. with its relatively cheaper currency. South Korea's current account will run a surplus and its capital financial account will necessarily run a deficit because $CA = -FA$.

The balance of trade impacts currency exchange rates as supply and demand can cause currency values to fluctuate. If a country exports more than it imports, its currency demand will consequently increase. If a country imports more than it exports, its currency demand will necessarily decrease. It is important to note that under a fixed or pegged exchange rate system money does not adjust as readily as it would under a floating exchange rate regime.

How Changes in Demand and Supply in Foreign Exchange Market Affect the Equilibrium Exchange Rate

The foreign exchange market is no different than the market for any other good and service. If there is an increase in demand, the price and quantity of a currency increases. If there is a decrease in demand, the price and quantity of a currency decreases. When supply increases, there is a decrease in price and increase in quantity; when supply decreases, there is an increase in price and decrease in quantity.

Fiscal Policy and Monetary Policy and What They Influence

Government policies have benefits and costs. Suppose that the United States is mired in a recession. If President Donald Trump and Congress agree on increasing government spending and decreasing income taxes, aggregate demand will increase, increasing both the real output and the price level. The real interest rate will increase and therefore increase the demand for U.S. currency, which will appreciate its value.

Recall that an increase in the budget deficit will also increase the demand for loanable funds in the loanable funds market. Real interest rates will increase as a result of the crowding-out effect. Businesses that would have happily expanded their business at 5 percent might be reluctant to do so at 7 percent. While there is increase in the *total* amount of loanable funds, there is a decrease in the quantity of loans in the private sector. Q_3 represents the amount of private loans while Q_2, represents the total amount of loans taken out. $Q_2 - Q_3$ represents the amount of loans with the higher real interest rate, or the crowding-out effect.

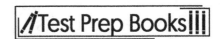

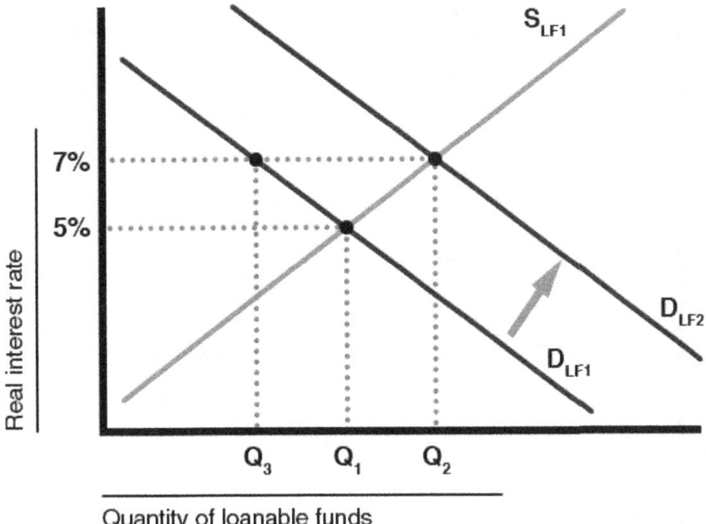

With interest rates now higher, worldwide investors will now be attracted to the relatively higher interest rates found in the United States. The demand for U.S. currency will therefore increase and the value of the dollar will appreciate.

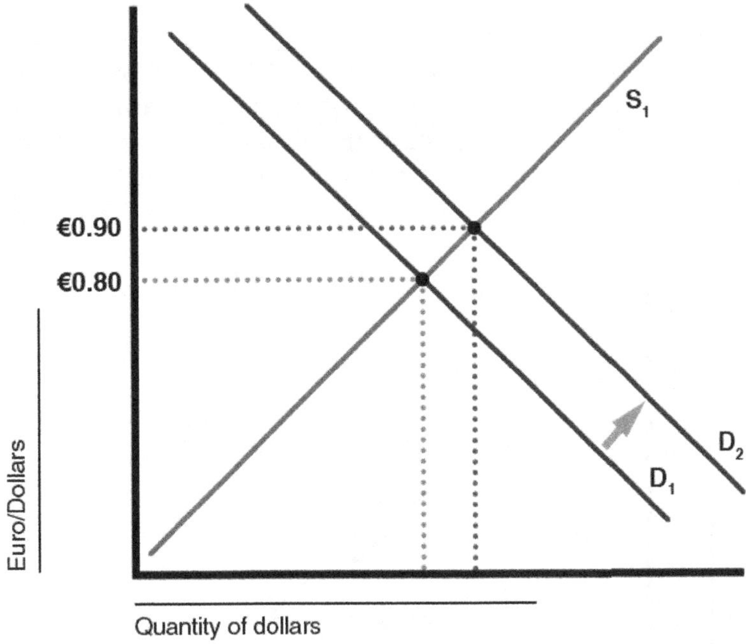

Expansionary fiscal policy will have the same impact as expansionary monetary policy in terms of the AD/AS graph, but the interest rate impact will lead to the opposite impact in terms of interest rates and exchange rates. The nominal interest rate will decrease when the money supply increases. The lowered interest rates will make the U.S. dollar relatively less attractive than other currencies, so the dollar will depreciate in value.

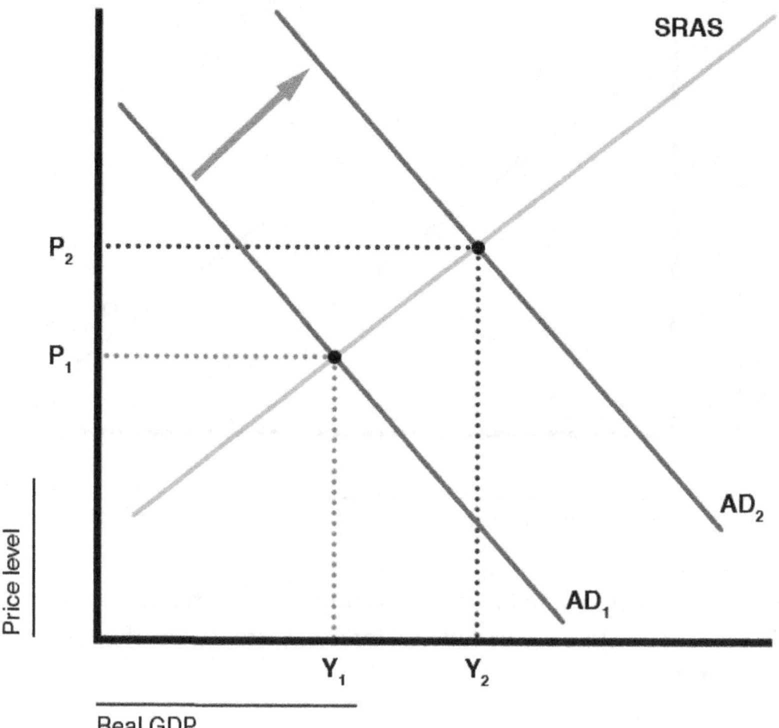

The difference comes in the subsequent graph that is impacted. Federal Reserve actions affect the money market graph. The loanable funds graph is the proper graph to analyze when fiscal policy is implemented. An increase in the money supply affects the money market graph, shifting the MS curve to the right. The nominal interest rate decreases with the increased availability of money in the economy.

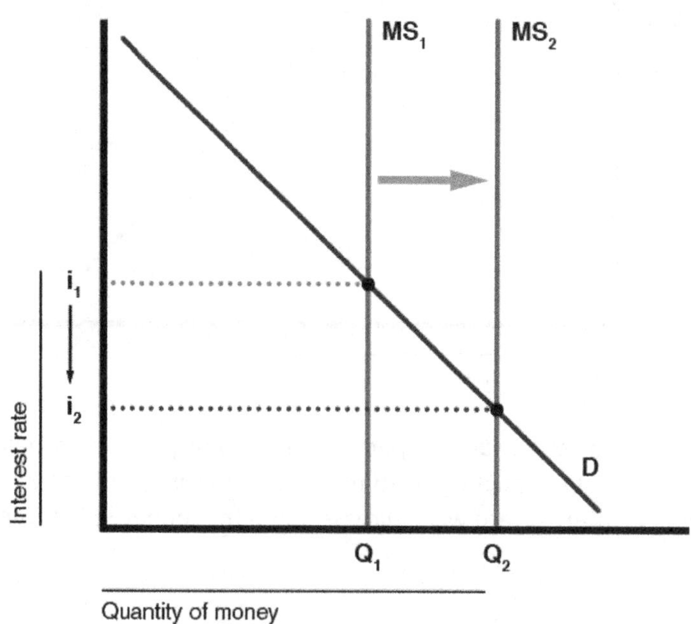

With interest rates now lower, investors in Europe are less inclined to invest in American assets due to the lowered interest rate. There is now a decreased incentive to put money into American markets when the decrease in U.S. interest rates has now made European assets relatively more attractive. Europeans are now less likely to demand U.S. dollars, so the demand for dollars will shift to the left and the dollar will depreciate in value.

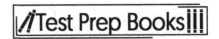

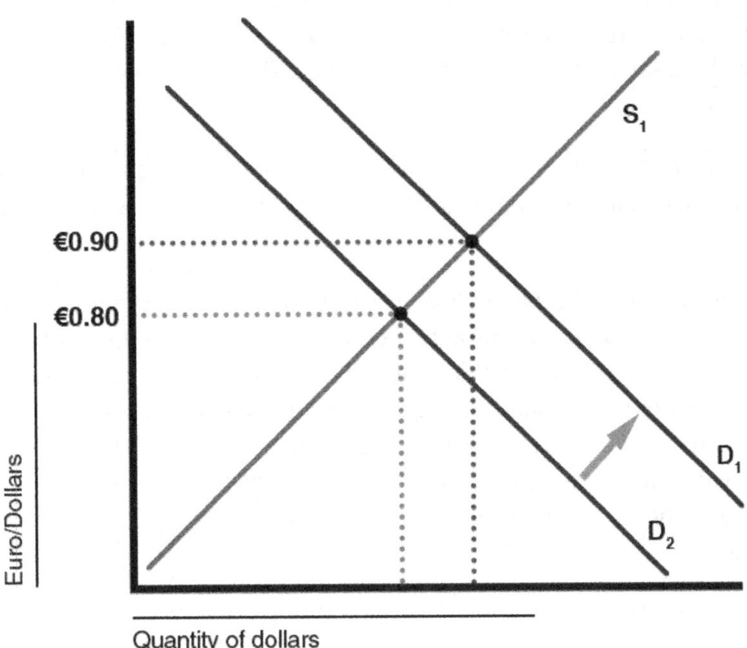

Changes in the Foreign Exchange Market and Net Exports

Changes in the Value of a Currency

Should the United States pursue government policy that creates a strong or a weak dollar? This is a normative question, so there is really no right or wrong answer. We can, however, examine both scenarios and see what the impact would be on the country's net exports and aggregate demand.

If the demand for the dollar increases, there will be an increase in the value of the dollar. The dollar will have appreciated. This is great news, right? Not so fast. If the dollar is now more expensive relative to other currencies worldwide, this will make it difficult for American businesses to compete on the world market when cheaper alternatives are present. Recall the macroeconomic equation, $Y = C + I + G + NX$. When exports go down, NX decreases, which means that Y goes down. Aggregate demand has decreased as a result of the dollar's appreciation. What's good for American travelers abroad is bad for American businesses that export its goods.

If the demand for the dollar decreases, there will be a decrease in the value of the dollar. The dollar will have depreciated. This is terrible news, right? Not so fast. If the dollar is now cheaper relative to other currencies worldwide, this will make it easier for American businesses to compete on the world market when American products are relatively cheaper than products made abroad. Let's go back to the macroeconomic equation, Y = C + I + G + NX. When exports increase, NX increases, which means that Y goes up. Aggregate demand has increased as a result of the dollar's depreciation.

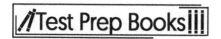

Real Interest Rates and International Capital Flows

Differences in Real Interest Rates Across Countries

We live in an interconnected world in which there is a free flow of capital between countries. When there are arbitrage opportunities, investors from foreign countries will take advantage in order to make themselves better off. High interest rates in a country will attract money from outside countries and will consequently increase the demand for its domestic currency. This, of course, assumes that the currency is flexible rather than fixed.

In an open economy, differences in real interest rates across countries change the relative values of domestic and foreign assets. Financial capital will flow toward the country with the relatively higher interest rate.

Interest rates vary in each and every country. Real interest rates are determined by the intersection of supply and demand in the loanable funds market. In countries where the supply of loanable funds is relatively greater than the demand for loanable funds, the real interest rate will tend to be low. Conversely, in countries where the demand for loanable funds exceeds its supply, real interest rates will be high. Investors in countries with the relatively low real interest rates will hunger after the returns found in the countries with the relatively high interest rates. Individuals worldwide seek to make themselves better off, and therefore financial capital will flow from low interest rate economies to high interest rate economies.

Central Banks

Let's imagine a world with only two countries: Hungary and Libya. In Hungary, interest rates are relatively high at 6 percent. In Libya, interest rates are relatively low at 4 percent. In a world in which there are no capital flows between the two countries, Hungary money would stay in Hungary while Libya money would stay in Libya. However, if money were allowed to flow from one country to another, what would happen? Would Hungary money flow to Libya or would the reverse be true? Would Libya money find its way into Hungary? Let's take a look.

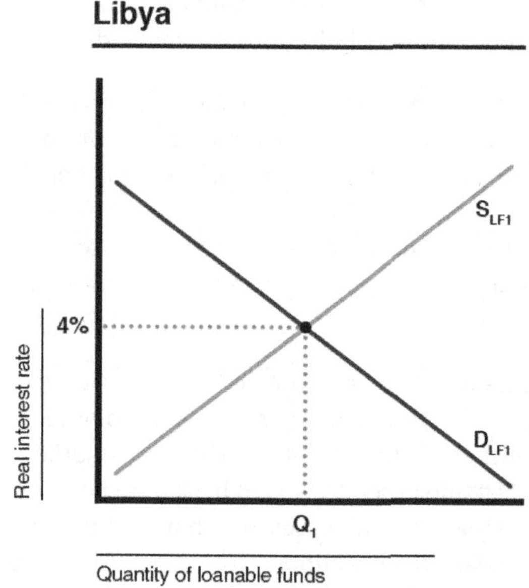

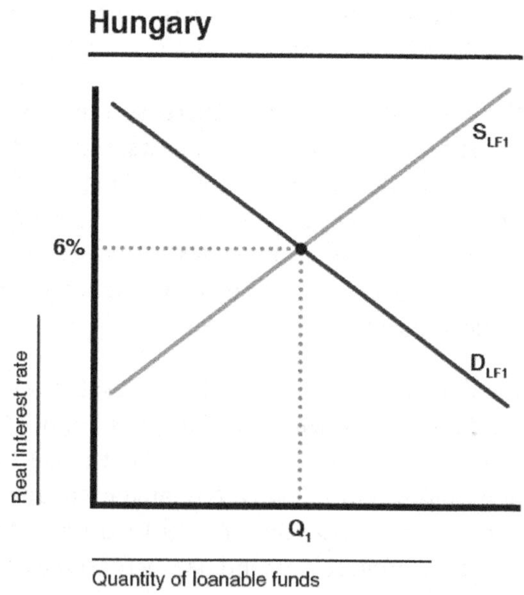

Economic theory indicates that the interest rate of 4 percent in Libya and 6 percent in Hungary will not hold. If there are no restrictions or barriers between lenders and borrowers from both countries, Hungarian borrows will be hungry for loans from Libyan lenders, who are attracted by the relatively higher Hungarian interest rates. Libya will send some of its loanable funds to Hungary. This capital inflow will increase the quantity of loanable funds supplied to Hungarian borrowers. This influx of loanable funds will decrease the interest rate in Hungary. Simultaneously, there will be a reduction in funds available in Libya, pushing the interest rate higher in the low-interest country of Libya. International capital flows will bring the high Hungarian interest rates and low Libyan interest rates into an equilibrium in which there exists no gap between the two countries. Exchange benefits the traders.

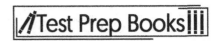

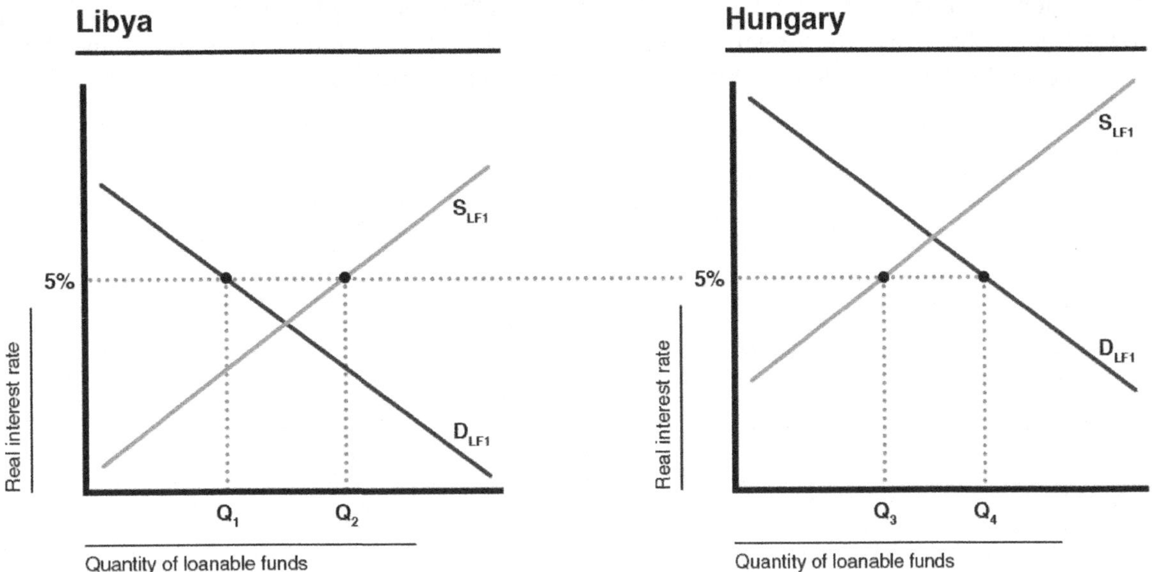

Assuming that there is a free flow of capital between both countries, interest rates will settle in at 5 percent. There will be capital inflow into Hungary and capital outflow out of Libya. $Q_2 - Q_1$ represents the amount of capital that flows out of low-interest Libya while $Q_4 - Q_3$ represents the amount of capital that flows into high-interest Hungary. However, the newfound reality with the international interest rate is that both countries will now have the exact same interest rate in the loanable funds market. Just as there is an international flow of goods and services, there exists an international flow of capital between countries. Capital flows from countries with low interest rates, like Libya, into countries with high interest rates, like Hungary.

Countries that have rapidly growing economies tend to have more investment opportunities than countries with slow rates of growth. These rapidly expanding economies will have a higher demand for capital and thus offer higher returns to investors than countries with slower rates of growth if capital cannot flow freely from country to country. Once barriers of capital flow are lifted, capital tends to flow from slowly growing economies to the countries that have higher rates of growth.

In the late nineteenth and early twentieth centuries, the U.S. economy was growing rapidly. As the population increased and expanded westward, the ensuing Industrial Revolution created a demand for investment spending on business expansion. Meanwhile, Great Britain was slowing down as industrialization had taken place in the earlier part of the nineteenth century. Britain had the excess supply of capital, and the United States had the excess demand. There was capital outflow from low-interest Britain, and capital inflow to high-interest United States.

It is important to keep in mind that the loanable funds model shows the *net* capital flows between countries. It would be way too simplistic to say that money flows from low-interest Libya to high-interest Hungary, or only that the British lend money to Americans. The interest rate, while a huge determinant of capital flow, is one of many determinants of individual decisions on investing. Individuals might seek diversification in both domestic and foreign stocks. While a stock market crash might affect equities worldwide, investors might hedge their bets by putting money in both European and American stocks. In addition, political risk in certain countries may dissuade investors from piling money into an unstable region that might bring about double-digit growth. While the growth rate might be significantly less in the United States than the growth rate in some South American countries for example, investors might simply opt for the safe albeit low interest rates found in the United States.

Microeconomics: Supply and Demand

Demand

Factors Related to Consumer Decision Making and the Law of Demand

Imagine walking by a car dealership and seeing the newest Lamborghini model on the floor of the dealership. For a moment, you imagine yourself pulling up to prom with your date in this nice ride. When you return to reality, you think about how much you would like to have this car but realize there is no way you can afford the $350,000 price tag. Your desire for this Lamborghini is not an example of demand. Just because a person has the desire to have something does not mean they have a demand for it. In economic terms, **demand** is when a person has the desire to have a good or service and they have the ability to pay for it.

The law of demand is different from demand. The **law of demand** states that the higher the price of a good, *ceteris paribus*, the less demand there will be for that good. ***Ceteris paribus*** is a Latin phrase that means "all other things held constant." This concept should be very easy to relate to because as consumers we think like this almost daily. When you go to the store and anticipate the price of your favorite candy will be $2 and then upon entering the store you realize the candy is on sale for $.50, nobody would suspect your demand for that product to decrease. Rather, most people would assume your demand for this product will most certainly increase. That is assumed to be true as long as nothing else in the situation has changed. But if your second favorite candy is next to it and they are giving it away, then everything else in the situation was not held constant (*ceteris paribus*), and the law of demand would not apply here because your demand for your favorite candy would likely decrease.

The law of demand can be illustrated in two distinct ways: a demand schedule and a demand curve. Both of these illustrations represent the identical situation.

Demand Schedule	
Price of Cowboys T-Shirt	**Quantity Demanded**
$25	25
$15	75
$9	150
$4	300
$3	450

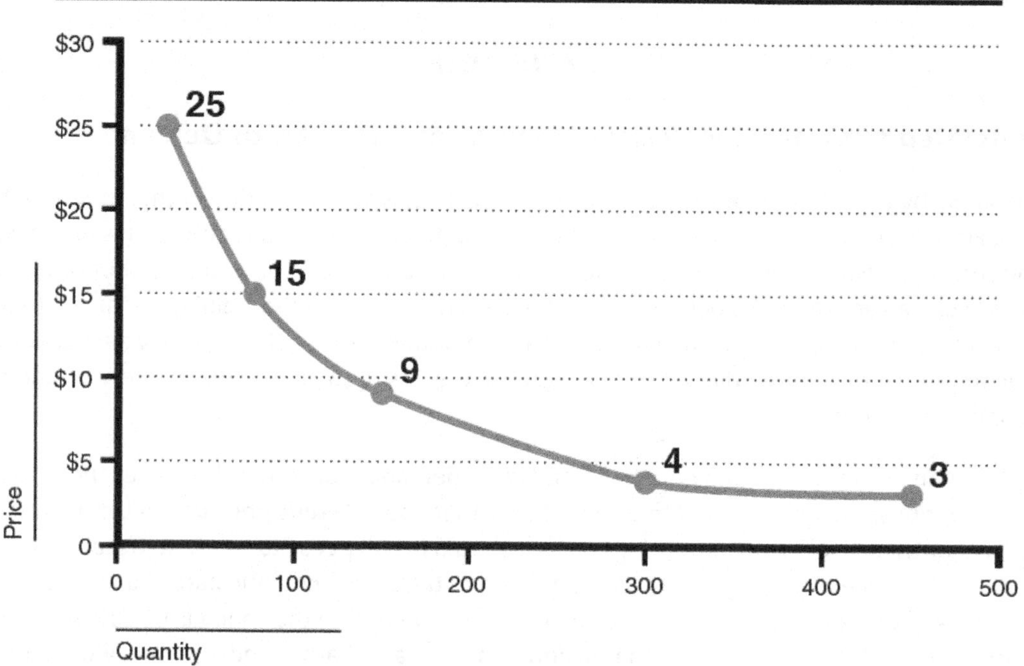

You will notice that price and the quantity demanded have an inverse relationship. This means that as the price goes up, the quantity demanded goes down. When the price goes down, the quantity demanded goes up. This shows a product that is functioning according to the law of demand.

Relationship Between Price and Quantity Demanded

A demand curve is meant to illustrate the relationship between price and quantity demanded. When the price goes up or down, the actual curve stays in the same place, but points on the curve move depending on the price. However, price is not the only thing that causes the quantity demanded to increase. Take, for example, the Dallas Cowboys sports team referenced above. If they have a winning record, it is likely that the demand for the jersey will increase, even if the price was not lowered. If a nonprice factor causes the demand to increase or decrease, it causes the entire demand curve to shift outward. The illustration below shows the demand curve moving outward.

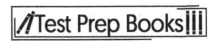

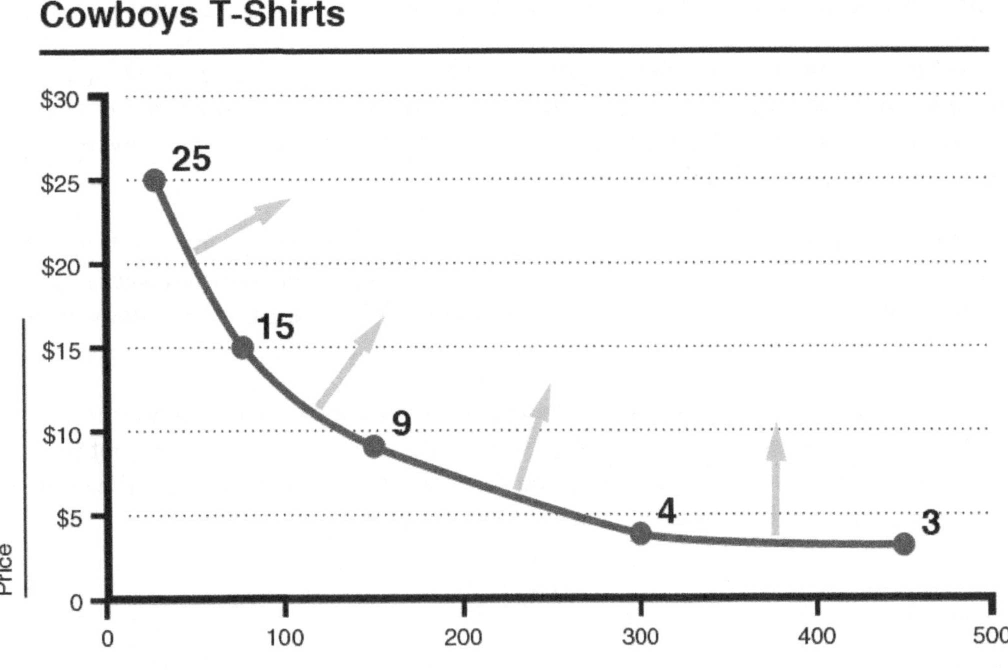

When the demand curve moves outward, it means the demand for this particular good or service has increased without changing the price. If it moves downward, the quantity demanded for this product has decreased despite no change in the price. In the example of Cowboy T-shirts, a successful team usually results in more people becoming fans and supporting the team. If the team went on a long losing streak, it is likely that the pride of fans would be lessened and the quantity demanded for the T-shirts will be less.

Buyers' Responses to Changes in Incentives and Constraints

There are a host of variables that shift the entire demand curve. These can be easily remembered by using the mnemonic device **TRIBE**. This mnemonic is explained below.

- **Tastes**. This means that, for whatever reason, the taste of consumers changed. In our example with the T-shirts, the taste of consumers for sports memorabilia changes as a team wins or loses. Other things that can change taste include advertisements that entice buyers to raise the quantity demanded and social media influencers giving a certain persona to a good or service.

- **Related goods (price of)**. Sometimes the demand for a product changes because the price of a subsitute good changed. A **substitute** is a good or service that can be used in the place of another good or service. If the prices of subsitutes change, the entire demand curve of a product will change. If the price of tacos stays the same, one would think that the demand for tacos will remain unchanged. But if the price of chicken nuggets is cut in half, the quantity demanded for chicken nuggets will increase, and the quantity demanded for tacos will decrease. This decrease will occur because a substite good's price was changed.

- **Income**. When a person's income changes, the quantity demanded for goods and services will usually change as well. A person's demand to go out to eat will rise if their income rises. This example illustrates that, without affecting the price of eating out, the demand for this increased. If a person's income decreases, their demand to go out to eat will also decrease.
- **Buyers (number of)**. If a large manufacutring warehouse was unexpectedly built in a neighborhood and within a couple years the population doubled, it would shift the demand curve outward. If people left a particular city, the demand curve would shift inward. Population affects the quanity demanded.
- **Expectations**. If buyers expect the price of a good or service to change in the future, the quantity demanded in the present will change. If I learn that a refrigerator I want is going to be on clearance in one week, my demand for that product will be less now. The demand curve shifts to the left because of my expectations.

Each of these variables can cause the entire demand curve to shift one direction or another. The important thing to remember about quantity demanded is that a change in price does not cause the entire curve to shift but rather is the relationship the demand curve is measuring. For the entire demand curve to shift, a variable outside of price must cause this change.

Supply

Law of Supply

It is generally easier for most people to think about the law of demand because it is from the perspective of a consumer. To understand supply, it is important to think from the perspective of a producer (usually thought of as a business owner). Fundamental to shifting our understanding is the realization that people want to be compensated for their work, and a business owner will work more to supply a certain product if they know they can sell it for a higher price.

Take, for example, a business owner who has provided forty hours of work this week and is called to work another ten hours over the weekend. At the normal rate, the business owner does not want to supply this much labor. But if a customer offers to pay him double the normal rate, the business owner is likely to supply their services for the additional income.

This example demonstrates the principle of the **law of supply**. The law of supply states that, *ceteris paribus*, producers are willing to supply more as the price increases for the good or service.

Relationship Between Price and Quantity Supplied

If a company is willing to pay a person $8 per hour for their work, the worker will be willing to supply a certain amount of labor at this price. But if the company offers $20 per hour, the law of supply says a person will supply more of their labor to a company at that price. The law of supply can be illustrated in two ways: a supply schedule and a supply curve. Examples are below.

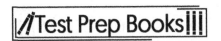

Price of Labor	Quantity of Labor Supplied
$5	3 hours
$8	8 hours
$12	16 hours
$17	25 hours
$20	30 hours

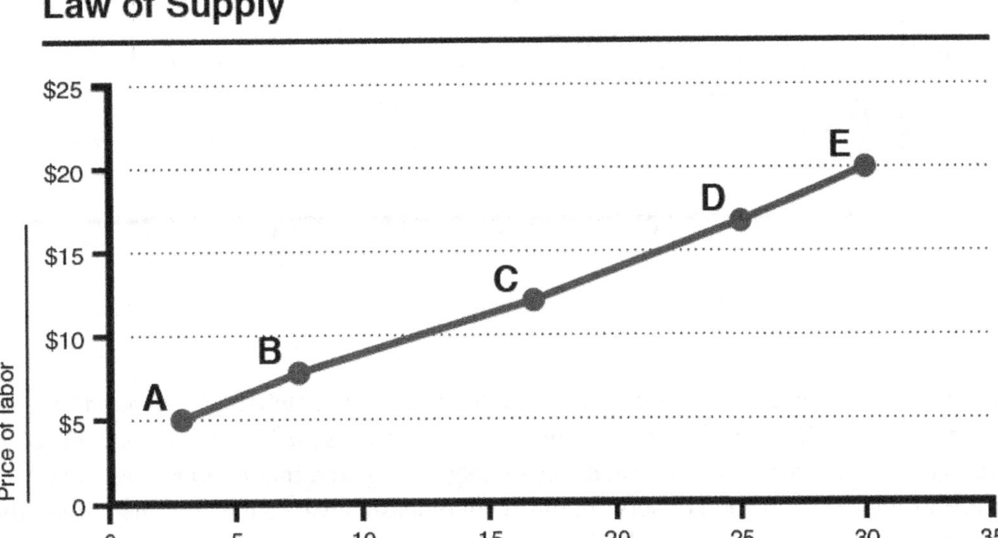

Both of these illustrations represent the law of supply. The price and quantity supplied have a positive relationship with one another. This means that as the price increases, the quantity supplied increases. When the price decreases, so does the quantity supplied.

Producers' Responses to Changes in Incentives and Technology

The entire supply curve can also shift if various things happen that cause suppliers to produce more without changing the price. One of the primary reasons for this is a change in technology. This means that some advance has been made in one part of the process of production that allows suppliers to spend less on production or produce more at the same price. When technology advances, it causes the entire supply curve to shift to the right, as demonstrated in the graph below.

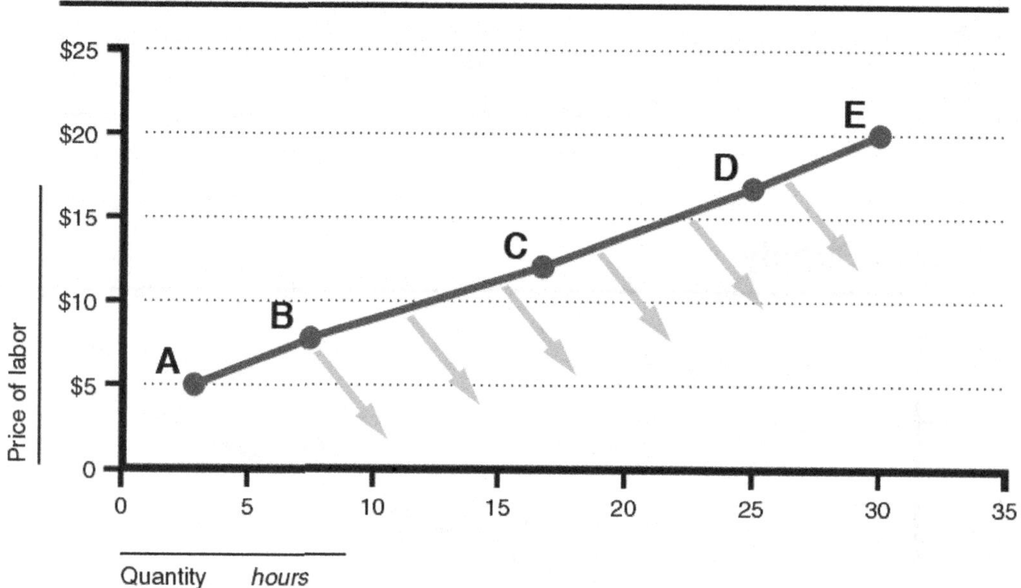

The advancement in technology has a noticeable benefit to consumers when the demand for a certain product has increased. If the demand for a product increases, *ceteris paribus*, the consumer will have to pay more for a good or service. But if a form of technology is invented that enables suppliers to lower the cost of producing a certain good or service, this technological advance in supply can offset the increase in price, which is usually the result of a greater demand.

Price Elasticity of Demand

Price Elasticity of Demand and Measures of Elasticity

Not all goods and services are equally demanded by consumers. For various reasons, some goods and services are highly sensitive to changes in price and others are not. This concept is known as **price elasticity**. If a good or service is extremely sensitive to price change, that good or service has an **elastic demand**. Elastic means that a small price increase results in a substantial decrease in the amount of goods or services demanded.

Measures of Elasticity and the Impact of a Given Price Change on Total Revenue

For example, if a certain brand of green beans (Green Giant) raises its price by 20 percent, buyers will likely consume much less of this brand of green beans. This is because most people don't notice a difference between the tastes of green beans produced by different companies. If Green Giant raises their prices, the likelihood is that people would substitute this brand with an alternative brand. The same is true of airfare. If a person is looking to fly with Delta Airlines but notices the price of Delta flights has risen, it is likely they will use a different airline because the quality of the services are similar.

The opposite of an elastic demand is an inelastic demand. An **inelastic demand** is when the demand for a particular good or service is not sensitive to change. This generally means there are not many available substitutes for this good or service.

For example, if the price of gasoline doubled over night, the demand for this product will not change substantially. Although the demand would be affected, it would not have as substantial of a change as most other products. Another example of an inelastic service would be important medical procedures. If the price of heart surgery increases substantially overnight, it is going to have little to no effect on the demand for this service. The reason for this is the lack of available substitutes. If somehow an alternative form of fuel is created or an alternative way to address heart problems is invented, these inelastic products would become elastic.

Calculate Measures of Elasticity

The **price elasticity of demand** is the ratio of the percent change in the quantity demanded to the percent change in price. The formulas below show how to calculate it:

$$\%\ Change\ in\ quantity\ demanded\ = \frac{Change\ in\ quantity\ demanded}{Initial\ quantity\ demanded} \times 100$$

and

$$\%\ Change\ in\ price = \frac{Change\ in\ price}{Initial\ price} \times 100$$

When the price of zoo admission is $15, ten thousand people visit the local zoo each week. When the price rose by $1, it decreased the number of visitors by one hundred visitors. To calculate the elasticity of demand for zoo admission fees, use the formulas below:

$$\%\ Change\ in\ quantity\ demanded = \frac{-100\ tickets}{10{,}000\ tickets} \times 100\ =\ -1\%$$

$$\%\ Change\ in\ price = \frac{\$1}{\$15} \times 100 = 6.67\%$$

$$Price\ elasticity\ of\ demand = \frac{1\%}{6.67\%} = 0.15$$

The larger the percentage change, the more responsive the good or service is to a price change. In the case above, the zoo admission was not very responsive to a $1 increase in the price, which means it has a reasonably inelastic demand. If the measure of elasticity is above 1, economists usually consider the product elastic. If it is below 1, the product is considered inelastic. Because the price of this product only rose by 5 percent ($1) and there are not many places you can go for a cheap price to see wild animals; it is a reasonable assertion that the demand for this product is inelastic.

Price Elasticity of Demand Depends on Certain Factors

One common feature of all elastic products is the availability of substitutes. Recall that a substitute is a good or service that can be used as an alternative to a good or service. A substitute for an iPhone would be an Android phone. A substitute for chicken might be pork or ground beef. Although each of these products differs slightly, they ultimately can be used to accomplish similar things. If there is a significant amount of goods or services that can be substituted for a good or service, it has an elastic demand. This means a small increase in price results in a significant decrease in the quantity demanded.

If there are a few substitutes, the product has an inelastic demand. Gasoline is one product that has an inelastic demand. Because most cars, small lawn mowers, and airplanes, run solely on gasoline, the price can be increased, and it will not have a significant decrease in demand.

Impact of a Given Price Change

The elasticity of a good or service has a tremendous impact on the total revenue of a business. **Total revenue** is the total value of sales of a good or service. To calculate the total revenue, multiply the number of goods that are sold times the price of each unit. For example, if a movie theater sells 450 movie tickets in one night and each movie ticket costs $11, the total revenue is $4,950.

If a business wants to raise their total revenue, they must understand how raising their price will affect the amount of goods or services they sell. The law of demand says that increasing the price will lower the quantity demanded; therefore, businesses need to know how significant the quantity demanded will decrease. By knowing this, they can raise or lower the price of their product to maximize their total revenue.

For example, if an airline company wants more revenue, they may think they can raise the price and their revenue will increase. However, because this product is elastic, the airline company actually learns that the demand for their product fell so drastically that the additional increased revenue may be offset by the decrease in overall flights demanded.

The table below illustrates a coffee company selling their most popular drink on the weekend. If the regular price of a specific coffee drink is $2 and the quantity demanded is 650 drinks, the total revenue is $1,300 for the weekend. If the owner wants to increase revenue, he might think increasing the price of the drink to $2.50 will lead to an increase in revenue. In reality, the elastic demand of the drinks leads to a substantial decrease in revenue.

Price	Quantity Demanded	Total Revenue
$1.00	1000	$1000
$1.50	800	$1200
$2.00	650	$1300
$2.50	350	$875
$3.00	275	$825

An obvious reason for this elastic demand is the availability of substitutes. Because other companies sell similar drinks, an increase in the price leads to a substantial decrease in the quantity demanded.

If a higher price leads to an increase in total revenue, the demand for a good is likely more inelastic. If a higher price leads to a decrease in the total revenue, the demand for a good is elastic. If a higher price leads to no increase or decrease, the demand is **unit elastic**.

Price Elasticity of Supply

Price Elasticity of Supply

Price elasticity of supply is how a change in the price affects the quantity supplied of a good or service. This is most easily understood when a company raises the price of something in order to increase total revenue. If a company is able to increase the price of something and the good or service is inelastic, the total revenue of that company will substantially increase. Because a company is receiving an increase in total revenue, competitors will likely increase the quantity supplied in order to increase their own total revenue.

If the supply of a good or service is elastic, when producers increase the price, the quantity supplied will also increase. Products that tend to be elastic are ones that have easily available resources to create the good. For example, hamburgers comprise resources that are readily available to producers, and therefore increasing the output is not too difficult. If the supply of a good is inelastic, it is much more difficult for businesses to change their quantity supplied in the short run. These types of goods generally involve resources that are difficult to manufacture quickly, such as gold, silver, oil, and other natural resources.

Measures of Elasticity and the Impact of a Given Price Change on Total Revenue or Total Expenditure

The elasticity of supply measures the extent to which the supply of a good or service is affected when the price increases. In other words, *how much* will the supply be affected? There are three types of elasticity that can be measured:

- **Elastic**. Supply is considered elastic when the price of a good increases and the quantity supplied increases by a higher percentage than the price. Example: The price of cups increases by 15 percent and the supply increases by 25 percent.
- **Inelastic**. Supply is considered inelastic when the price of a good increases and the quantity supplied is less than the percentage change in price. Example: The price of cups increases by 15 percent and the supply increases by 5 percent.
- **Unit elastic**. Supply is considered unit elastic when the price of goods and the supply increase at the same percentage rate. Example: The price of cups increases by 15 percent and the supply increases by 15 percent.

When the price of a good or service changes, it can have a multitude of effects on the supply of that good as well as total revenue and total expenditures. If the price of an item increases and the supply of that item is elastic, the total revenue and total expenditures will increase because they are producing a higher percentage of goods and services. If the price of an item increases and the supply is inelastic, the total revenue and total expenditures will decrease because they proportionally produce less of that good or service. In other words, if the price increases 15 percent and the supply only increases 5 percent, the total expenditures and revenue will decrease.

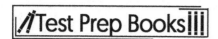

Calculate Measures of Elasticity

To calculate the price elasticity of supply, use this formula:

$$Price\ elasticity\ of\ supply = \frac{\%\ change\ in\ quantity\ supplied}{\%\ change\ in\ price}$$

If the elasticity is 1, the price elasticity of supply is unit elastic. If the elasticity is less than 1, the price elasticity of supply is inelastic. If the elasticity is greater than 1, the price elasticity of supply is elastic.

For example, if the price of hot dogs rises by 15 percent and the change in the quantity supplied also rises by 15 percent, the price elasticity of hot dogs is unit elastic. If the number of hot dogs supplied increases by 25 percent and the price of hot dogs only rises 15 percent, the supply is elastic. If the number of hot dogs supplied increases by 5 percent and the price rises 15 percent, the supply is inelastic.

Price Elasticity of Supply Depends on Certain Factors

The price elasticity of supply of a specific product is contingent on various factors, including the following:

- **The availability of alternative inputs**. This refers to the availability of input goods (the combined goods required to produce the final product). If substitute goods can be used easily and are readily available, the supply will be elastic. If the input goods are not easily substituted, it is inelastic.
- **Mobility of capital and labor**. If the factors of production needed to produce a good or service are versatile, the supply is elastic. For example, if a piece of equipment can be used to produce multiple goods or services, its ability to increase supply is high.
- **The price of alternative inputs**. If a different raw material is going to be used to produce a good or service but that alternative raw material is much more expensive than the original, the elasticity of supply is inelastic. If the alternative good is comparable in price to the original input, the elasticity of supply is elastic.

Elasticity can be Measured for any Determinant of Demand and Supply

Price is not the only determinant of supply and demand that can have its elasticity measured. Remember that elasticity is the measure of how responsive one variable is to a change in a different variable. Because things other than price affect supply and demand, these other variables also have an effect on the elasticity of a good or service. In other words, if other variables in the marketplace change, what sort of impact will that have on the supply or demand of a good or service?

One variable that can have an impact on the demand of a product is the income of a population. If the overall income of a community rises for various reasons, this can cause one of two things to happen regarding the demand for a product. If a product is an inferior good and the income of the community rises, it is likely that the demand for this product will decrease. An **inferior good** is something that people generally want less of if their income rises. Examples include bus rides, cheap restaurants, and generic brands of food.

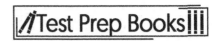

These goods or services are different from normal goods. **Normal goods** are things people desire more of when their income rises. Examples might include clothes, shoes, and vacations.

Income Elasticity of Demand

In order to determine whether a good is inferior or normal, economists use a formula that measures the income elasticity of demand. The formula is:

$$Income\ elasticity\ of\ demand = \frac{\%\ change\ in\ quantity\ demanded}{\%\ change\ in\ income}$$

If the income elasticity of demand is a positive number, the good is a normal good. If the income elasticity of demand is a negative number, the good is an inferior good.

In addition to determining whether a good is normal or inferior, economists also determine whether the demand is income elastic or income inelastic. A good is elastic if the number is greater than 1. In other words, when the income of an individual rises, the demand for income-elastic goods or services rises faster than the income. This usually means this good or service is a luxury enjoyed by the wealthy. If the number is less than 1, it is a normal good, but it has an inelastic demand. These usually include goods and services that are necessities, such as clothing, food, and gasoline.

Cross-Price Elasticity of Demand

Another factor that influences the demand for a good or service is the price of other goods and services. **Cross-price elasticity of demand** measures how changing the price of one good or service affects the quantity demanded for another good or service. The formula below shows how this is measured:

$$Cross - price\ elasticity\ of\ demand = \frac{\%\ change\ in\ quantity\ of\ A\ demanded}{\%\ change\ in\ price\ of\ B}$$

The important information we can determine from this equation is whether the items being cross-compared are substitutes or complements. Again, a **substitute** is a good or service that can be used in place of another good or service, such as an iPhone for an Android phone. This differs from a **complement**, which is a good or service that is most often used in conjunction with another good or service. For example, baseball cleats and baseball pants are examples of complement goods.

If the cross-price elasticity of demand between goods A and B is negative, the goods are complements. This means that if the price of hot dogs rises, it is likely people will buy fewer hot dog buns, which leads to a negative number. If the number is positive, it shows they are substitutes for one another. For example, if the price of iPhones increases and the quantity demanded for Androids increases, the items are substitutes for one another. The higher the positive number, the more closely connected the two products are as substitutes. If the number is positive but very small, goods A and B likely have a minimal ability to be substituted for one another.

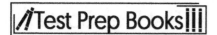

Market Equilibrium, Disequilibrium, and Changes in Equilibrium

Market Equilibrium, Consumer Surplus, and Producer Surplus

Market equilibrium is the price at which the number of goods and services produced equals exactly the number of goods and services supplied. For example, imagine a man selling cotton candy at a baseball game. He made exactly eighty sticks of cotton candy and spends the entire game walking around the stadium selling them for $3 per stick. After the game, all of the fans are leaving the stadium, and he is left with just one stick of cotton candy. As he is returning to the cafeteria to finish his day, the last fan in the stadium runs up and buys the last stick. This would be an example of someone reaching **equilibrium price**, which is the price wherein the demand for the product or service equals the supply of that product or service. Nobody else has a desire for cotton candy, which means all of the consumers who are willing to pay for cotton candy at that price have bought it. The man was willing to produce a certain amount of cotton candy for $3 and is left with none to throw away or take home for himself.

How Equilibrium Price, Quantity, Consumer Surplus, and Producer Surplus for a Good or Service are Determined

Below is the supply-and-demand curve for the example above. The blue line is supply, and the orange line is demand. The point at which they intersect is the **point of equilibrium**. This means the equilibrium price was found at $3.

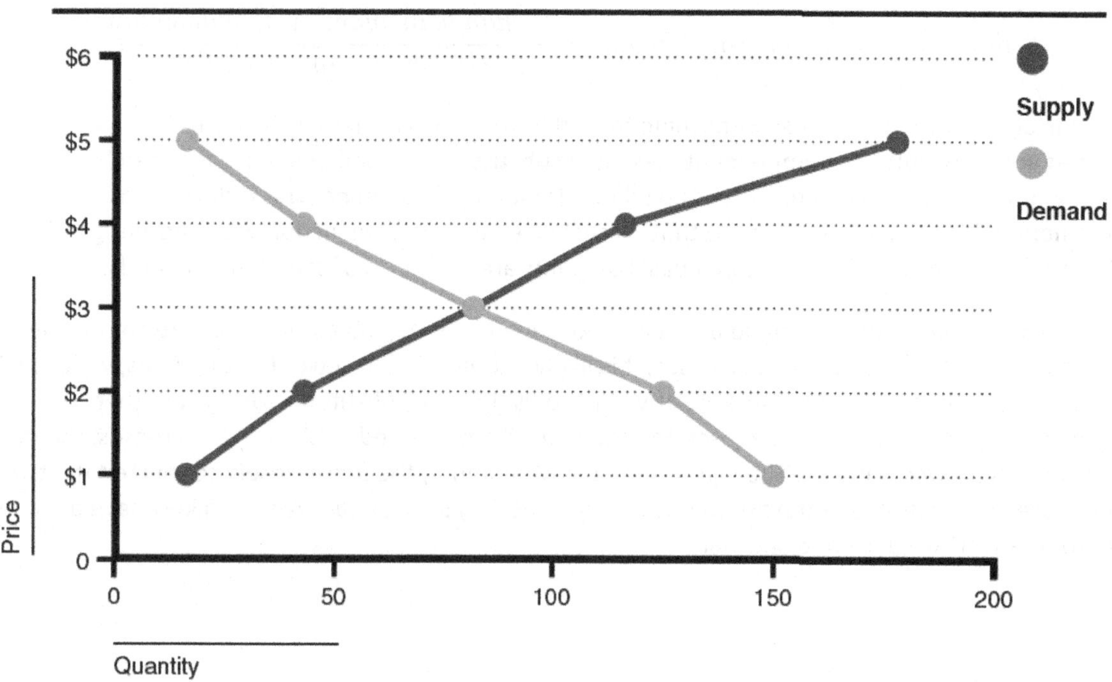

The equilibrium price is determined at the price that producers are willing to produce an amount of goods or services at the same point that consumers will demand the goods and services. The price where producers and consumers are at a perfect match, or in other words, the amount demanded is the precise amount supplied, is the equilibrium price. This is not set by governments or producers but is the point at which a multitude of factors together find a common balance.

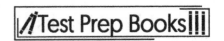

The **consumer surplus** is the difference between the price consumers are willing to pay for a good or service and the actual price they pay. This is illustrated on a demand curve in the area between equilibrium price and the top of the demand curve. The **producer surplus** is the difference between the equilibrium price and the bottom of the supply curve.

Calculate Areas of Consumer Surplus and Producer Surplus at Equilibrium

The previous example will help calculate the consumer surplus and producer surplus. Casey has 3 T-shirts of her favorite basketball team she is willing to sell. Rebekah loves basketball and is willing to pay $20 for the T-shirt. Melissa, who likes basketball but isn't quite as big a fan as Rebekah, is willing to pay $17 for the T-shirt. Landry likes basketball but a little less than Rebekah and Melissa. He is only willing to pay $15 for the T-shirt. Ideally, Casey would sell each T-shirt at the maximum price each person is willing to pay. But she doesn't know how much each person is willing to pay, so she sets the price of the T-shirts at a place she thinks will sell all three T-shirts but maximize her profit. She sets the price at the equilibrium price of $15, and each of the T-shirts is sold.

The consumer surplus is the amount of money consumers saved between what they actually paid and what they were willing to pay. In this example, Rebekah saved $5, and Melissa saved $2, which means the total consumer surplus was $7. If a producer can find a way to sell the T-shirts at different levels to different people, they may be able to maximize their profit. Industries often do this when they target children, senior citizens, or students for certain promotional deals. They recognize that these demographics have a lower overall demand for a good or service, and therefore they charge less. By doing so, they minimize the consumer surplus and maximize the profit of the company.

Conversely, **producer surplus** (also known as **economic surplus**) is the difference between the price producers are willing to sell a good or service for and the higher price they charged for the good or service. In this example, if Casey was willing to sell each T-shirt for $7 but ended up selling each one for $15, that means her producer surplus was $8 per T-shirt, for a total of $24 producer surplus.

The graph below illustrates the concepts of producer and consumer surplus in a supply-and-demand curve.

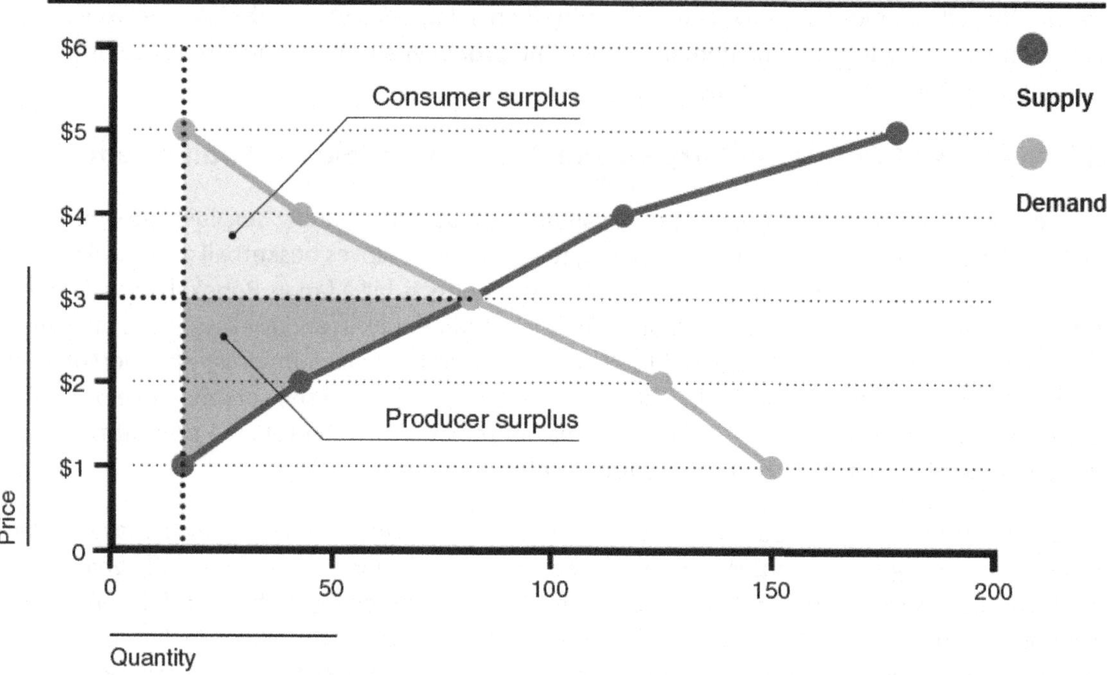

Disequilibrium and Changes in Equilibrium

As discussed, the equilibrium price is the price at which the producers are willing to supply the exact amount of a good consumers demand. Producers do not have any additional goods or services they are willing to produce at that price, and consumers do not demand another unit of the good or service at that price. The equilibrium price is the optimum price for an efficient economy. Unfortunately, the equilibrium price is rarely ever reached.

A **surplus** is when producers supply more of a good or service than what is demanded by consumers at a specific price. If we consider the example from earlier regarding cotton candy, imagine if the producer would have set the price of cotton candy at $4 instead of $3. The graph below shows that at $4 per stick, he would have gladly worked additional hours to make more than eighty sticks of cotton candy. He was willing to make 115 sticks. But because the price is higher than equilibrium, only forty people are willing to pay the higher price. This means there was a surplus of seventy-five units of cotton candy. The higher price led to a lower demand for this product, and he would have been left with additional units of cotton candy.

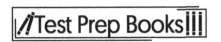

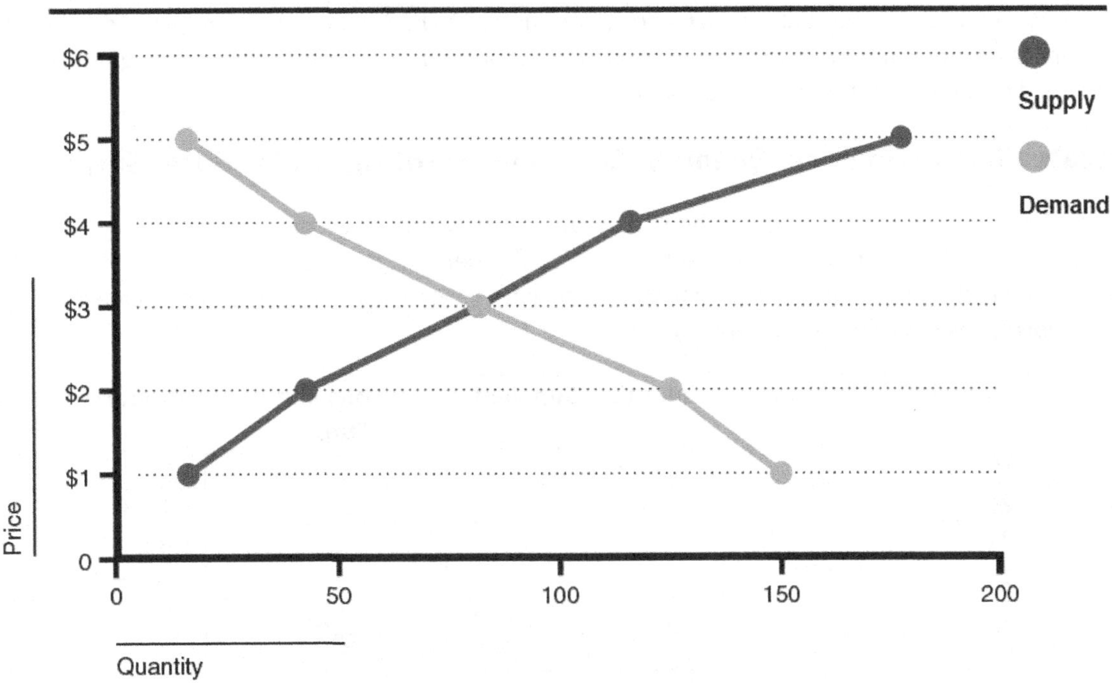

The opposite of a surplus is a shortage. A **shortage** is when consumers demand more of a product than what producers supplied at a specific price. If the cotton candy man would have priced his sticks of cotton candy at $2 per stick, the demand would have risen to 120 units. But for that price, he is only willing to supply forty sticks of cotton candy. This means there will be a shortage of eighty sticks of cotton candy at the baseball game.

Changes in Underlying Conditions and Shocks to a Competitive Market

Changes in the price and quantity demanded for goods and services generally have a predictable pattern. But there have been times when the marketplace experienced a demand shock, which had a tremendous and immediate impact on the price and quantity of goods and services. A **demand shock** is when the aggregate demand curve radically shifts by a sudden change in various areas. This can happen positively or negatively.

The most well-known negative demand shock in the United States came in the late 1920s during the Great Depression. Unexpectedly, wealth disappeared because of the collapse of the stock market, consumer confidence decreased drastically and suddenly, and the availability of factors of production decreased because of high unemployment. The most well-known positive demand shock came shortly after this in the 1940s when the U.S. government substantially increased spending at the start of World War II.

A negative demand shock is going to cause individuals and businesses to slow down spending because of the uncertainty in the economy. As a result of the decrease in quantity demanded, businesses will lower prices. This means the consumer surplus and producer surplus will decrease because businesses are more desperate to sell goods and services to avoid going out of business, and consumers are much less willing to pay higher prices, which lowers their consumer surplus.

A positive demand shock leads to the opposite effect. It causes the aggregate demand curve to shift right and the aggregate price level to increase as well. This is because the quantity demanded for the product has increased substantially, which allows producers to charge more for their product. Because consumers have more money to spend, the consumer surplus and producer surplus are higher than if consumers didn't have a lot of money to spend.

Calculate Changes in Price, Quantity, Consumer Surplus, and Producer Surplus

The chart below shows the price, quantity demanded, quantity supplied, consumer surplus, and producer surplus of a sports video game and a store's sales per day. It is the most recent edition of the game, but the technology, rosters, and features of the game are nearly six months old because the specific sports season ended six months ago.

Price	Quantity Demanded	Quantity Supplied	Consumer Surplus	Producer Surplus
$5	30	0		
$10	24	3		10 × 3 = $30
$15	21	8		5 × 5 = $25
$20	**15**	**15**		**Total = $55**
$25	9	26	5 × 6 = $30	
$30	4	35	5 × 5 = $25	
$35	0	49	**Total = $55**	

These sales continued until a newer version of the game came out. This newer version has the updated rosters for each team, newer technologies that make the game more enjoyable, and different features that enhance the quality of the picture. As a result of this new game, the market conditions have changed. There is a newer edition of the game that came out, and consumers prefer it to the old edition. Immediately after the release of the game, the supply and demand of the old game changes. The new chart is below.

Price of Old Edition	Quantity Demanded	Quantity Supplied	Consumer Surplus	Producer Surplus
$5	25	0		
$10	18	0		
$15	13	0		
$20	9	2		20 × 2 = $40
$25	**5**	**5**		**Total = $40**
$30	1	8	5 × 4 = $20	
$35	0	11	**Total = $20**	
$40	0	14		
$45	0	20		

Because something in the market changed, the overall supply and demand of the product changed. Rather than stock their stores with games that are out of date, game retailers would prefer to sell newer games. As a result, they are only willing to supply the older games at a higher price because they would prefer to sell the newer games. Most consumers are no longer willing to pay a higher price for the older game because they prefer the newer edition.

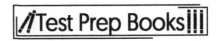

As a result of these changes, the consumer surplus and producer surplus decrease substantially because the overall willingness to supply this game and the demand for this game have diminished.

Effects of Government Intervention in Markets

Forms of Government Price and Quantity Intervention

The government can have a tremendous impact on a marketplace if it chooses to intervene. One such intervention is known as a **price ceiling**. A price ceiling is when the government imposes a limit on the price producers can charge for a specific good or service. This type of government intervention is usually done in a democracy because the public's perception of what will help alleviate the problem is different from what will actually fix the problem.

For example, during the 1970s, President Nixon imposed a price ceiling on gasoline. This meant that gas stations could not charge more than $1 for gasoline regardless of demand. Because the price ceiling was set below the equilibrium price, the result was a shortage of gasoline. If the producers were allowed to raise the price of gasoline, consumers would have demanded less of this product and the producer would have been willing to supply more at the higher price. But because the government intervened in the marketplace and prevented the equilibrium price from being met, it led to a shortage. Practically, this meant that gas stations had long lines with waits of more than an hour, and they sold out of gas in just a fraction of the normal time. When they ran out of gas, many gas stations chose to close for the day to eliminate variable costs rather than order more gasoline for such a small profit margin. The result of any price ceiling is a shortage.

A price ceiling is not the only type of government intervention that can cause problems in a marketplace. A **price floor** is when the government sets a minimum price a producer can charge for their good or service. The result of this government intervention is a surplus.

The most well-known price floor is the **minimum wage** law, which requires people to charge a minimum rate for their labor regardless of the job. This has a particularly harmful effect on less skilled people, such as the young and disabled, who are trying to develop the skills necessary to participate in the labor market. When the government raises the price, they are allowed to charge for their labor, and it very often "prices them out of the labor market." This means the benefit they bring to the company is less than the wage they are required to charge (the minimum wage) the company for their labor. Many companies choose not to hire someone for the position or automate the labor by using technology. The result of this government intervention is a surplus of labor, which is also known as **unemployment**.

When the government intervenes in a market, the result is often a series of inefficiencies that disallow consumers and producers to maximize the amount of mutually beneficial transactions.

How Government Policies Alter Consumer and Producer Behaviors

When the government decides to implement an economic policy, it has an effect on the marketplace and results in a change in behavior by the consumer, producer, or both. If the government decides to impose an excise tax on rental cars, it will have a tremendous impact on the willingness of producers to supply rental cars.

For example, before any excise tax on rental cars was implemented, the average rental car cost at Los Angeles Airport (LAX) was $130 per week. When this was the weekly rate, the airport rented out 3,400 rental cars per week on average. The government decided to implement a "rental car tax" that would charge an additional $40 per week on any rental vehicles. Because of the increased tax burden, the incentives for both rental cars and consumers have changed.

After the rental car tax was added, companies were willing to provide 2,500 rental cars but only if they were paid $155 for the weekly rate ($115 for the rental car companies and $40 for the new tax).

The rental car companies were incentivized to provide fewer cars because of the tax, and the consumers were discouraged from renting cars because of the additional cost. The result of the excise tax is to drive a wedge between the consumer and the producer, lowering the quantity supplied by the producer and raising the cost paid by the consumer.

The outcome of this excise tax is to make the rental car market in Los Angeles much less efficient in satisfying consumers and producers of rental cars. Furthermore, the total revenue of rental car companies will be lower, and the number of people willing to purchase complement goods (such as flights to Los Angeles and gasoline at local gas stations) will also decrease.

Calculate Changes in Market Outcomes Resulting from Government Policies

If a local government imposes a minimum wage law, the supply-and-demand schedule may look something like the chart below.

Price of Labor	Quantity Supplied	Quantity Demanded	Surplus (Unemployment)
$9	500	500	0
$10	650	450	200
$11	750	400	350
$12	900	300	600
$13	1200	225	975

The impact of raising the minimum wage law on quantity supplied is an increase in the number of people interested in working at that price. However, if the government raises the minimum wage law, businesses will demand fewer people work at that price. The result is an increase in unemployment. Unemployment is a type of surplus that can be caused by a price floor set below the equilibrium price.

Deadweight Loss Represents the Losses to Buyers and Sellers

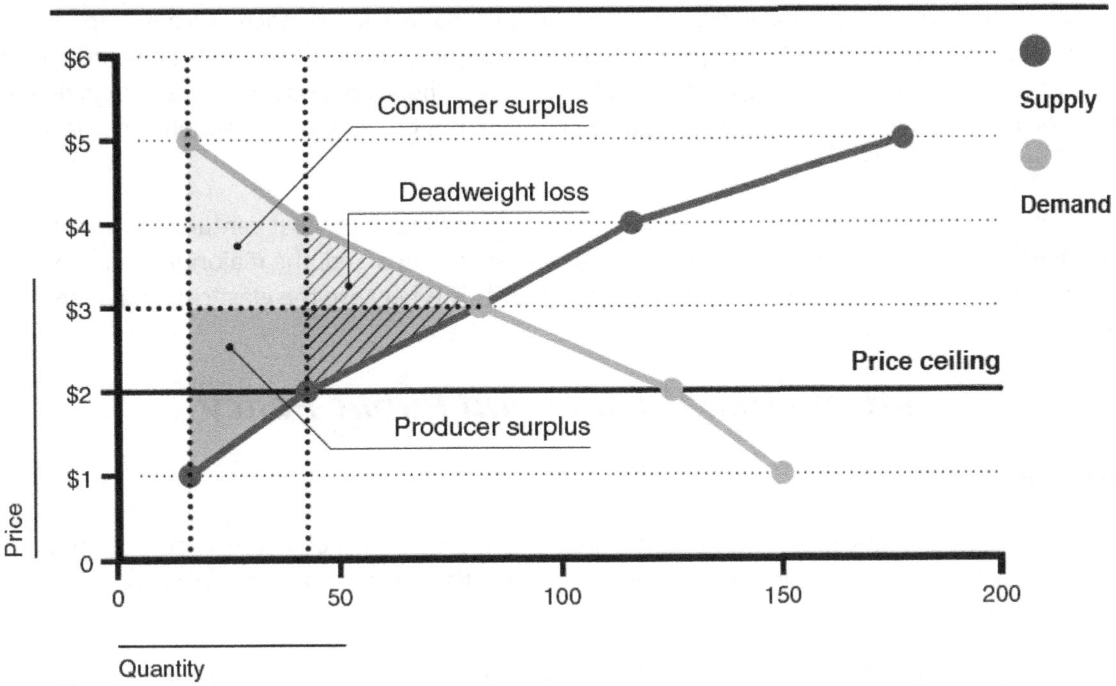

The chart above shows the concept of a deadweight loss. A **deadweight loss** is the economic inefficiency caused by government policies that prevent the price from reaching equilibrium. The specific government policy that caused the above-listed deadweight loss is a price ceiling.

In the chart, producers are willing to supply approximately eighty units of this good at the price of $3, and consumers are willing to purchase eighty units at the same price. However, the government implemented a price ceiling, which disallowed producers from selling the product for more than $2. At the price of $2, producers were only willing to supply forty units of the good. If the producers would have been allowed to charge $3 for the good, they would have supplied forty more units of the good, and all of those units would have been demanded by consumers. Because these additional forty transactions were disallowed due to government policy, it was a deadweight loss.

Good economic policies should be designed in a way that minimizes the deadweight loss to producers while simultaneously accomplishing the objective of the government. A deadweight loss can occur as a result of various government policies, which include subsidies, taxes, price ceilings, price floors, and monopoly pricing.

Incidence of Taxes and Subsidies Imposed on Goods Traded in Perfectly Competitive Markets

When the government intervenes in a marketplace to either tax, regulate, or subsidize a good or service, it does not impact the consumers and producers equally. In other words, sometimes the producer will bear the larger burden of government interference, and other times the consumer will bear the larger burden. This is known as the tax incidence. The **tax incidence** is the way the tax burden is divided between producers and consumers.

As a review, a perfectly competitive market is a hypothetical marketplace where the ideal conditions are met for a competitive marketplace and perfect efficiency of that market is reached. To determine who will bear the majority of the burden for government interference, one must first determine how elastic and inelastic supply and demand are for the good or service. When supply is more elastic than demand, consumers bear more of the cost for the tax. When demand is more elastic than supply, producers bear more of the cost for the tax.

For example, electricity has become a necessary part of life in the twenty-first century. Because the government and producers know that electricity has an inelastic demand, the majority of any tax imposed on electricity will be passed on to the consumer. This is because the elasticity of demand is lower than the elasticity of supply.

International Trade and Public Policy

Tariffs and Quotas

One revenue source for governments is the use of tariffs. A **tariff** is a tax on goods or services that are imported from another country. When a nation imposes tariffs, there are multiple effects on international trade.

From the standpoint of other nations, tariffs put foreign competitors at a substantial disadvantage. This is a disadvantage because they must either add the additional tax onto their product, take less revenue from the sale of their product, or a combination of the two. This gives a definitive advantage to their domestic competitor because they do not have to charge their customers the additional cost of the tariff or lose the additional revenue like the foreign nation does.

An additional advantage a government can give to domestic producers is imposing an import quota on other nations. An **import quota** is when the government limits the amount of goods or services that can be imported over a specified period of time. This is often done to limit a nation's dependence on foreign nations for specific goods and services they consider vital to the economy. For example, if a nation became dependent on a particular foreign nation for oil and for some reason the relationship with that foreign nation became tense, the foreign nation could use this as leverage to harm a nation. As a result of the potential volatility, a nation protects itself by placing import quotas on the other nation. This encourages the nation to depend on domestic producers rather than exclusively foreign producers.

How Markets are Affected by Public Policy Related to International Trade

All nations make public policy decisions that affect the economy. **Public policy** is any decision by government in accordance with laws and customs. It is common for governments to make a multitude of public policy decisions that affect trade with other nations.

These public policy decisions can affect an entire economy or just a specific market in an economy. For example, if a nation imposes a 10 percent tariff on all goods entering the nation, it will likely have an equal effect on all marketplaces. But if a 10 percent tariff is put on a specific commodity entering the country from a specific nation, it may affect the market substantially because people could use substitutes instead.

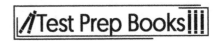

For example, if the U.S. Congress imposes a 25 percent tariff on corn, it will cause the cost of corn to rise and the quantity demanded to decrease. Many consumers will likely substitute another vegetable because of the additional cost. Notice that this one policy decision impacts the corn market as well as the market for every other substitute. If, in addition to the 25 percent tariff on corn, the U.S. Congress imposes an import quota for all non-corn vegetables, the market for vegetables will be affected again by these public policies.

Because these policies give an advantage to domestic farmers, there will be a higher demand for labor in the agricultural market, which will affect the labor market in agriculture and other competing blue-collar labor markets.

The government's attitude toward international trade has a significant impact on the economy. For example, consider a nation that does not have a significant amount of natural resources. If the government of this nation severely limits international trade, the equilibrium price will be much higher because the resources available to the market are limited. But if this same nation increases international trade, the market will be supplied with more and the cost will be lower. The cost will continue to decrease if these neighboring nations have an abundance of these natural resources and can supply them at a cheaper cost.

Calculate Changes in Market Outcomes Resulting from Public Policy Related to International Trade

Below are two supply-and-demand schedules. One illustrates a nation that disallows international trade, and the other illustrates the same nation that allows for international trade.

No International Trade (Oil)		
Price (in dollars)	**Quantity Supplied (in millions)**	**Quantity Demanded (in millions)**
$1.00	2 gallons	35 gallons
$1.50	9 gallons	30 gallons
$2.00	16 gallons	26 gallons
$2.50	22 gallons	22 gallons
$3.00	27 gallons	12 gallons
$3.50	30 gallons	5 gallons

International Trade (Oil)		
Price	Quantity Supplied (in millions)	Quantity Demanded (in millions)
$1.00	8 gallons	35 gallons
$1.50	16 gallons	29 gallons
$2.00	25 gallons	25 gallons
$2.50	30 gallons	22 gallons
$3.00	40 gallons	14 gallons
$3.50	55 gallons	6 gallons

Because more producers of oil were allowed entry into the marketplace, the supply of oil at a particular price also moved up. Notice in the No International Trade table that, without foreign producers of oil, the nation would only produce 2 million gallons of oil for $1. But when other oil producers are allowed in the marketplace, that suddenly increases the supply to 8 million gallons of oil at the same price.

Also notice the point at which both tables hit equilibrium price. If no trade is allowed, the equilibrium is reached at 22 million gallons of oil at $2.50 per gallon. If trade is allowed, equilibrium is reached at 25 million gallons of oil at only $2 per gallon. The obvious benefit of trade is that more people are able to enjoy oil, more companies can profit from the sale of oil, and consumers pay a smaller price for the oil they consume.

Microeconomics: Production, Cost, and the Perfect Competition Model

The Production Function

Key Terms Relating to Production and Cost

The relationship between factors of production and output is known as the production function. Mathematically, the production function is described as $Q = f(L, K)$ which means that quantity (*Q*) is produced from labor and capital. Although other factors exist, labor (*L*) and capital (*K*) are the only two inputs generally used in production functions. For example, it might take 5 units of labor (*L*) to make a T-shirt and 2 units of capital (*K*) to make that same T-shirt.

It is important to note different terms regarding the production function. A **fixed input** is an input that cannot change over time, and a **variable input** refers to an input that can be changed over time. The **long run** represents a timeframe in which all costs are variable, whereas the **short run** deals with at least one cost that is fixed. The **total product (TP) curve** below shows the relationship between the increase in the factor of production (labor or capital) and the corresponding increase in TP (quantity).

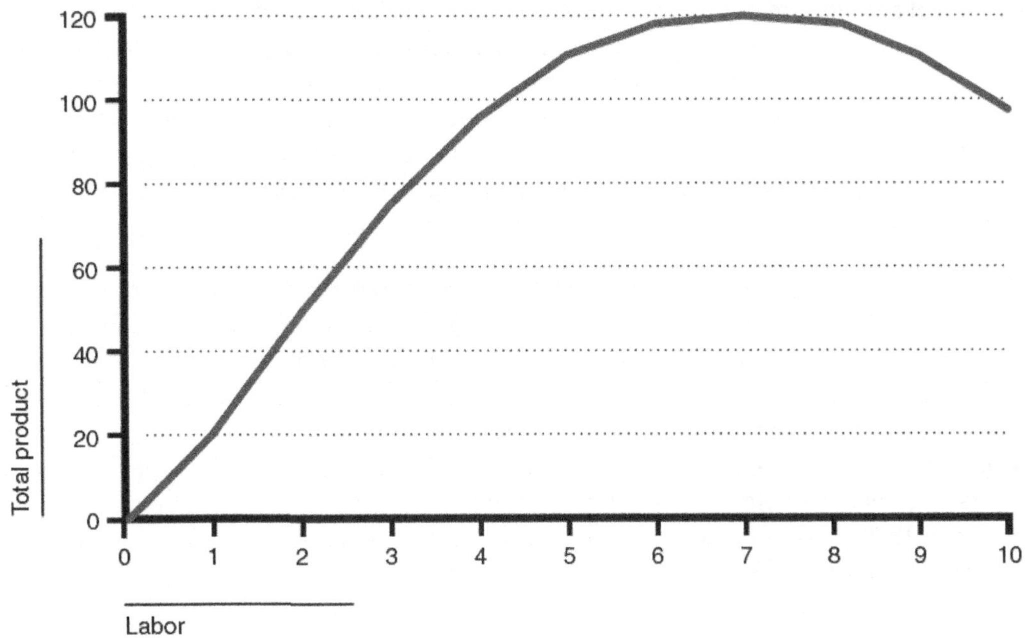

Total Product (TP) Curve

Although the curvature of the TP curve will vary depending on each product, the TP will generally follow a similar pattern. The total will at first increase at an increasing rate, then increase at a diminishing rate, and then actually decrease in output. Economic theory (and common sense) dictates that firms should continue hiring labor when the rate of production is increasing and stop hiring if the total output is decreasing.

How Production and Cost are Related in the Short Run and Long Run

The **marginal product of labor (MPL)** or (MILK) refers to the additional quantity of output produced by using one unit of either labor or capital. For those who are more mathematically inclined, $MPL = \Delta Q/\Delta L$ when input is labor, and $MPK = \Delta Q/\Delta K$ when input is capital. Although either labor or capital can be used to demonstrate MP, for the sake of simplicity, labor will be used as the preferred input of choice.

Increasing marginal returns means that as an additional unit of labor is hired, not only does the TP (quantity) increase, the *rate* of production increases as well. Let's imagine that Eugene is the CEO of Trader Paul's, and he is in charge of hiring labor. His first worker, Hannah, produces 5 rolls of toilet paper. If Eugene hires Peter, who is able to produce 9 rolls of toilet paper, Trader Paul's is experiencing increasing marginal returns of labor because the average rate of production went from 5 rolls of toilet paper to 7 rolls of toilet paper with Peter's hiring.

Diminishing marginal returns means that as an additional unit of labor is hired, the TP (quantity) increases, but the *rate* of production decreases. Now, let's assume Eugene hires two more workers, Cathy and Chanmi. Cathy can produce 4 rolls of toilet paper, whereas Chanmi can only churn out 2 rolls. Both Cathy and Chanmi represent diminishing marginal returns of labor because the average rate of production went down to 6 and 5, respectively, with their hiring.

Negative marginal returns means that as an additional unit of labor is hired, not only does the rate of production decrease but the TP (quantity) decreases as well. Now let's assume that Eugene hires a fifth worker, Penny. Unfortunately for Eugene, Penny is not the most competent employee. She constantly distracts the other workers, has a short attention span, and is also a kleptomaniac who hoards toilet paper! The total amount of production before Penny's hiring was 20 rolls of toilet paper. After her hiring, the production falls to 10 rolls. Penny's MPL is a woeful −10 rolls of toilet paper. The average rate of production for Trader Paul's plummets from 5 rolls of toilet paper to 2 rolls of toilet paper.

Let's use a basketball analogy to highlight increasing marginal returns, diminishing marginal returns, and negative marginal returns. Suppose that the Los Angeles Lakers decide to build their team from scratch with only one of its existing players, Kyle Kuzma. If the Lakers add Lebron James to its team, the NBA's top superstar, they would experience increasing marginal returns. If they decide to add a player who will improve the team but not at the same rate as an all-time great like Lebron James, they can add Dwight Howard, who represents diminishing marginal returns. Howard adds to the total output but certainly not at an increasing marginal rate. If the Lakers sign Kevin Hart, a five-foot-four comedian with no professional basketball experience to the team, they would experience negative marginal returns and quite possibly lose every game they play!

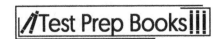

Measures of Productivity and Short-Run and Long-Run Costs

Estevan is the CEO of Taco Town Enterprises and wants to know when his company experiences increasing marginal returns, diminishing marginal returns, and negative marginal returns regarding hiring workers (holding all other inputs constant).

No. of Workers	TP	MP
1	10	10
2	22	12
3	40	18
4	48	8
5	52	4
6	54	2
7	53	-1

The first three workers Estevan hires represent increasing marginal returns because the MPL increases each time a new worker is hired, from 10 to 12 to 18. The average rate of production increases from 10 to 11 to 13.3—hence, increasing marginal returns of labor. The next trio of hires (workers 4–6) have an MPL of 8, 4, and 2, respectively. The average rate of production from the three workers declines from 12 to 10.4 to 9, which represents diminishing marginal returns of labor. The seventh and final worker has an MPL of −1, meaning that their hiring leads not only to a lower average rate of production (7.6) but also to a reduced total output.

Short-Run Production Costs

Key Terms Relating to Production and Cost

In the short run, there are costs that do not change. These costs are referred to as **fixed costs (FCs)**. Rent would be the prime example of an FC because businesses generally pay rent regardless of the amount of output they produce. If businesses close during the summer months, they generally will still pay rent despite not actively selling products. **Variable costs (VCs)** are costs that change depending on the amount of output that is produced. For example, the amount of baseball gloves produced at a sporting goods store would be a VC. During the baseball season, more gloves would be produced than during the winter months. The **total cost (TC)** is the sum of the FC and VC. The resulting equation would be $TC = FC + VC$. By dividing quantity on both sides of the equation, it necessarily follows that $average\ total\ cost\ (ATC) = average\ fixed\ cost\ (AFC) + average\ variable\ cost\ (AVC)$.

Marginal cost (MC) is the additional cost of producing additional output, or the change in TC from making one more item. Because the FC (by definition) does not change, one could also find the change in VC from making one more item in order to find the MC. As production increases, the MC, AFC, AVC, ATC, TC, and VC will change as total output changes, but the FC remains constant regardless of the output. Meanwhile, the AFC curve never slopes upward. As quantity increases, the AFC curve becomes increasingly closer to the x-axis without ever touching it, as shown below.

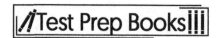

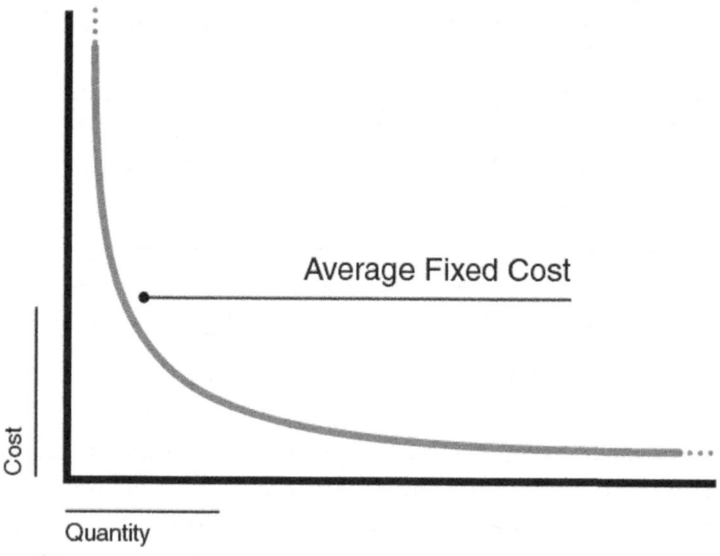

AFC Curve

How Production and Cost are Related in the Short Run and Long Run

Constant MC means that the additional cost remains the same regardless of the output. Imagine that Jim makes staplers and the TC of the first stapler is $10, the TC of two staplers is $20, the TC of three staplers is $30, and the TC of four staplers is $40. The MC of the first, second, third, and fourth staplers would be $10.

Very few, if any, firms produce all of their goods at a constant MC. When firms initially start producing a good, they will have increasing marginal returns of labor, and when production of that good increases, there will be diminishing marginal returns of labor. Increasing MPL corresponds with a decreasing MC curve, whereas diminishing MPL matches with an increasing MC curve. The resulting MC curve strongly resembles Nike's "Just Do It" logo, as shown below.

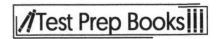

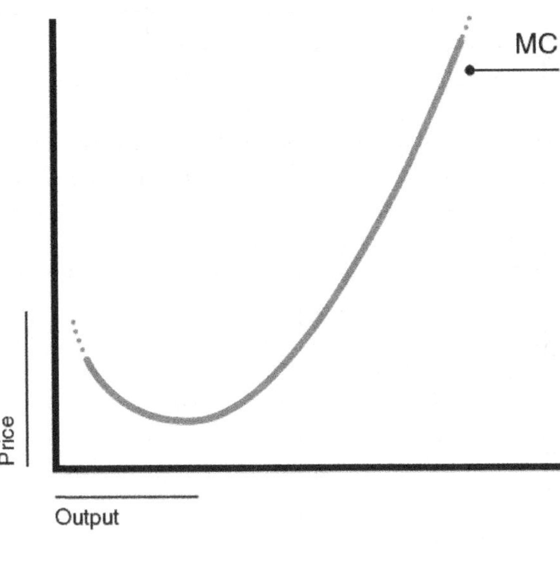

MC Curve

Calculate Various Measures of Productivity and Short-Run and Long-Run Costs

Peter is a carrot farmer who wants to figure out the MC, ATC, AVC, and AFC of various outputs of carrots for his business given that he only knows the FCs and VCs. The daily cost of rent (FC) is $50, and the VC is given. Let's help Peter figure out the rest.

Quantity	FC	VC	TC	MC	AFC	AVC	ATC
0	$50	$0					
1	$50	$10					
2	$50	$14					
3	$50	$21					
4	$50	$32					
5	$50	$45					
6	$50	$60					

Perhaps the easiest part of the chart to fill out would be the TC because the only thing required to do so would be to follow the TC equation where $TC = FC + VC$. The totals would equal 50, 60, 64, 71, 82, 95, and 110.

Quantity	FC	VC	TC	MC	AFC	AVC	ATC
0	$50	$0	$50				
1	$50	$10	$60				
2	$50	$14	$64				
3	$50	$21	$71				
4	$50	$32	$82				
5	$50	$45	$95				
6	$50	$60	$110				

Finding the MC requires taking the TC of the current quantity and subtracting the TC from the previous quantity. In equation format, it would look like this: $MC_n = TC_n - TC_{n-1}$. The MC of 0 would not be filled in with any number because one cannot go from a negative quantity to 0. The MC values for the remaining cells would be 10, 4, 7, 11, 13, and 15. Notice that the firm initially experiences decreasing MCs, but starting with the third carrot, increasing MCs exist. Peter could also find that same MC for each quantity by taking the current VC and subtracting the previous VC: $MC_n = VC_n - VC_{n-1}$.

Quantity	FC	VC	TC	MC	AFC	AVC	ATC
0	$50	$0	$50	-			
1	$50	$10	$60	$10			
2	$50	$14	$64	$4			
3	$50	$21	$71	$7			
4	$50	$32	$82	$11			
5	$50	$45	$95	$13			
6	$50	$60	$110	$15			

The AFC is the only cost curve that never increases. Because the FC does not change, any additional quantity serves to reduce the AFC curve by spreading the quantity out. The AFC would be blank when 0 quantity is produced. The initial AFC would be 50 because $50 \div 1 = 50$. But then the subsequent AFC totals would be 25, 16.7, 12.5, 10, and 8.3. Recall that the AFC is the only cost curve that will continuously decrease in value and therefore never slope upward.

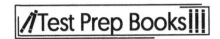

Quantity	FC	VC	TC	MC	AFC	AVC	ATC
0	$50	$0	$50	-	-		
1	$50	$10	$60	$10	$50		
2	$50	$14	$64	$4	$25		
3	$50	$21	$71	$7	$16.70		
4	$50	$32	$82	$11	$12.50		
5	$50	$45	$95	$13	$10		
6	$50	$60	$110	$15	$8.30		

The AVC is found by taking the VC and dividing the quantity, or $VC \div Q$. The AVC cell at 0 quantity will also be blank because when a firm does not produce anything, the VC will be $0, unlike the FC, which is the same regardless of the amount of production. The AVC at 1 would be 10, decrease to 7, stay at 7 for one more quantity, and then increase to 8, 9, and 10.

Quantity	FC	VC	TC	MC	AFC	AVC	ATC
0	$50	$0	$50	-	-		
1	$50	$10	$60	$10	$50	$10	
2	$50	$14	$64	$4	$25	$7	
3	$50	$21	$71	$7	$16.70	$7	
4	$50	$32	$82	$11	$12.50	$8	
5	$50	$45	$95	$13	$10	$9	
6	$50	$60	$110	$15	$8.30	$10	

The ATC is the TC divided by the quantity, or $TC \div Q$. However, there is another means to calculate the ATC. One could simply add the AFC and AVC totals: $ATC = AFC + AVC$. The ATC at 0 quantity would (like MC, AFC, and AVC) still be blank. The ATC at 1 is 60, and then it continues dropping to 32, 23.7, 20.5, and 18.3. Peter's company is operating on the downward sloping portion of the ATC and continues to do so. Whereas the AFC will continue to do so in perpetuity, the ATC, however, will eventually slope upward as the MC increases.

Quantity	FC	VC	TC	MC	AFC	AVC	ATC
0	$50	$0	$50	-	-	-	
1	$50	$10	$60	$10	$50	$10	$60
2	$50	$14	$64	$4	$25	$7	$32
3	$50	$21	$71	$7	$16.70	$7	$23.70
4	$50	$32	$82	$11	$12.50	$8	$20.50
5	$50	$45	$95	$13	$10	$9	$19
6	$50	$60	$110	$15	$8.30	$10	$18.30

When drawing the cost curves on a graph, there are a few points to consider. Very rarely will the AFC curve be depicted on a graph alongside the ATC and AVC curves. Because $ATC = AFC + AVC$, the equation can be rearranged such that $AFC = ATC - AVC$. The AFC is typically recognized as being the vertical distance between the AFC and AVC. Another key point when drawing the cost curves is that the ATC and MC will always cross the ATC at the minimum point. When the MC is above the ATC, the ATC is increasing. Conversely, when the MC is below the ATC, the ATC is decreasing. The figure below illustrates this concept.

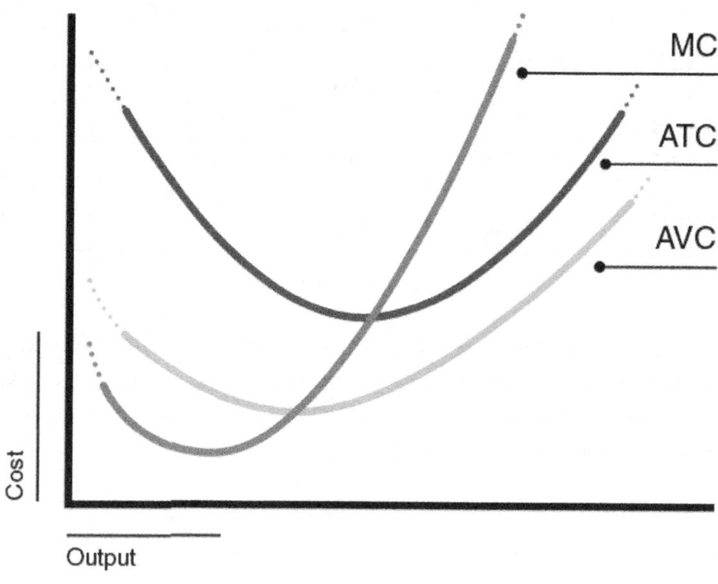

Cost Curves

Long-Run Production Costs

Key Terms Relating to Production and Cost

Constant returns to scale means that an increase in input will result in the same proportionate increase in output. For example, if 10 units of labor produces 2 T-shirts, doubling the units of labor will produce exactly twice the amount, or 4 T-shirts. Or if 4 units of capital produces 2 T-shirts, doubling the units of capital to 8 would yield a total of 4 T-shirts.

Increasing returns to scale means that output increases by more than the same amount of input. For example, if a company doubles the amount of capital and production, the output might triple or quadruple in production. Firms would have a huge incentive to increase their production level if they could operate with increasing returns to scale.

Decreasing returns to scale means that a company will return less than a proportional increase in output compared to its input. For example, if a company triples the amount of inputs but only doubles the output, they would be experiencing decreasing returns to scale.

So, what's the difference between decreasing returns to scale and diminishing marginal returns? Whereas input is fixed in the case of diminishing marginal returns, the same cannot be said for decreasing returns to scale. There is no assumption that only one input is fixed when dealing with returns to scale. Both capital and labor can be increased to determine whether the returns to scale is constant, increasing, or decreasing.

How Production and Cost are Related in the Short Run and Long Run

In the long run, there is no FC. All costs are variable because firms can adjust their inputs. If a company signs a one-year rental lease, for example, the monthly rent would be considered an FC in the short run. However, the business could decide to adjust costs so that even rent would be considered a VC in the long run. Usually, increases in technology cause firms to adjust production methods in order to stay economically viable.

The long-run ATC (LRATC) can be described as either economies of scale, diseconomies of scale, or constant returns to scale, as shown in the figure below.

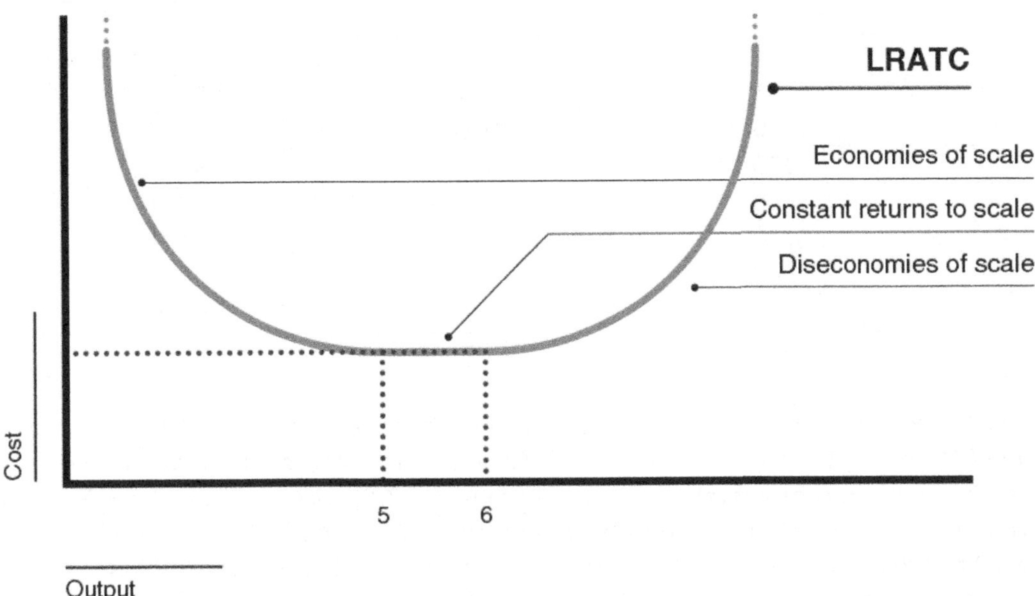

Economies of scale occurs when the ATC decreases as businesses produce output. Natural monopolies operate on the economies of scale portion of the ATC and have a competitive advantage over competing businesses because the MC of each additional output serves to further lower the ATC. It is more efficient to have one firm produce the entirety of output rather than many firms competing to produce the same product. Water and electricity are examples of industries that benefit from economies of scale.

When firms experience diseconomies of scale, the ATC increases as production increases. This occurs because businesses are producing output at a quantity where the MC is increasing when production increases. As businesses increase in size, it is common for firms to experience growing pains and operate at a higher ATC than when the output is at a lower level.

Constant returns to scale occurs when businesses have the same ATC when they increase the level of production. For example, if Paul produces 100 boots at an ATC of $20 and produces an additional 50 boots, he will continue to produce at an ATC of $20. The ATC remains at a constant level.

The minimum efficient scale (MES) is the lowest point on the LRATC in which a firm produces its product. There are many variables when determining the MES, and because all costs are variable in the long run, firms must reevaluate their production decisions to accommodate a variety of situations. An industry with a high MES typically only contains a few large firms and is therefore associated with high barriers to entry. On the other hand, if the MES is low, there tend to be lower barriers to entry and a higher number of firms that compete in the industry.

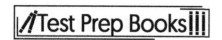

Calculate the Various Measures of Productivity and Short-Run and Long-Run Costs

Assume that Kyoung Kim is operating a hand sanitizer business and wants to operate at the MES. He wants to know at what point in the production process he is experiencing economies of scale, constant returns to scale, and diseconomies of scale.

Quantity	TC	MC	ATC
0	$100	-	-
10	$120	$2	$12
20	$130	$1	$6.50
30	$135	$0.50	$4.50
40	$150	$1.50	$3.75
50	$170	$2	$3.40
60	$200	$3	$3.30
70	$230	$3	$3.30
80	$260	$3	$3.30
90	$350	$9	$3.90
100	$500	$15	$5

Kyoung's hand sanitizer business is experiencing economies of scale for the first 60 hand sanitizers because the ATC steadily declines from 12 to 6.5 to 4.5 to 3.75 to 3.4 to 3.3. Between 60 and 80 bottles, the business experiences constant returns to scale because the ATC stays constant at 3.3. This is the MES. Most firms will attempt to produce within this range of output. If Kyoung increases production within the 80 to 100 range, the ATC will increase to 3.9 and then 5.0 because the MC has increased sharply in this range of production.

Types of Profit

Various Types of Profit

Adam Smith wrote in his landmark book, *An Inquiry Into the Nature and Causes of the Wealth of Nations,* that it "is not from the benevolence of the butcher, the brewer, or the baker that we expect our dinner, but from their regard to their own interest. We address ourselves, not to their humanity but to their self-love, and never talk to them of our necessities but of their advantages." The concept of profit is what motivates businesses to risk capital. A business that makes profit is successful; a business that cannot maintain profit is not successful and will eventually go out of business.

The most basic type of profit is **accounting profit**, or the money a business has left over after expenses. For example, if David opened up a bakery called Mak Café and had total revenues (TRs) of $1,000,000 with TCs of $900,000 for the year, his accounting profit would be $100,000 because the profit is the TR minus the TC ($1,000,000 – $900,000).

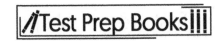

Economic profit takes the opportunity cost of an individual's decision into account. Let's say that David was also an accomplished lawyer and that his decision to pursue a career in the bread business means that he forgoes an annual salary of $150,000 as an attorney.

$$Economic\ profit = accounting\ profit - opportunity\ cost$$

$$-\$50{,}000 = accounting\ profit\ (\$100{,}000\ from\ Café\ Mak - opportunity\ cost\ (\$150{,}000\ as\ an\ attorney)$$

This means that even though David is making an accounting profit of $100,000 at Café Mak, he is incurring an economic loss of $50,000 because of his decision. Or, alternatively, David's economic profit is -$50,000.

Let's suppose that David sees increased business at Café Mak through a combination of increased marketing and customer satisfaction and now sees an annual revenue of $1.50 million but also increased costs of $1.35 million. Now, his accounting profit will have increased to $150,000 because $1.50 million (TR) minus $1.35 million (TC) equals $150,000. David could have made the same amount of income as a lawyer; therefore, his economic profit would now equal $0. This is referred to as **normal profit**, meaning that David's accounting profit is *exactly* equal to his opportunity cost.

How Firms Respond to Profit Opportunities

Economic profit (or loss) provides businesses the necessary barometer to determine whether or not to enter or exit a business. If there is any level of economic profit, firms will enter the industry. The resulting increase in the supply of firms will cause economic profit to lessen. Conversely, economic loss will cause firms to exit the industry. The resulting decrease in the supply of firms will cause economic loss to dissipate.

Let's examine the secondary market for Dodger Stadium giveaways. The Dodgers will hand out a stadium giveaway, such as a bobblehead, T-shirt, gnome, or jersey, on selected home baseball games. Some enterprising fans will take the items they have received at the game and sell them on sites like eBay. When there are very few sellers in the marketplace, the ability to profit handsomely exists. If, for example, an individual was the only seller of a Vin Scully bobblehead, he or she would be poised to earn a healthy dose of economic profit. However, when other sellers flood the market, economic profit is driven out so that sellers only receive normal profit.

Now let's look at the market for Korean BBQ restaurants to examine how economic loss might drive out competitors. Let's say that owners of Korean BBQ restaurants are collectively experiencing economic loss. The loss is a signal to individual firms to exit the industry. Hence, the supply of firms will decrease and drive out the loss in the long run. The equilibrium price for the entire Korean BBQ industry will increase, but the equilibrium quantity will decrease because there are now fewer firms competing in the marketplace.

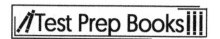

Calculate a Firm's Profit or Loss

Imagine that Austin goes into business selling alarm clocks and wants to figure out his profit (or loss) from selling various quantities. Each alarm clock sells for \$10. The cost numbers are detailed in the chart below. MR = marginal revenue.

Quantity	FC	VC	TC	MR	TR	Profit
0	\$12	-	\$12	\$10	\$0	
1	\$12	\$7	\$19	\$10	\$10	
2	\$12	\$10	\$22	\$10	\$20	
3	\$12	\$15	\$27	\$10	\$30	
4	\$12	\$25	\$37	\$10	\$40	
5	\$12	\$40	\$52	\$10	\$50	

When a firm produces nothing in the short run, the TR is \$0. The profit, however, is not \$0 because a firm that does not produce anything still has to pay the FC, usually rent. In this case, the profit would be $\$0 - \$12 = -\$12$. The profit at quantity 1, 2, 3, 4, and 5 would be –\$9, –\$2, \$3, \$3, and –\$2, respectively.

Quantity	FC	VC	TC	MR	TR	Profit
0	\$12	-	\$12	\$10	\$0	–\$12
1	\$12	\$7	\$19	\$10	\$10	–\$9
2	\$12	\$10	\$22	\$10	\$20	–\$2
3	\$12	\$15	\$27	\$10	\$30	\$3
4	\$12	\$25	\$37	\$10	\$40	\$3
5	\$12	\$40	\$52	\$10	\$50	–\$2

Profit-Maximizing Rule

The profit-maximizing rule of $MR = MC$ applies to businesses in all market structures. When the MR equals the MC, profit is maximized. A firm's decision on production is based on marginal behavior and not FCs, TCs, or TR. Recall Austin's alarm clock business. Using the same information from the previous chart, when one finds the MC numbers, the MR = MC rule dictates the optimal quantity of alarm clocks Austin will produce.

Quantity	FC	VC	TC	MC		MR	TR	Profit
0	\$12	-	\$12	-		\$10	\$0	-\$12
1	\$12	\$7	\$19	\$7		\$10	\$10	-\$9
2	\$12	\$10	\$22	\$3		\$10	\$20	-\$2
3	\$12	\$15	\$27	\$5		\$10	\$30	\$3
4	\$12	\$25	\$37	\$10	=	\$10	\$40	\$3
5	\$12	\$40	\$52	\$5		\$10	\$50	-\$2

Profit-Maximizing Level of Production

At the first quantity, the MR of 10 exceeds the MC of 10, so it makes sense to produce. The second alarm clock will only cost an additional $3 to make while the MR stays constant at $10, so it's a no-brainer to produce the second clock. The MC of the third quantity is still only $5 compared to the still constant MR of $10, so it makes sense to continue making more alarm clocks. The MC equals the MR at quantity 4. Austin will stop because $MR = MC$; he has reached the point of profit maximization. The previous quantity of 3 will also yield the same level of profit, but keep in mind that production decisions are based on *marginal* decisions and not overall profit. It's the process that matters and not the end result. If, however, one is erroneously making production decisions based on overall profit, a good rule of thumb is that in the case of a tie, the benefit of doubt should go to the quantity with the *higher* level of production. In either case, Austin is better off producing 4 (not 3) alarm clocks.

Firms' Short-Run or Long-Run Decisions

In the short run, firms make decisions on whether to stay in business or not based on VCs and not TCs. A firm may have the incentive to stay in business even it is not profitable. For example, let's assume that Marty runs a laser tag business and pays a one-time licensing fee of $1,000. The following chart shows the rationale as to why Marty might still want to stay in business despite losing money. Marty charges $22 per laser tag event.

Qty.	FC	VC	TC	MC	AFC	AVC	ATC	MR	TR	Profit
0	$1000	$0	$1000	-	-	-	-	$22	$0	-$1000
1	$1000	$20	$1020	$20	$1000	$20	$1020	$22	$22	-$998
2	$1000	$25	$1025	$5	$500	$12.50	$512.50	$22	$44	-$981
3	$1000	$35	$1035	$10	$333.30	$11.70	$345	$22	$66	-$969
4	$1000	$50	$1050	$15	$250	$12.50	$262.50	$22	$88	-$962
5	$1000	$70	$1070	$20	$200	$14	$214	$22	$110	-$960
6	$1000	$100	$1100	$30	$166.70	$16.70	$183.30	$22	$132	-$968

The same $MR = MC$ rule applies even when the numbers do not look pretty. The profit-maximizing quantity (qty.) for Marty is 5 even though the profit is -$960. The alternative of shutting down leads to a profit of -$1000, so producing 5 laser tag events is preferable to shutting the business down. In this particular case, the MC of the fifth laser tag event is $20, whereas the MR is $22. Because the sixth laser tag event exceeds the MR of $22, Marty should stop at the fifth quantity. Because the price is less than the ATC, Marty's laser tag business is unprofitable. However, because the price is greater than the AVC, he should still stay in business. Or, alternatively, because the TR is greater than the VC, it makes sense for Marty to continue operations because the amount of revenue he will get from continued operations exceeds the cost of running his business from that point in time. Unfortunately, Marty's $1,000 licensing fee is an unrecoverable cost. In other words, it's a "sunk" cost. There's no use crying over spilled milk. Marty overestimated his ability to overcome such a relatively large FC. Unfortunately, he is unable to create a time machine, travel back into time, and advise his past self to forgo venturing into the laser tag business.

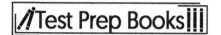

Perfect Competition

Characteristics of Perfectly Competitive Markets and Efficiency

There are four different market structures: monopoly, oligopoly, monopolistic competition, and perfect competition. A **monopoly** is a market structure with only one firm selling an undifferentiated product. An **oligopoly** is when a few firms sell either differentiated or undifferentiated products. Firms competing in **monopolistic competition** do so by selling differentiated products with many other competing firms. Finally, **perfect competition** is a market structure in which there are a lot of firms selling undifferentiated products.

There are two defining characteristics of perfect competitive firms. First, each individual firm cannot affect the market price of the firm. There are simply too many firms for one firm to affect the market price. For example, no individual wheat farmer is capable of changing the market price of wheat because his or her market share is negligible. The second prerequisite for a perfectly competitive market is that the product being sold is a **commodity**. Any attempt to raise the price of wheat will be firmly rebuffed by buyers who are able to buy the exact same good from Joe or Jane Farmer as they can from Jim or Jill Farmer. Individual firms are price takers.

Any individual firm can enter the market when profit exists. In a monopoly, barriers to entry preclude businesses from encroaching upon the profits found in that particular market structure. No such barriers exist in perfectly competitive firms (see figure below). Firms in perfect competition have no market power because each individual's market share is so miniscule. Profit serves as an incentive for enterprising firms to swoop in and take profit in the market.

In the long run, firms will have no economic profit. On the side-by-side graphs shown below, the graph on the right depicts the market for wheat. The graph on the left is an individual firm's costs and revenue for wheat. In the short run, economic profit exists, but firms will eventually enter because no barriers to entry exist and economic profit will return to $0.

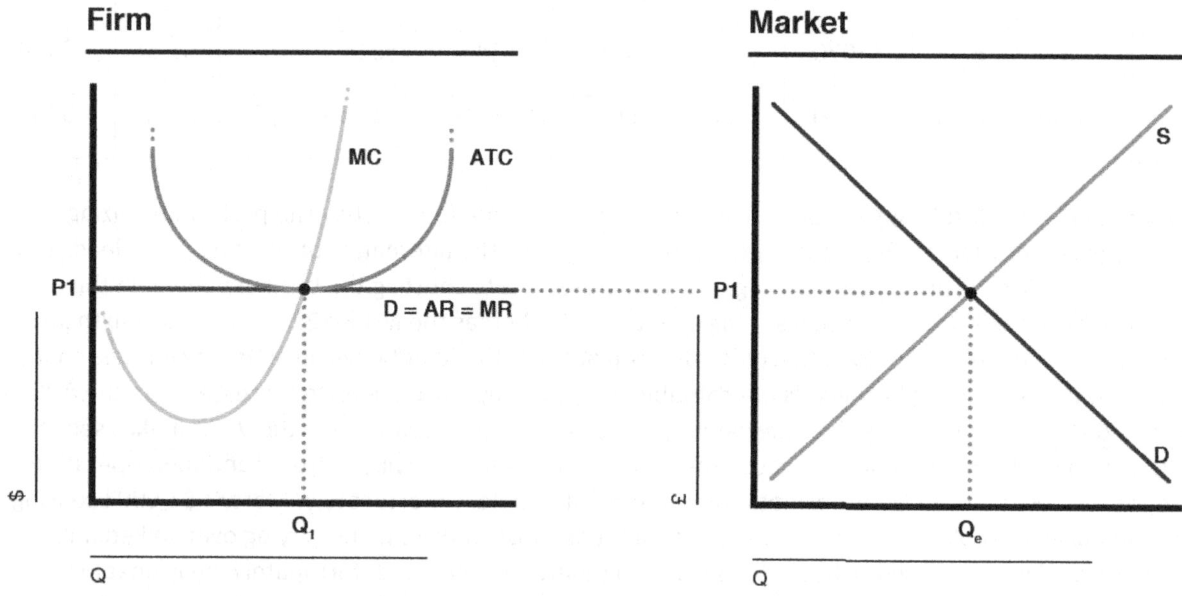

Economic profit is not a long-term sustainable situation for a firm in a perfectly competitive market. Because the price exceeds the ATC, economic profit exists. Firms will act on this "information" that there is above-normal profit and enter into the industry. There are no barriers to entry in perfectly competitive markets, so the entrance of new firms will eventually drive out the economic profit.

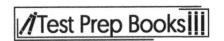

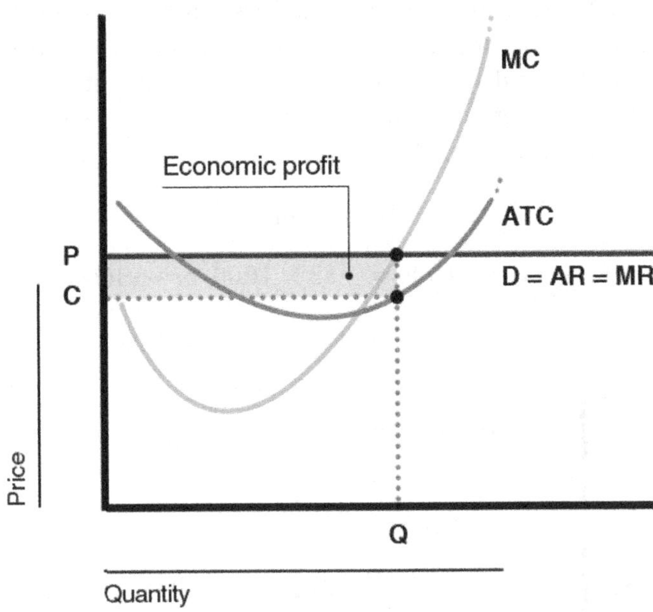

Firms would love the ability to dictate the price of their products on the open market. For example, let's say that Brown Paper Bag Company considers raising the price of their brown paper bags from $1.00 for a pack of 20 bags to $1.50. Here's the problem. Brown paper bag producers are a dime a dozen. There are 20,000 other brown paper bag companies that are selling their product at exactly $1.00 for that same 20-pack. Customers do not care who they are buying brown paper bags from because the product is identical. In fact, Brown Paper Bag Company cannot even afford to raise the price of its product to $1.01 because the demand curve is perfectly elastic.

Equilibrium and Firm Decision Making

In perfectly competitive markets, firms are both **allocatively efficient** and **productively efficient**. What that means is that the interaction of producers and consumers, through Adam Smith's "invisible hand," produces at a point that is both best for society and the individual producer.

Allocative efficiency means that no deadweight loss (DWL) exists. The intersection of the MC with the demand curve is the point of allocative efficiency because $price = MC$ at that juncture. Alternatively, another way to define allocative efficiency is finding the point in which consumer and producer surplus is maximized.

Productive efficiency is found at the minimum point of the ATC. On the production possibilities frontier, productive efficiency is equivalent to any point on the PPF graph. Any point underneath the PPF graph is inefficient and implies that firms are underproducing their goods or services. Firms that are perfectly competitive find themselves both allocatively efficient and productively efficient at the profit-maximizing point.

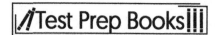

Economic Profit in Perfectly Competitive Markets

The economic profit (or loss) is the area between the price and the ATC curve. If the price exceeds the ATC, there is economic profit. If the ATC exceeds the price, there is economic loss.

In the graph below, the shaded area represents economic loss. Note that labeling the rectangular area as "economic profit" is also acceptable because it is negative economic profit. However, labeling the area as "economic loss" serves to avoid any confusion as to whether or not economic profit exists. Alternatively, one could determine that the economic loss is $3,000. Or, the economic profit is –$3,000. The formula to find the economic profit would be:

$$(price - ATC) \times (quantity)$$

$$(\$7 - \$10) \times 1000 = -\$3 \times 1000, \text{ or } -\$3000$$

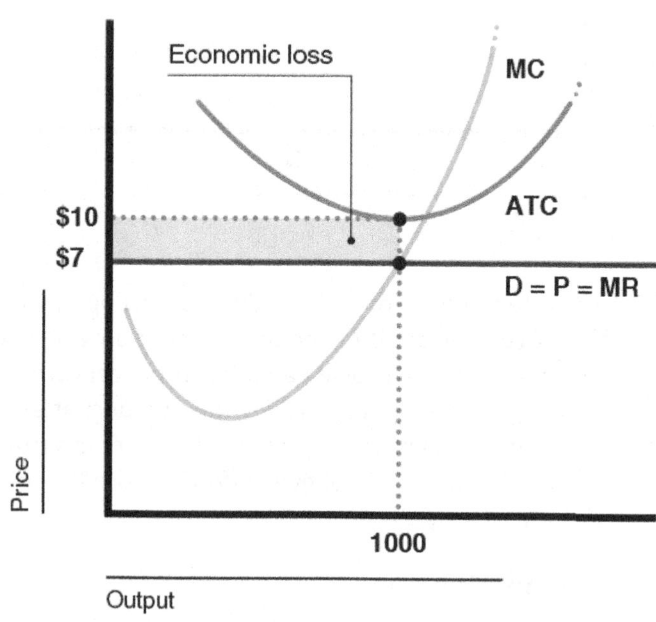

Microeconomics: Imperfect Competition

Introduction to Imperfectly Competitive Markets

Imperfectly Competitive Markets and Inefficiency

Firms rarely operate in perfectly competitive markets. Markets do not always function efficiently. In theory, everything functions equally and fairly. But the reality is that the real world is different from the world of perfect competition. Companies simply do not sell the exact same product. Some firms are able to control and manipulate the prices of their products, which is something that is not possible in a perfectly competitive environment.

In perfect competition, firms have equal market share. Each individual company does not have the ability to affect the market price of its product, even by a penny. In imperfect markets, that is certainly not the case. Pepsi and Coca-Cola, for example, certainly have greater market shares than other soda companies and wield a disproportionate amount of influence in their industry. Another factor at play that makes perfect competition more of a utopian concept than actual reality is that perfect information about prices and products is simply not available to all buyers. And finally, high barriers to entry (or exit) exist to make markets both imperfect and inefficient.

Monopoly, Oligopoly, Monopolistic Competition, and Monopsony

A **monopoly** is when a single seller exists in the marketplace. An **oligopoly** is when a few firms control the industry output. Firms compete in **monopolistic competition** when there are many buyers and sellers, and these sellers offer differentiated products to the masses. In contrast, their perfectly competitive counterparts sell identical products to their buyers. A **monopsony** is when there is only one buyer of either a good or a service.

Lowering Prices

A monopolist, like a firm in any other market structure, would love to charge as high a price as possible in order to maximize his or her profits. Firms in perfect competition cannot lower the price because they are price takers. Not so with monopolists. They are **price makers** capable of dictating the price they set in the marketplace. The quandary, however, lies with the fact that when the monopolist sells additional goods, it must lower the item's price in order to sell more of its product. As shown in the figure below, its marginal revenue (MR) will decrease when output increases.

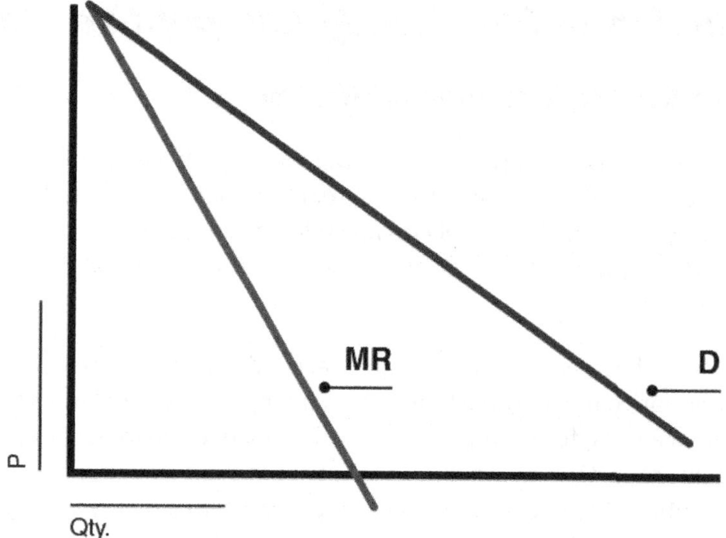

Leo is an entrepreneur who sells Rubik's Cubes in Taiwan. He sells his first Rubik's Cube for $10 and therefore receives a total revenue (TR) of $10, which is exactly the same as his MR of $10. If Leo sells a second Rubik's Cube, he must lower the price to $8. The TR is now $16, and the MR drops down to $6.

Now, let's say that Leo sells the third Rubik's Cube. He encounters the same problem as he did before. In order to motivate the third buyer to purchase his Rubik's Cube, Leo must lower the price of all Rubik's Cubes to $6. The TR is now $18 compared to a $16 TR when two Rubik's Cubes are sold. The MR of the third Rubik's Cube is $2. A fourth Rubik's Cube would fetch a price of $4. The TR would decrease back to $16, so $MR = -\$2$, which means $MR = MC$ has passed the point of revenue maximization. A profit-maximizing monopoly will always produce on the demand curve where the MR is positive (or the portion of the demand curve that is elastic). Because the TR decreased when the price decreased, the demand is inelastic when the MR is negative.

Quantity	Price	TR	MR
1	$10	$10	$10
2	$8	$16	$6
3	$6	$18	$2
4	$4	$16	-$2

Consumers and Producers Respond to Prices

Perfectly competitive firms produce at the allocatively efficient point; monopolistic firms do not. Perfectly competitive firms are not more naturally altruistic than their counterparts in a monopoly. Both types of firms are in the business of maximizing profit. It just so happens that the profit-maximizing point coincides with the allocatively efficient point for perfectly competitive firms. That's not the case for the monopolist.

A monopolist will produce at Qf where $MC = MR$ and charge Pf. The economic profit is the shaded area below the demand curve and above the ATC, or $(Pf \times Qf) - (ATC \times Qf)$, which is TR minus total cost

(TC). The monopolist will gladly take the economic profit that exists when the price is greater than the marginal cost (MC).

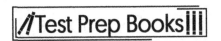

The point of allocative efficiency for a monopoly is where $MC = P$ at Qs. Monopolists have no incentive to produce at that point because the MC exceeds the MR. Even though the MR is still positive and economic profits still exist at that point, no profit-maximizing firm will willingly produce more output if it decreases profit. Monopolists simply do not care that the allocatively efficient yields no deadweight loss (DWL) and that consumer and producer surplus is maximized. A monopolist is in the business of doing what's best for its company, not what's best for society.

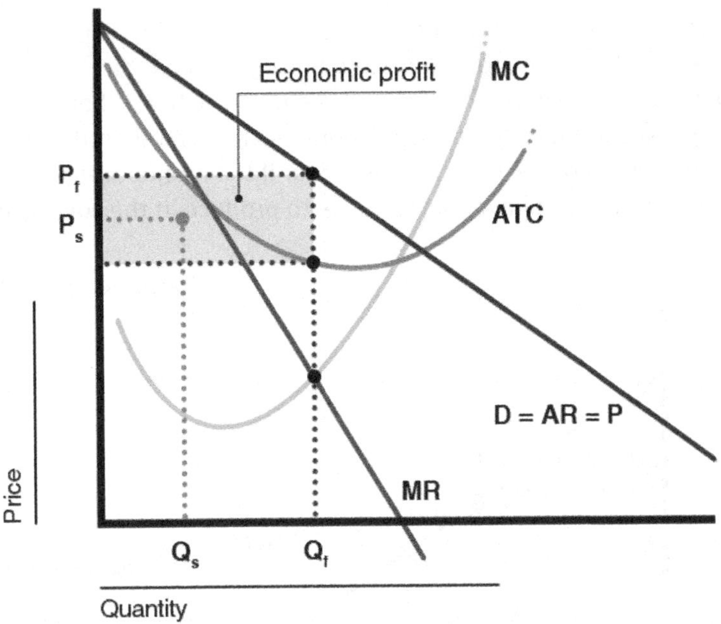

Barriers to Entry

In perfect competition, economic profit serves as an incentive for firms to enter. As the supply of firms increases, economic profit dwindles away to nothing in the long run. So, why doesn't that happen in a monopoly? Whereas firms competing in a perfectly competitive market have no barriers to entry, the opposite is true in a monopoly. High barriers to entry prevent competitors from threatening the profits of the existing monopolist.

Major League Baseball (MLB) is an example of a government monopoly. In *Federal Baseball Club v. National League* (1922), one of the teams from the failed Federal League in the mid-1910s sued MLB for having a monopolistic hold on baseball. Although the defendants (MLB) were initially held liable, the Supreme Court upheld a Court of Appeals ruling that overturned the verdict. In a unanimous decision written by Chief Justice Oliver Wendell Holmes, the Court argued that the Sherman Antitrust Act did not apply to baseball because it did not involve interstate commerce. No other professional sport has been given the same type of free rein to run as a monopoly. In theory, an upstart league could try to supplant MLB as the preeminent baseball league in the country, but the barriers to entry include a century of historic baseball accomplishments ingrained within a country's psyche as well as the full backing of the Supreme Court of the United States of America. Talk about high barriers to entry!

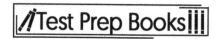

Monopoly

Equilibrium, Firm Decision Making, Consumer Surplus, Producer Surplus, Profit, and Deadweight Loss

In a monopoly, DWL exists. Because firms do not produce at the allocatively efficient point, consumer and producer surplus is not maximized. The consumer surplus is the area below the demand curve but above the price. The producer surplus is the area above the MC (which serves as the de facto supply curve) but below the price. The DWL represents the "lost" area of production.

The graph below shows the profit-maximizing price (Pf) and quantity (Qf), consumer surplus, producer surplus, and the DWL. This particular monopoly is experiencing an economic loss but is still acting rationally because profit maximizing in this case means the quantity that is being produced is loss minimizing. If the monopolist continues to produce, additional losses will accrue and the rectangular-shaped economic loss area will increase. DWL will disappear if the monopolist produces where the $MC = P$, but the monopolist does not have the incentive to produce at the socially optimal point.

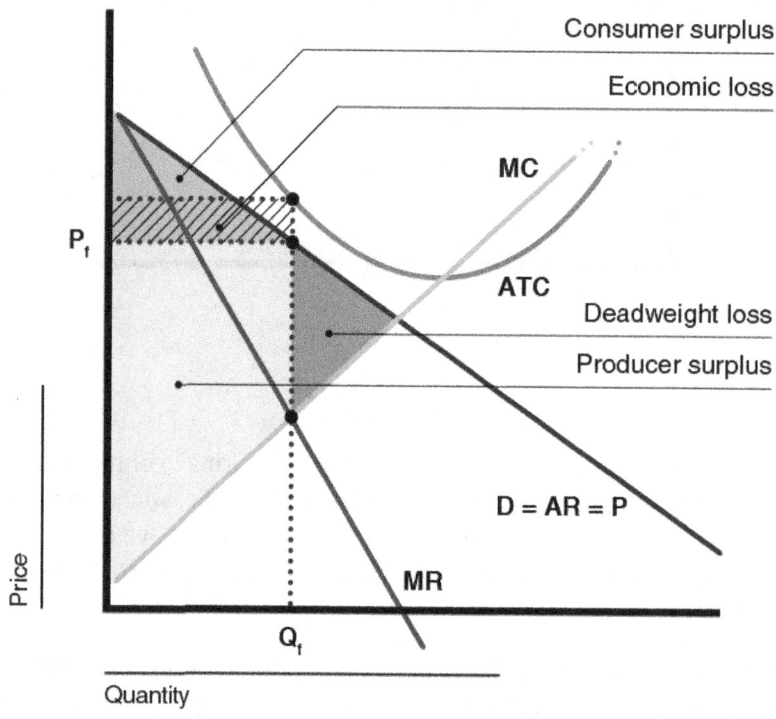

Areas of Consumer Surplus, Producer Surplus, Profit, and Deadweight Loss in Imperfectly Competitive Markets

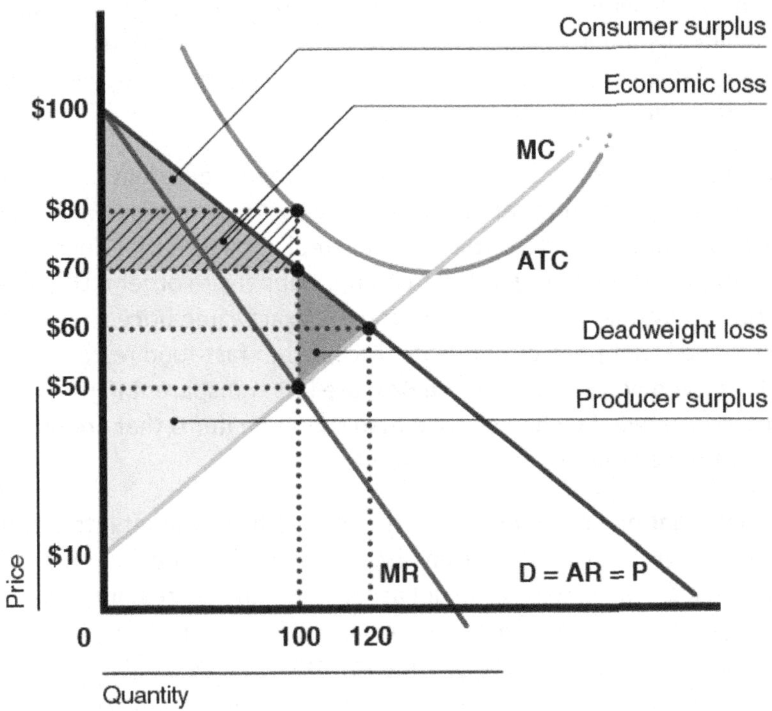

The numeric calculations for the monopoly graph above are as follows:

Consumer surplus: $(\$100 - \$70) \times (100) \div 2 = \$1500$

Producer surplus: $(\$50 - \$10) \times (100) \div 2 + (\$70 - \$50) \times (100) = \$2000 + \$2000 = \$4000$

Economic profit: $(\$70 - \$80) \times 100 = -\$1000$ or economic loss of \$1000

DWL: $(\$70 - \$50) \times (120 - 100) \div 2 = \$200$

The ability to calculate the total amount of consumer surplus, producer surplus, economic profit, and DWL is contingent on the monopoly graph containing specific numbers. In the absence of numbers, it is sufficient to shade the requisite area and label accordingly. However, if numbers are provided, the two simple formulas of $length \times width = total\ area\ of\ a\ rectangle$, and $½(length \times width) = total\ area\ of\ a\ triangle$ can be used to calculate the labeled areas of the graph.

Price Discrimination

Prices in Imperfectly Competitive Markets

The idea that the MR curve of a monopolistic firm is below the demand curve rests on the assumption that the monopolist can only charge a single price for its product. But what if a firm can sell its product to different groups of people at varying prices? This is known as **price discrimination**.

The first type of price discrimination is referred to as **first-degree price discrimination**. Imagine if Apple knew *exactly* what price each and every consumer was willing to pay for its new iPhone. Every item sold would match a consumer's maximum willingness to pay for the new phone. Consumers would lose all its consumer surplus to the producer in the form of additional profit. Apple would not exactly be "ripping off" its consumers if it had this supernatural ability of assessing consumer demand because consumers would willingly purchase items at relatively higher prices; however, market power would have shifted considerably to the producer in this hypothetical scenario.

Second-degree price discrimination occurs when companies charge different prices for quantities of goods (or services) that are consumed at varying levels. The best way to provide an example of how second-degree price discrimination works is to give an example of a firm that does *not* employ second-degree price discrimination: In-N-Out Burger. If a customer happens to order a Double-Double, french fries, and a medium coke individually, he or she will pay the exact same price as a Double-Double combo because In-N-Out Burger does not price discriminate. Most other fast-food restaurants, including McDonald's, Burger King, Wendy's, and Jack in the Box, are less transparent in their pricing in that individual menu items are charged at a higher price than the same items that are purchased as part of a combo meal. That's what price discrimination is all about.

Third-degree price discrimination occurs when sellers can classify its market into distinct categories. For example, some restaurants will offer senior citizen discounts based on the idea that individuals in a particular age bracket are less willing to pay top dollar for food. And so, restaurants will offer discounted pricing to those who might be living on a fixed income. One reason Denny's might offer a senior citizen discount but Nike offers no reduced pricing to its shoe-loving elderly population is that meals are difficult to resell. Shoes, on the other hand, can be resold easily, and offering senior citizens Nike Air Jordan discounts would result in a disproportionate number of older folks deciding to become "sneakerheads." At the minimum, teenagers would insist on taking Grandma or Grandpa to Foot Locker to take advantage of any available discounts!

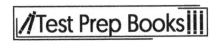

Calculate Areas of Consumer Surplus, Producer Surplus, Profit, and Deadweight Loss

A monopolist that perfectly price discriminates does not create additional DWL. However, the consumer surplus is transferred over to the producer in the form of additional profit.

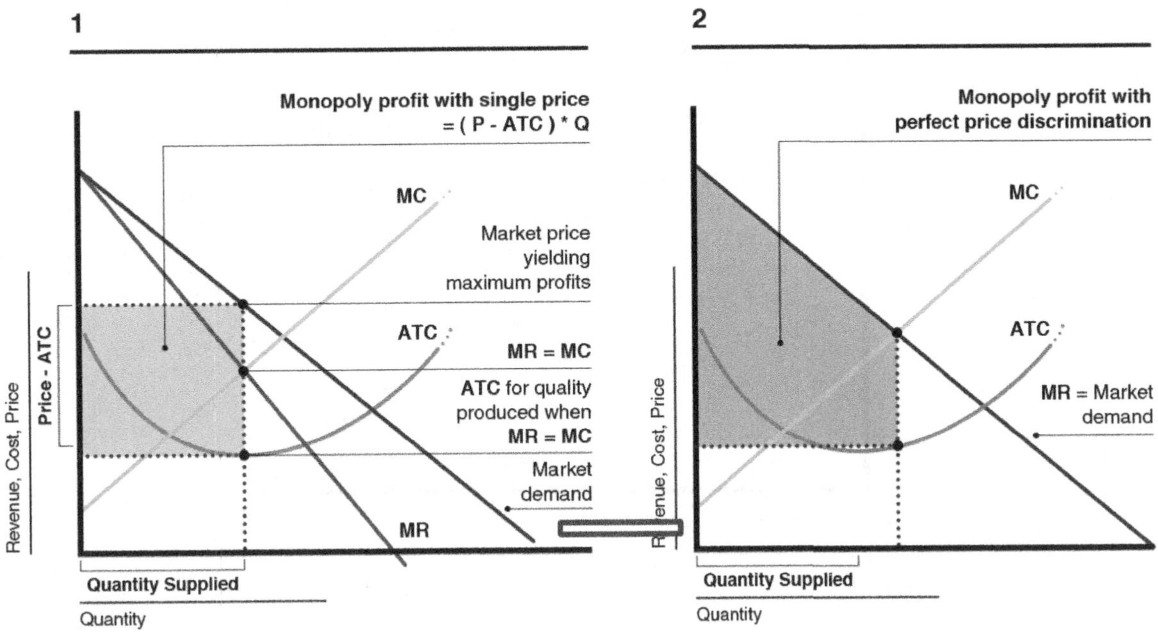

The above graph shows a typical monopoly graph with economic profit represented as the rectangular area, or $(P - ATC) \times Q$. The area below the demand curve but above the price is the consumer surplus. If a monopolistic firm has the power to perfectly price discriminate, the market demand curve and MR curve become one and the same (as seen in graph 2). The same profit-maximizing rule is employed in determining the quantity. However, because the new MR curve is now the demand curve, a monopolist will supply more of its good. All the consumer surplus will be transferred to the producer in addition to the consumer surplus that is gained from the elimination of DWL. A monopolist perfectly price discriminates for the purpose of increasing his or her economic profit. The unintended consequence, however, is that the monopolist increases its production to reach the socially optimal (or allocatively efficient) point because DWL is now a thing of the past.

Monopolistic Competition

Monopolistic Competitive Firm

A **monopolistically competitive firm** competes in an environment that is not quite a monopoly or perfectly competitive market. The graph of a monopolistically competitive firm looks extraordinarily similar (if not identical) to that of a monopoly making zero economic profit, as shown in the figure below. However, it would be disingenuous to claim that monopolistically competitive markets are closer to monopoly than perfectly competitive markets. The reality is that monopolistic competition is sort of a hybrid of these two market structures.

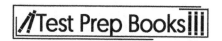

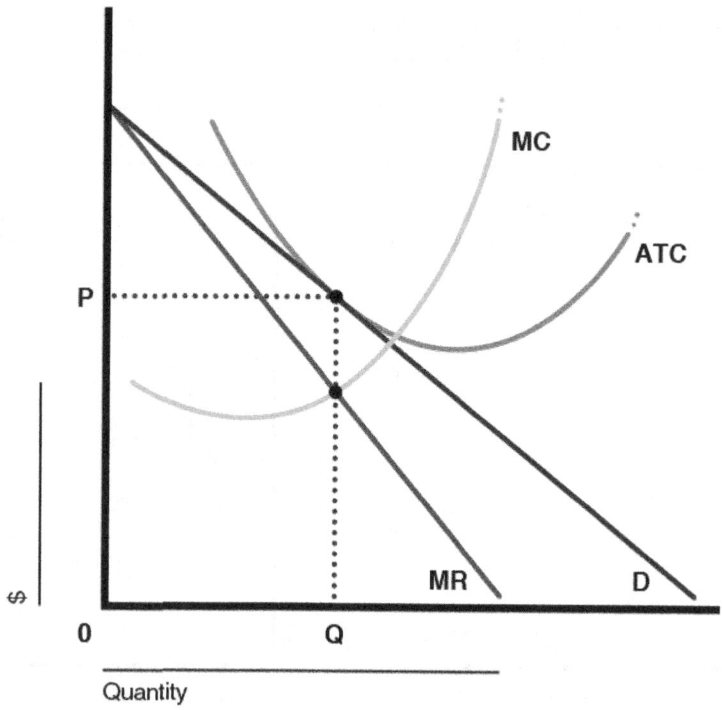

The only difference between a monopoly graph with $0 economic profit and a monopolistically competitive graph in long-run equilibrium is that the latter graph is slightly more elastic than the former. The reason is that monopolistically competitive firms are subject to competition that does not concern their counterparts in a monopoly market structure. Therefore, items in a monopoly tend to be more inelastic than items in monopolistic competition. Whereas firms in perfect competition sell identical products, product differentiation is a defining characteristic in monopolistically competitive models.

What makes perfectly competitive and monopolistically competitive markets similar is that there is no economic profit in the long run. Firms in monopolistic competition may produce an inefficiently low quantity, but they make only a normal profit (accounting profit but not economic profit), just like firms in perfect competition. And unlike a monopoly in which a firm has no competitor, firms in monopolistic competition and perfect competition find themselves competing with large numbers of firms to maximize profit and gain market share.

Monopolistically competitive firms, in the long run, make no economic profit. But, as shown in the figure below, just like in a monopoly market structure, firms in monopolistic competition can make a profit (or loss) in the short run.

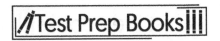

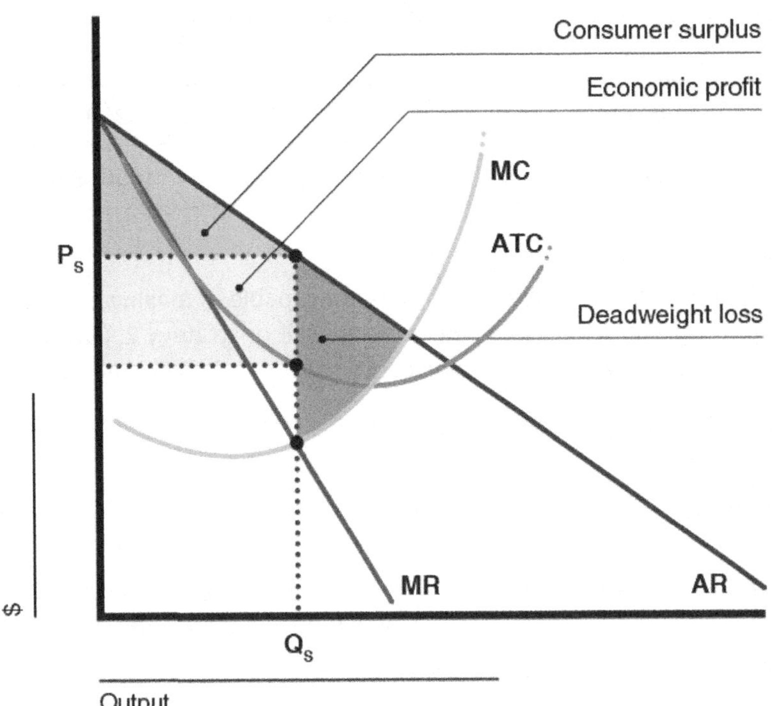

The area below the demand curve and above the price represents the consumer surplus. In this short-run equilibrium, economic profit exists, which is the area below the demand curve but above the price. The DWL is the almost triangular-shaped figure sandwiched between the profit-maximizing price, socially optimal point, and where $MR = MC$. The existence of economic profit in the short run serves as a signal to firms to enter into the market. And because there are low barriers to entry in monopolistic competition, the onslaught of firms entering the market will eventually drive away all economic profit so that only normal profits remain.

Oligopoly and Game Theory

Concepts Relating to Oligopolies and Simple Games, Strategy, and Player

An oligopoly is a market structure in which a few firms dominate. The phone industry is an example in which the top two players (AT&T and Verizon) dominate the marketplace. An often overlooked oligopoly is the comic book industry. Marvel and DC Comics comprise the bulk of superhero-related content that has been published over the years. It would take a lot to topple the likes of Batman, Superman, or the Avengers.

The study of **game theory** is comfortably ensconced in the oligopoly unit. Game theory examines individual decision making within a group context. Simple two-player games would not work in a perfectly competitive, monopolistically competitive, or monopoly context. Too many firms exist in either perfect competition or monopolistic competition for collusion to take place. And in monopoly, the role of interdependence is non-existent because, by definition, only one firm exists.

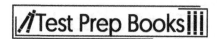

		Player B	
		Strategy 1	Strategy 2
Player A	**Strategy 1**	A ($100, $100)	B ($200, 0)
	Strategy 2	C ($200, 0)	D ($50, $50)

In the simplest game theory model, only two individuals are capable of making a choice between two alternatives. Player A (the x-player) can choose either strategy 1 or strategy 2. Player B (the y-player) can choose either strategy 1 or strategy 2. The resulting combination of choices yields box A, box B, box C, or box D.

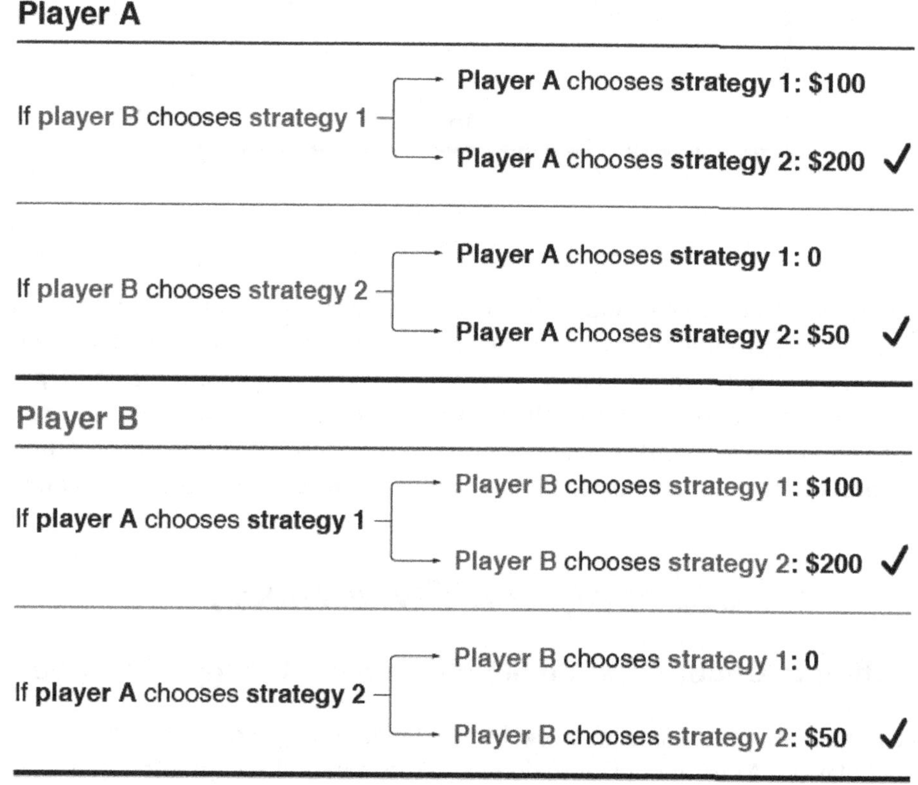

Dominant strategy means that an individual will choose the same option regardless of what the other individual decides. If player B opts for strategy 1, player A will profit $100 by choosing strategy 1 and $200 by choosing strategy 2; strategy 2 beats strategy 1. If player B chooses strategy 2, player A is left with $0 by choosing strategy 1 but makes $50 by choosing strategy 2. Yet again, strategy 2 beats strategy 1. Player A has a dominant strategy of choosing strategy 2.

Because player B (the y-player) faces the exact same scenario as player A, player B also has a dominant strategy of choosing strategy 2. In either scenario (player A choosing strategy 1 or strategy 2), player B maximizes his own profit by choosing strategy 2. Both players have a dominant strategy of choosing strategy 2, so the result is box D. This is referred to as the **Nash equilibrium**. Neither player has an incentive to switch his or her strategy even if the other person switches his or her play. Both players are better off staying put by choosing strategy 2.

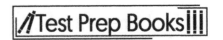

This particular game is a **prisoner's dilemma** because if both players choose strategy 1, the overall profit will be better than if they choose individually what's best for themselves. If both players choose strategy 1, each player will walk away with $100 in profit. The problem, however, is that players do not choose the combined boxes; each player can only control his or her play. If player A chooses strategy 1, player B's best option is strategy 2, and player A walks away with nothing. And if player B chooses strategy 1, player's A's best option is strategy 2, and player B walks away with nothing. What a dilemma! (A prisoner's dilemma, that is.)

Strategies and Equilibria in Simple Games

A game theory situation in which both players have a dominant strategy with the Nash equilibrium yielding a situation worse than the collusive output (prisoner's dilemma) is only one of a multitude of scenarios. Let's look at a game theory matrix in which two high school students sell boba on campus. They are the only two boba sellers at school, so they have to operate in an oligopoly market structure.

		Cassie	
		High	Low
Miley	High	A ($400, $500)	B ($300, $600)
	Low	C ($200, $400)	D ($500, $800)

Miley is the x-player, and Cassie is the y-player. Box A yields a profit of $400 for Miley and $500 for Cassie. Box B provides Miley with $300 and Cassie with $600. Box C gives a paltry $200 for Miley and an unexciting $400 for Cassie. Box D nets $500 for Miley and a whopping $800 for Cassie. Keep in mind, however, that the participants do not collectively decide to choose box A, B, C, or D. Miley and Cassie can only control their individual decisions to go high or too low.

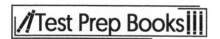

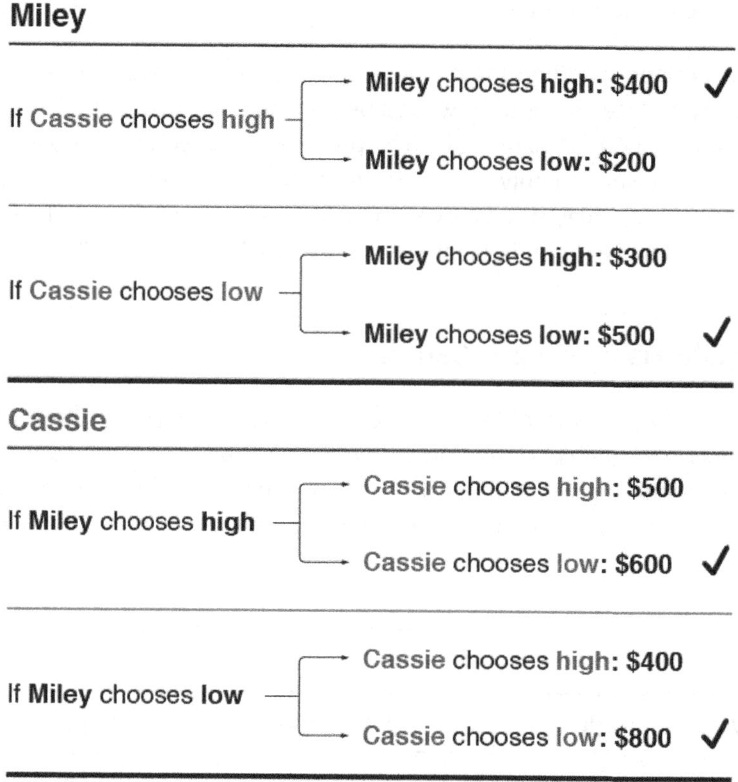

Miley does not have a dominant strategy. If Cassie chooses high, Miley is better off going high because $\$400 > \$200$. If Cassie decides to sell low, Miley makes more money by also going low because $\$500 > \$300$. Cassie, on the other hand, has a dominant strategy of going low. If Cassie chooses high, going low is the better option because $\$600 > \$500$. If Miley goes low (which Cassie hopes will happen), Cassie will also go low and make $800 instead of a relatively paltry $400 profit.

So, what will happen if Cassie and Miley both know the figures in the game theory matrix? Well, Cassie has the competitive advantage because she will play her dominant strategy, and Miley will simply have to follow suit. Cassie will go low, and then Miley will have to determine whether to go high and profit $300 or go low and generate $500 in earnings. The choice is simple for Miley, so she will go low. Box D represents the Nash equilibrium because that is where box players optimize their individual game strategies.

Nash equilibrium

The **Nash equilibrium** is a situation in which no participant can gain by changing his or her strategy after considering his or her opponent's choice. The Nash equilibrium, heretofore, has resided in a single box.

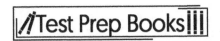

This is not always the case. Let's look at a game theory situation in which there is a Nash equilibrium of more than just one combination of points. Let's call this game "Video Game Wars."

		Microsoft	
		Early	Late
Sony	Early	A ($4 million, $4 million)	B ($7 million, $8 million)
	Late	C ($10 million, $10 million)	D ($3 million, $6 million)

Microsoft and Sony have to make a decision on when to release their new game consoles. They can either choose early or late. If both choose early or both choose late, their profits will collectively be less than if one releases early and the other releases late. The optimal solutions occur if Sony and Microsoft stagger the release of their new consoles such that one releases early and the other releases late.

Microsoft

If Microsoft chooses early	Sony chooses **early: $4 million**	
	Sony chooses **late: $8 million**	✓
If Microsoft chooses late	Sony chooses **early: $10 million**	✓
	Sony chooses **late: $6 million**	

Sony

If **Sony** chooses **early**	Microsoft chooses early: **$4 million**	
	Microsoft chooses late: **$10 million**	✓
If **Sony** chooses **late**	Microsoft chooses early: **$7 million**	✓
	Microsoft chooses late: **$3 million**	

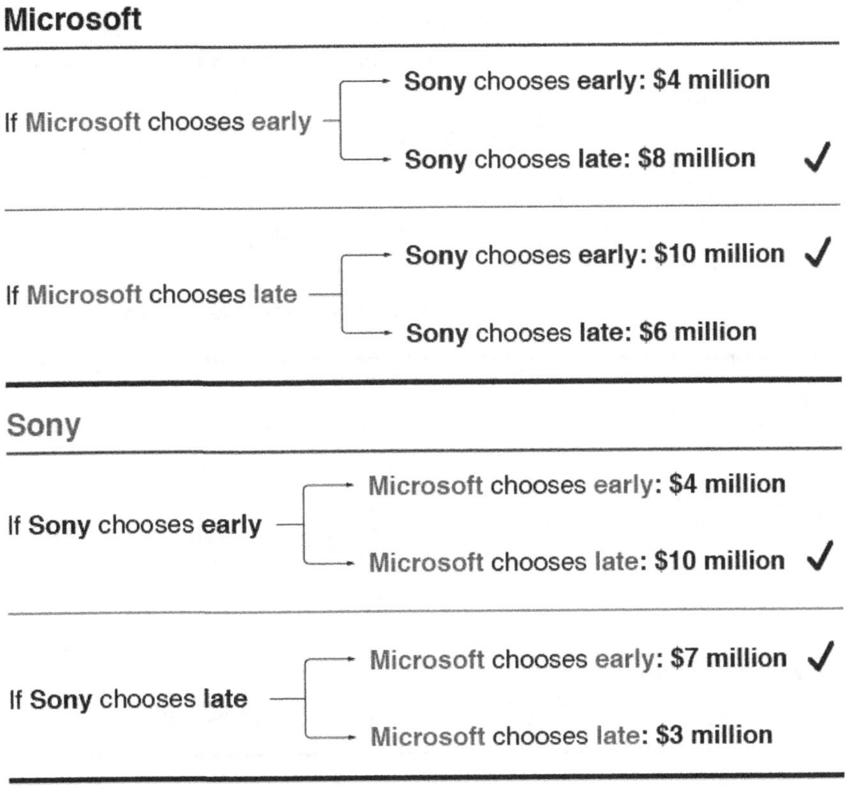

Neither Microsoft nor Sony has a dominant strategy. If Sony chooses early, Microsoft is better off choosing late. If Sony choose late, Microsoft should choose early. This is also the case with Sony. If Microsoft opts to go early, $\$10 > \$4\ million$, so Sony should choose late. If Microsoft opts to go late, $\$7\ million > \$3\ million$, so early is the better of the two options for Sony. The Nash equilibrium, therefore, resides in box B and box C. Both parties now have a clear incentive to switch their strategy if the other company changes from early to late or late to early.

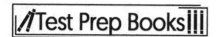

Calculate the Incentive Sufficient to Alter a Player's Dominant Strategy

Now, assume that the government has decided to provide a $5 million subsidy to game console producers who release early. Does that alter what Microsoft or Sony will do? Let's rewrite the game theory matrix to reflect the added incentive to release early.

		Microsoft	
		Early	Late
Sony	Early	A ($9 million, $9 million)	B ($12 million, $8 million)
	Late	C ($10 million, $15 million)	D ($3 million, $6 million)

Now that $5 million has been added to each early entry, the situation has changed. Let's take a look.

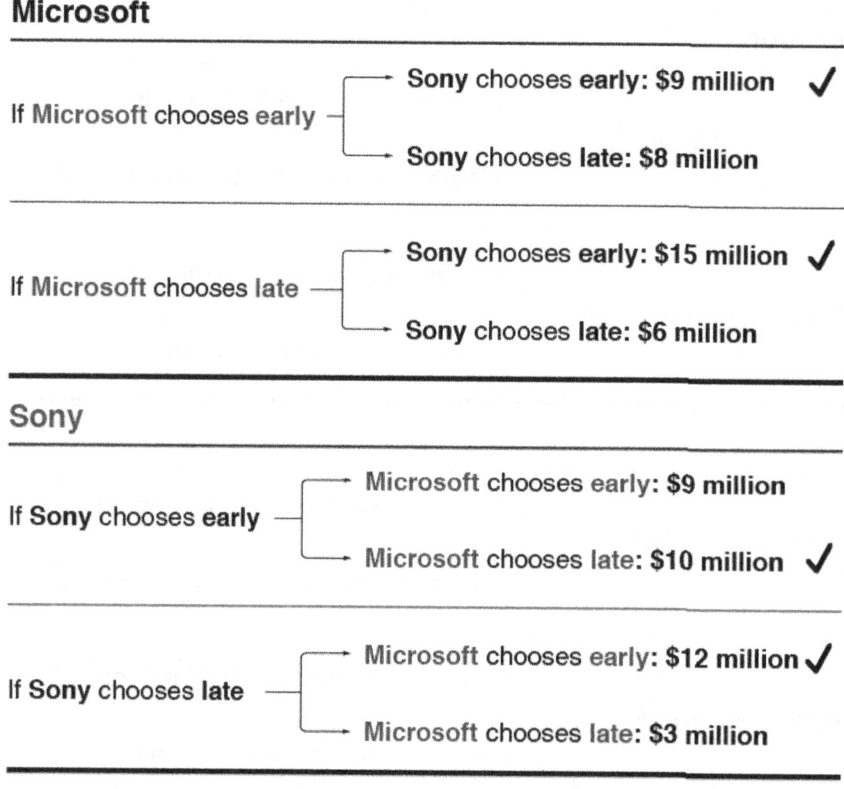

Microsoft now has a dominant strategy. The $5 million subsidy has motivated the company to choose early even when Sony chooses early; $9 million (choosing late) is more than $8 million (choosing early), and $15 million (choosing early) is now much more attractive than $6 million (choosing late). Microsoft will now choose early no matter what.

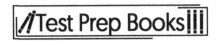

With this changed game theory matrix, Sony will disregard the universe in which Microsoft chooses late. Microsoft will go early 100 times out of 100. So now, Sony must choose between early ($9 million) or late ($10 million). Sony will choose late, and the resulting Nash equilibrium will be box C.

Oligopolists Have Difficulty Achieving the Monopoly Outcome

In a classic prisoner's dilemma, firms will choose the result that is not optimal for the group. The best solution comes when both firms act *against* their individual self-interest, which will produce the highest collective profit. In real life, there are similar constraints that prevent oligopolists from making the most money for the industry. The Organization of the Petroleum Exporting Countries (OPEC) would make the most money collectively if member countries would simply agree to limit total output. But countries think about what's best for themselves and not what's best for all the member countries of OPEC. When one country decides to produce more oil than was originally agreed upon, other countries will follow suit and flood the market with more oil, which benefits to serve consumers in the form of lower prices. In the United States, this type of collusive behavior is illegal. Coke and Pepsi would suffer a variety of legal consequences if they colluded to jointly raise prices of soda to increase profit.

Nevertheless, oligopolists enjoy a greater ability to raise prices than their counterparts in monopolistic competition or perfect competition. When there are so few firms in an industry, it goes to reason that there would be a considerable amount of pricing power within a small group of powerful companies. So, firms in oligopolies will raise the price of their products even if it means losing some customers because the goal of any business is not to maximize the number of customers, maximize revenue, or even maximize the quantity of goods sold. The goal of any business in a monopoly, perfectly competitive market, monopolistically competitive market, and oligopoly is to simply maximize profit. That's the long and short of it.

Microeconomics: Factor Markets

Introduction to Factor Markets

Concepts Relating to Factor Markets

The **factor market** is a market in which business firms purchase the factors of productions (land, labor, and capital) from households in order to produce goods and services. **Land** is all of the natural resources that can be used for supply. Gold, oil, and timber are considered natural resources; **rent** is the income derived from natural resources. **Labor** is the paid work performed by individuals who have varying levels of skill, motivation, and education. **Wages** are the income that households receive from work performed. **Capital** refers to man-made goods that are used in the production of consumer goods, and income from capital goods is referred to as **interest**.

Some economists acknowledge a fourth factor of production: entrepreneurship. An **entrepreneur** is an individual who is willing to take the risks inherent in the marketplace and combines the three factors of production (land, labor, and capital) in order to produce a good or service that households will want to purchase. Income that entrepreneurs make is called **profit**.

The **circular flow diagram** is a simplified depiction of how firms and households interact in both the factor and the product markets. In the factor market, households are the sellers and business firms are the buyers. Izabella Morales partakes in the factor market when she goes to work at the daycare center as a babysitter. Her employer, Ashley's Angelic Infants, is impressed with Izabella's amazing ability to take care of little children, so the marginal benefit that her company derives exceeds the marginal cost associated with hiring Izabella, who has an impressive amount of human capital.

Households sell their land, labor, and capital to businesses in exchange for rent, wages, interest, and profit. In the **product market**, the reverse of the factor market is true: households are the buyers of goods and services, while business firms are the sellers. When Adrian Loper, a sophomore in high school, goes to buy strawberry milk boba at the Porras Palace of Bobas, he makes a sales payment in exchange for a good. The interaction of buyers and sellers in both the factor and product markets creates a circular flow of the economy.

Incentives matter. Households make decisions to sell land, labor, and capital in the factor market based on whether the rent, wages, and interest payments are high enough to make it worth their time. Similarly, a firm's decision to hire *x* number of workers or employ *y* number of capital stems from how productive the factor is, how much the item sells for, and the cost of the factor.

Relationship Between Factors of Production, Firms, and Factor Prices

The **marginal revenue product** is the marginal product of labor times the price of the product. The **marginal factor (or resource) cost** is the additional wage that is paid to a worker. If the wage rate does not change based on the amount of labor hired, the wage rate is the same as the marginal factor cost. However, this is not always the case. If the wage of an additional worker is higher than the existing wage rate, then the wage rate will necessarily increase as a result of a new, more expensive worker's hire because the employer will now have to pay that same wage rate to all current employees. Ultimately, the goal for a firm is for its marginal factor cost to equal its marginal revenue profit ($MFC = MRP$) in order to maximize profit.

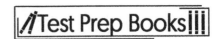

Calculate the Marginal Revenue Product and Marginal Resource Cost

Suppose Susan owns a t-shirt factory called Susan's T-Shirt Factory. The number of t-shirts that she produces depends on several factors. How many t-shirts does each worker produce? What is the price that the t-shirt is selling for? And finally, what is the wage that each t-shirt worker makes? Let's assume that she sells t-shirts in a perfectly competitive market and that she also hires workers in a perfectly competitive labor market.

Susan, like most entrepreneurs, is in the business of maximizing profit. The item that she sells just happens to be t-shirts, and her concern is hiring the optimal number of workers in the factor market. Let's assume that she can hire between one and five workers. The first worker that she can hire, Andrew, can make 5 t-shirts in one hour of work. Andrew's **marginal product of labor (MPL)**, which is the amount of additional output from hiring one unit of labor is 5. The second worker, Bernie, would increase the total production to 15 t-shirts for the hour. Bernie represents **increasing marginal returns**, which means that his hiring has caused an increase in the rate of production which necessarily means that the total production has increased as well. The MPL increased from 5 to 10.

The third and fourth workers would represent **diminishing marginal returns**, meaning that their hiring has resulted in a decrease in the rate of production while increasing the total amount. Charles, the third worker, would increase the total to 18 t-shirts, while Daniel, the fourth worker, would increase the total to 20 t-shirts. Their marginal products of labor would be 3 and 2, respectively.

The fifth worker Susan is considering for Susan's T-shirt Factory, Jinhee, represents **negative marginal returns**, which means the *total* amount of production decreases as well as the rate of production. The total number of t-shirts produced would now be 15, so Jinhee's MPL is -5.

Now, let's assume that the price of a t-shirt is $5 while the wage for unskilled workers is $15 an hour. What would the optimal number of workers be in this particular situation? Let's take a look using the numbers from the table that follows.

Quantity of Workers	Total Number of T-Shirts	Marginal Product of Labor (per hour)	Price of T-shirts	Marginal Revenue Product	Wage (per hour)
0	0	0	5	0	15
1 (Andrew)	5	5	5	25	15
2 (Bernie)	15	10	5	50	15
3 (Charles)	18	3	5	15	15
4 (Daniel)	20	2	5	10	15
5 (Jinhee)	15	-5	5	-25	15

Without question, Andrew should be hired. His MRP is 25. Remember, the $MRP = MPL \times Price\ of\ the\ Product$, and $5 \times 5 = 25$. Also, the wage that Andrew is paid is only $15. Bernie's MPL of 10 yields an even higher MRP of 50, because his MPL of 10 multiplied by 5 = 50. When you have increasing marginal returns to labor, there is absolutely no question as to whether you should hire that next individual. The real question is whether or not a company should hire an individual if there exists diminishing marginal returns to labor. As with most things in life, the answer is, "It depends." Charles has an MPL of 3, so his MRP is 15, which equals the wage of 15. Because the $MRP = MFC$ (or wage), it makes sense to hire Charles, the third employee. Daniel's MPL is 2, so his MRP is 10, which is below the wage of 15. Because the $MRP < MFC$ (or wage), it does not make sense to hire Daniel, the third employee. Even though both Charles and Daniel have diminishing MPL, it only makes sense to hire Charles. Hiring Charles will increase profitability while hiring Daniel will decrease profitability.

Changes in Factor Demand and Factor Supply

Firms' and Factors' Responses to Changes in Incentives and Constraints

Changes in the factor demand stems from one of two factors.

$$Marginal\ Revenue\ Product\ (MRP) = Marginal\ Product\ of\ Labor\ (MPL) \times Price\ of\ the\ Product$$

As such, the marginal revenue product can increase or decrease depending on the 1) change of MPL, or 2) change of the price of the product. The **demand for labor** is the firm's MRP curve, so the Demand for Labor shifts when the MPL or the price of the product changes.

If the MRP shifts to the right, the quantity of labor increases but the wage stays the same in a perfectly competitive factor market because the wage is perfectly elastic. If the MRP shifts to the left, the quantity of labor decreases but the wage still remains the same in this scenario.

Suppose Shaw's Burger Shack is looking to hire the optimal quantity of workers. The number of workers that the owner hires in a perfectly competitive labor market would be at Q_1, which is where $MRP_1 =$ MFC. However, if there is a new technology that increases the productivity of unskilled workers, the MPL increases, which causes the MRP curve to shift to the right. The optimal quantity increases from Q_1 to Q_2. The wage, however, stays the same.

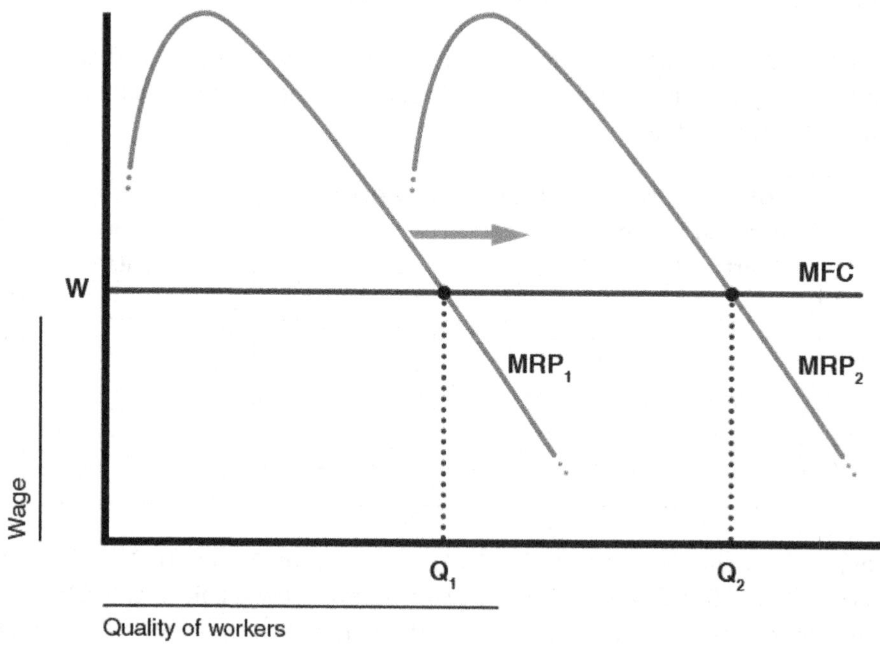

Suppose Taco Town is also looking to hire the optimal quantity of workers. The number of workers that Taco Town hires in a perfectly competitive labor market would be at Q_1, the point at which $MRP_1 =$ MFC. However, if the price of a taco drops from $5 to $3, then the MRP curve would shift to the left. The optimal quantity decreases to where $MRP_2 =$ MFC from Q_1 to Q_2. If either the MPL or the wage rate decreases, the MRP shifts to the left to ultimately decrease the number of workers hired in the industry.

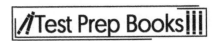

The wage rate, however, will stay exactly the same just like in the previous example with Shaw's Burger Shack.

Profit-Maximizing Behavior in Perfectly Competitive Factor Markets

Characteristics of Perfectly Competitive Factor Markets

In a perfectly competitive factor market, the **Marginal Factor Cost (MFC)**, which is the cost of adding one unit of labor, is constant. Laborers in a perfectly competitive factor market are referred to as wage-takers because they are unskilled laborers that take the wage given to them.

The **Marginal Revenue Product (MRP)** is the amount of money that a producer takes in from the sales of a particular product. As an equation:

$$Marginal\ Revenue\ Product\ (MRP) = Marginal\ Product\ of\ Labor\ (MPL) \times Price.$$

Alternatively, the Value of the Marginal Product of Labor (VMPL) is the additional value added by the labor of the worker. As an equation:

$$Value\ of\ the\ Marginal\ Product\ of\ Labor\ Prod\ (VMPL) = Marginal\ Product\ of\ Labor\ (MPL) \times Price.$$

Profit-Maximizing Behavior of Firms Buying Labor in Perfectly Competitive Markets

Let's examine a situation in which the MRP does not exactly equal the MFC. What happens if the MRP and MFC never intersect? Chris is in the business of maximizing profit. He sells basketballs for his company, Mamba Basketballs, and his concern is hiring the optimal number of workers in the factor market. Let's assume that he can hire between one and give workers. The first worker that he can hire, Jeff, can make 6 basketballs in one hour of work. Jeff's **marginal product of labor (MPL)**, which is the amount of additional output from hiring one unit of labor, is 6. The second worker, Kobe, would increase the total production to 14 t-shirts. Kobe represents **increasing marginal returns**, which means that his hiring has caused an increase in the rate of production, which necessarily means that the total production has increased as well. The MPL increased from 6 to 8.

The third and fourth workers represent **diminishing marginal returns**, meaning that their hiring has resulted in a decrease in the rate of production while increasing the total amount. Mark, the third worker, would increase the total to 19 t-shirts, while Dean, the fourth worker, would increase the total to 22 t-shirts. Their marginal products of labor would be 5, and 3, respectively.

The fifth worker, Bob, is a kleptomaniac. Chris did not conduct a thorough background check with Bob prior to his hiring. Bob represents **negative marginal returns**, which means the *total* amount of production decreases as well as the rate of production because while he does make one basketball per hour, he also pilfers two basketball in the process! The total number of basketballs produced would now be 21, so Bob's MPL is -5.

Now, let's assume that the price of a basketball is $3 while the wage for unskilled workers is $12 an hour. What would the optimal number of workers be for Mamba Basketballs? Let's take a look using the numbers from the table below.

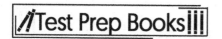

Calculate Measures Representing the Profit-Maximizing Behavior of Firms Buying Labor in Perfectly Competitive Markets

Quantity of Workers	Total Number of Basketballs	Marginal Product of Labor (per hour)	Price of Basketballs	Marginal Revenue Product	Wage (per hour)
0	0	0	3	0	12
1 (Jeff)	6	6	3	18	12
2 (Kobe)	14	8	3	24	12
3 (Mark)	19	5	3	15	12
4 (Dean)	22	3	3	9	12
5 (Bob)	21	-1	3	-3	12

Jeff definitely should be on the payroll. His MRP of 18 easily exceeds his wage of 12. Kobe's MPL of 8 yields an even higher MRP of 24. Kobe is a superstar, and his ability to make basketballs is legendary. His ability to produce basketballs is unparalleled, and there is no disputing that he is the greatest ever to produce Mamba basketballs. Mark has an MPL of 5, so his MRP of 15 exceeds the wage of 12. Dean's MPL is 3, and so his MRP is only 9. Because the MRP of 9 < MFC (or wage) of 12, Chris should not hire Dean. So even though both Mark and Dean have diminishing MPL, it only makes sense to hire Mark because Mark's MRP exceeds his MFC, whereas Dean's MRP is less than his MFC. In this particular example, because there is no point at which the MRP = MFC (or wage), the applicable rule would be to hire the number of workers in which the MRP is greater than the MFC (or wage) but before the MRP dips below the MFC (or wage).

Monopsonistic Markets

Characteristics of Monopsonistic Markets

Whereas a **monopoly** is a market with only one seller, a **monopsony** is a market in which there is only one buyer. A typical firm in a monopsonistic market will continue hiring workers until the marginal revenue product equals the marginal factor cost. However, a monopsonist does not pay its laborers where the $MRP = MFC$. Rather, the monopsonist pays a wage corresponding to the supply curve directly beneath the MFC curve. Whereas the **marginal revenue (MR)** curve in a monopoly graph is below the demand (D) curve in the product market, the **marginal factor cost curve (MFC)** is above the supply (S) curve in a monopsony graph. The monopolist is able to "overcharge" for its product; the monopsonist is able to "underpay" its workers.

In a perfectly competitive labor market, the marginal factor cost is a horizontal supply curve. The labor market is perfectly elastic because each firm is so small that hiring an additional worker will not impact the market wage one bit. This is not the case in a monopsony. The monopsonist faces an upward-sloping supply curve and every worker that it hires can potentially affect the market wage. Hence, the additional cost of hiring a new worker is the wage of the new worker and also the additional increase to the wages of the previously hired workers who were content with the lower wages. This makes for quite the dilemma for a monopsonist who wishes to hire more workers but simultaneously wants to keep labor costs down to a minimum.

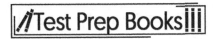

Profit-Maximizing Behavior of Firms Buying Labor in Monopsonistic Markets

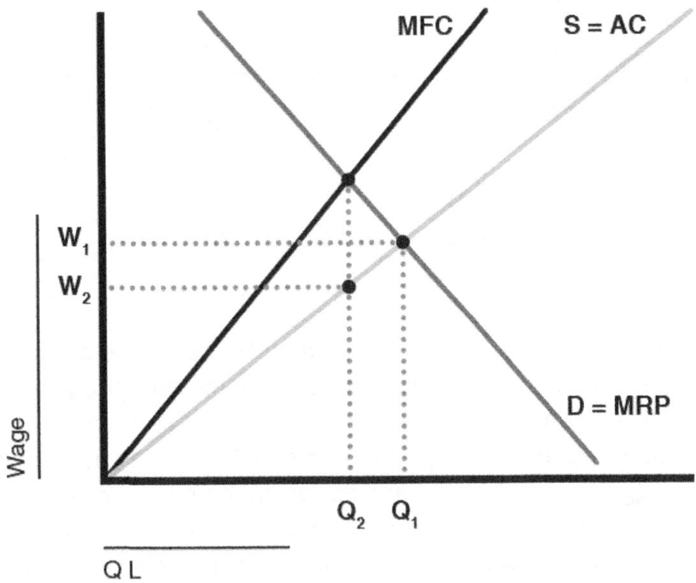

An example of a monopsony would be when there is only one employer in town that hires workers. Let's assume that it's a paper company named Paper Center. If Paper Center is the sole purchaser of workers in the labor market, it would have the ability to pay workers less than their actual productivity might dictate. Assume Paper Center hires a new worker, Jim Smith. If Jim's $MFC = MRP$, then Paper Center would no longer hire any additional workers because the optimal point of hiring workers is where $MRP = MFC$, but the wage paid to all workers would be at W2. The next job applicant, Dwayne Howard, makes a case to be hired as the new assistant regional manager at Paper Center, but there's a problem. Dwayne's MFC is higher than his MRP and profit-maximizing behavior dictates that you do not hire someone that decreases your profitability. The decision to hire Dwayne would be a net marginal loss for the monopsonist, as Paper Center would have to raise the wage for all its workers, cutting into the monopsonist's profit. A rational monopsonist would therefore choose to hire fewer workers in order to maximize profit. Hiring Dwayne would reduce deadweight loss, and hiring workers up to Q_1 would completely eliminate deadweight loss, but a monopsonist (without government intervention) would not voluntarily act in the best interests of society.

Calculate Measures Representing the Profit-Maximizing Behavior of Firms Buying Labor in Monopsonistic Markets

Let's assume that the only employer in the small town of Leverett, Massachusetts is the United States Postal Service (USPS). Workers have no real alternative in the labor market than to work for USPS. It simply would not be feasible for the workers to move to another geographic location. Homer, the postmaster of the Springfield branch, wants to hire the optimal quantity of laborers where Marginal Factor Cost (MFC) of Labor = Marginal Revenue Product (MRP) of Labor. The problem is that in order to attract more workers to work for the USPS, the monopsonist must not only pay the new workers the new wage, Homer must give a raise to all the current workers as well. Therefore, the marginal cost of labor (or marginal factor cost) will always be greater than the average cost of labor (supply of labor). Homer is incentivized to reduce costs by limiting the quantity of workers hired.

Here is a table depicting Homer's hiring dilemma.

Workers	Hourly Wage	Total Hourly Cost of Labor	Marginal Factor Cost	Marginal Revenue Product
1 (Bart)	5	5	5	75
2 (Maggie)	10	20	15	60
3 (Lisa)	15	45	25	55
4 (Marge)	20	80	35	50
5 (Milhouse)	25	125	45	45
6 (Krusty)	30	180	55	40
7 (Ned)	35	245	65	35
8 (Selma)	40	320	75	30

Let's take a look at the first worker, Bart. If Bart is hired, then Homer has to pay only $5 and receives $75 worth of benefit from his initial hire because Bart' MRP is 75. Homer definitely should hire Bart. In order to entice Maggie to enter the labor market, Homer must raise his wage to $10 to pay both Bart and Maggie, so Homer's MFC increases to $15. Maggie brings in $60 worth of goods, so her MRP is 60. The smart decision is to hire Maggie. Lisa and Marge are also worth hiring in the labor market. As the third and fourth workers, Lisa and Marge have an MFC of 25 and 35, respectively. And they bring in an MRP of 55 and 50, respectively. As long as the MRP is greater than the MFC, the logical, rational thing to do is hire the worker.

Bart recommends that Homer hires a friend he has known since the fourth grade. Does Homer hire Milhouse, the fifth worker? Let's take a look. In a world with just 4 workers, Homer spends $80 on hourly wages. Hiring Milhouse brings the total hourly cost of labor to $125 at an average wage of $25, so his marginal factor cost is $45. It's a steep marginal cost to pay. However, his MRP is $45 as well. So, yes, Homer hires Milhouse, but that's where Homer draws the line. Homer stops where the MFC = MRP. If Homer continues to hire more workers, the MFC will exceed the MRP, and his profitability on the margin will definitely decrease. Therefore, Homer will not hire the sixth, seventh, or eighth workers (Krusty, Ned, and Selma).

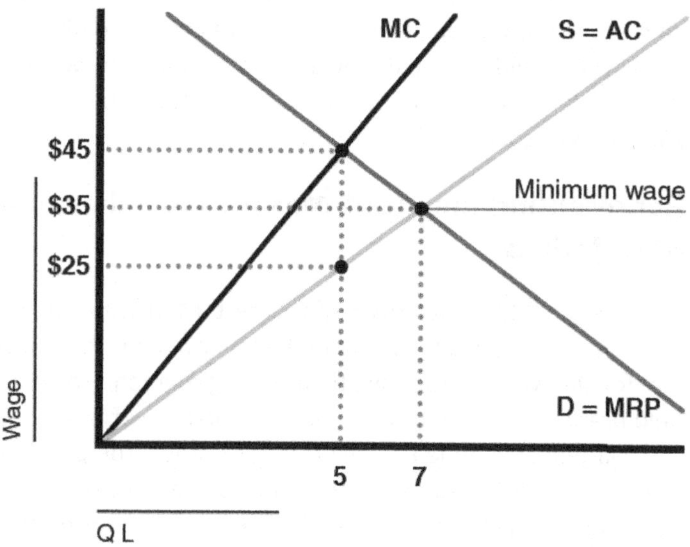

One way to combat a monopsony that "underpays" its workers is for the government to implement a minimum wage. In a perfectly competitive labor market, a binding minimum wage would serve to decrease the quantity of labor demanded while increasing the quantity of labor supplied. Hence, there would be a surplus of labor (or unemployment). A minimum wage in a monopsonistic market would not have the same effect. If the minimum wage is set to the market rate of $35, the minimum wage becomes the de facto marginal factor cost, and Homer is now properly incentivized to hire the sixth worker (Krusty) because Krusty's MRP of 40 now exceeds the new MFC of 35. And by the seventh worker (Ned) has an MRP of 35, Homer will also add Ned to the payroll because that is the point at which the (new) MFC = MRP. However, if the minimum wage is set above the market rate, then the business could simply choose to hire fewer workers if the MRP is less than the MFC.

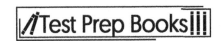

In this particular example, however, even if the minimum wage is set at $45, the monopsonistic firm would hire 5 workers, as that is where the MFC would now intersect with the MRP. In an unregulated market, 5 workers would have been hired as well. The difference in this scenario with a minimum wage of $45 is that the wage is $20 higher than it otherwise would have been. The best case that advocates of minimum wage have is that in imperfectly competitive labor markets, government intervention serves to not only provide higher wages to workers but also provides the proper incentives for a profit-maximizing monopsonist to pay their workers the prevailing wage rather than pocketing the profits for themselves. Money is essentially "transferred" from the capitalist to the working class.

Microeconomics: Market Failure and the Role of Government

Socially Efficient and Inefficient Market Outcomes

Social Efficiency

Every choice has a cost. However, the person that makes the choice is not necessarily the individual who bears the entirety of the costs. An **externality** is a side effect (good or bad) of a decision that is created by a separate third party. In the case of a **negative externality**, an individual chooses to produce too much of a relatively undesirable good (i.e., smoking). In the case of a **positive externality**, an individual chooses to produce too little of a relatively desirable good (i.e., college education).

Why would individuals, presumably rational agents, choose to underproduce or overproduce a product? The reason is that individuals do not make decisions based on producing a socially efficient outcome. Individuals act rationally by responding to market incentives that align with their own self-interested outcomes. The market equilibrium quantity represents the amount of a good that individuals will end up on through the magic of Adam Smith's "individual hand," the unintended social benefits of an individual's self-interested activity. But what happens when individuals act collectively as a society? **Social efficiency** refers to the optimal distribution of resources in society, taking into account all external costs and benefits, as well as internal cost and benefits.

Resource Allocation Efficiency

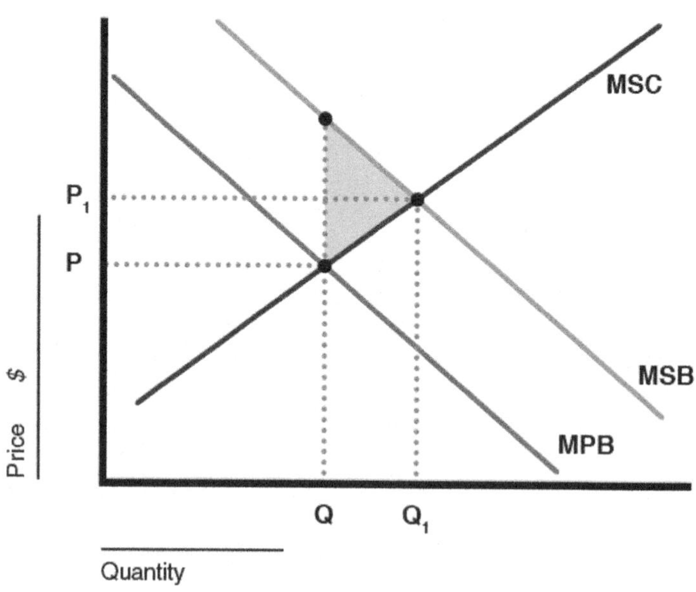

In the positive externality graph above, MPB = Marginal Private Benefit (or Marginal Benefit). MSC represents Marginal Social Cost, and MSB stands for Marginal Social Benefit.

$$Social\ benefit = Private\ benefit + External\ benefit$$

When individuals act in their own self-interest, they will produce where the $MPB = MSC$. The socially optimal point, however, is where $MSB = MSC$. The triangular area created by the "underproduced" quantity is referred to as the **deadweight loss (DWL)**. To incentivize the market to reach Q1, the government could provide a subsidy.

How Private Incentives Can Lead to Actions by Rational Agents that are Socially Undesirable Market Outcomes

Two powerful principles in the field of economics are: 1) people choose, and 2) every choice has a cost. What's implicit in these two principles is that people do things that make themselves better off; people are self-interested beings. When individuals make decisions, however, this individual desire to maximize profit or utility may come at odds with what other people want. Sometimes, individuals make decisions that adversely affect society, meaning that their decisions can lead to individually optimal outcomes at the expense of society.

Market Power

Market power refers to a company's ability to raise prices, which can lead to reduced output and loss of economic welfare. Market power is most prevalent in a monopoly market structure. Because there is only one firm in a monopoly, the monopolist wields complete control of prices. The monopoly is a "price-maker." A company can simply increase its prices by restricting the amount of goods it puts out on the market, which serves to increase demand for the product. An example of a company using (or abusing) its market power is Nike and how it releases a limited supply of Nikes and variants of Air Jordans to increase demand for its overall brand.

The term "sneakerhead" describes individuals who trade, collect, buy, and sell shoes. It's an industry that only exists because of Nike's incredible market power in the shoe industry. Nike is not only the most dominant player in the shoe market, it also creates an extremely powerful secondary market by restricting supply of its own shoes on the primary market. In one fell swoop, Nike could choose to kill the "sneakerhead" industry by increasing supply of its product in its initial release. But Nike does not do this, and the company has determined that the benefits of creating this secondary market outweigh the costs associated with losing control of its products in the secondary market.

In **perfect competition**, there are hundreds, and perhaps even thousands, of competitors selling a homogenous product. As such, firms that in this market structure are referred to as "price-takers." Because there are so many firms capable of selling the exact same product, firms in perfect competition have little to no market power. Firms that compete in an oligopoly have quite a bit more market power than do their counterparts in a perfectly competitive industry because of the relatively few number of firms competing in the industry. In **monopolistic competition**, firms have less market power than firms in an oligopoly because they are regulated by higher amounts of competition. For example, if a local dry cleaner raises its price by twenty percent, customers can simply choose to take their business to a neighboring competitor.

Reducing Market Inefficiencies

Most individuals agree that pollution is generally an **economic bad**. Whereas an **economic good** provides positive value to a consumer, an economic bad does the exact opposite. A "bad" represents negative value to the consumer. Because pollution is considered to be a "bad," it follows that the government should work toward reducing, or perhaps eliminating pollution altogether. There clearly is a benefit for policymakers to enact measures to limit pollution. Each state, for example, has varying regulations to control the amount of pollution it allows.

In the state of California, the Bureau of Automotive Repair (BAR) mandates regular measures of tailpipe emissions through smog checks. Owners of most vehicles in California are sent notices every two years that require them to obtain a smog check certification on their vehicles prior to getting their vehicles' registration renewed. Other states may or may not have more stringent regulations when it comes to pollution. Each state employs cost-benefit analysis in order to determine the amount of regulation in the economy.

Equilibrium Allocations in Imperfect Markets Relative to Efficient Allocations

Equilibrium allocation refers to where the equilibrium ends up in the absence of any regulation. In the case of a negative externality, individuals will produce a quantity where the private cost equals the private benefit. This market outcome is inefficient because individuals will ignore the external costs of their decisions and incur deadweight loss.

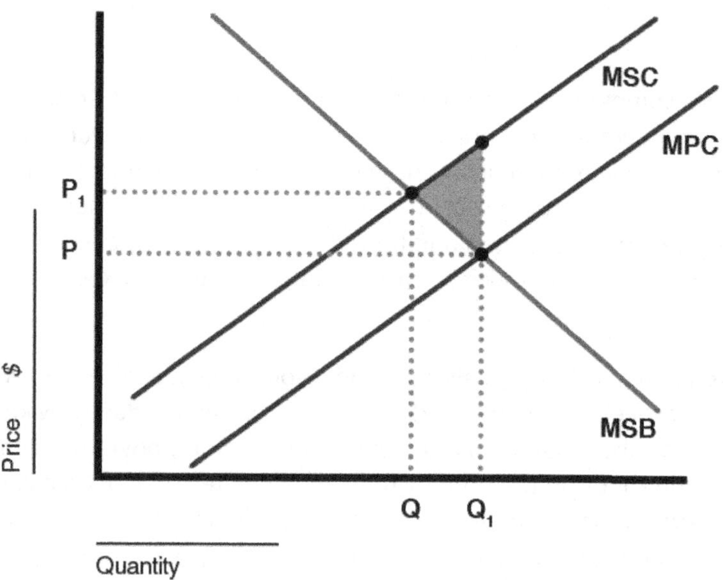

In the graph above, $MSB = Marginal\ Social\ Benefit$. MSC represents Marginal Social Cost, and MPB stands for Marginal Private Benefit (or Marginal Benefit). The $Social\ cost = Private\ cost + External\ cost$. When individuals act in their own self-interest, they will produce where the $MSB = MPC$. The socially optimal point, however, is where $MSB = MSC$. The triangular area created by the "overproduced" quantity is referred to as the deadweight loss (DWL). In order to discourage the market from reaching Q, the government might impose a tax.

Calculate Deadweight Loss

The deadweight loss in a negative externality is represented by the triangular box depicted in the negative externality graph for a pack of cigarettes shown below. Firms, left to market forces, would choose to produce at the market quantity. Society prefers that firms produce less quantity at the socially optimal quantity. The difference in what the market produces and what the socially optimal quantity is depicted as the DWL, or deadweight loss. In other words, smokers smoke *too* many cigarettes at too *low* of a cost.

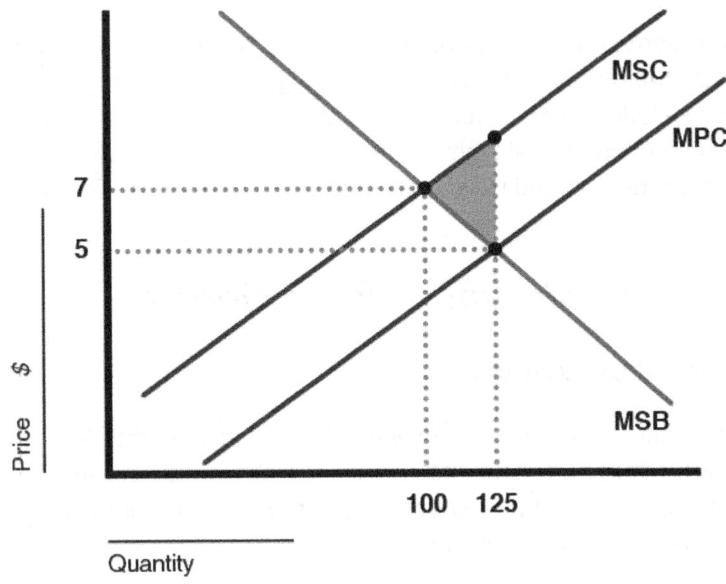

Individuals would prefer to purchase a total of 125 packs of cigarettes at $5, while society would prefer smokers pay a higher price of $7 and at the lesser quantity of 100 packs. Society prefers that smokers pay a higher premium for their actions. But, in the absence of any government regulation, smokers will continue smoking at the point where the $MPC = MPB$. The deadweight loss is depicted by the triangular box shown above. The actual formula to calculate the area is found through the equation:

$$Deadweight\ Loss = (P_2 - P_1) \times (Q_2 - Q_1)$$

$$DWL = (7 - 5) \times (125 - 100) = 2 \times 25 = \$50$$

Externalities

Externalities

Externalities are costs and benefits associated with third parties who did not choose to incur the costs or benefits. A **positive externality** is the benefit that a third party receives from a good such as higher education. For example, suppose Jade Armadillo decides to attend Stanford University for her undergraduate studies. The decision is based on her personal desire to further her education and increase her human capital. However, the skills and knowledge that she gains not only benefits Jade and her family but others as well because of the benefit that her education provides to society when she gets her degree in economics. That's the rationale that the government provides for the massive amounts of financial aid that it provides to millions of students every year.

How Public Policies Address Positive or Negative Externalities

Governments must determine the benefits and costs of implementing policies that either tax negative externalities or subsidize positive externalities. For example, the federal government provides billions of dollars in financial aid on the premise that college attendance acts as a positive externality. Similarly, the government has determined that smoking is a negative externality and so various public policy measures are enacted to reduce cigarette consumption through taxation or even to ban its use outright in public settings.

In the United States, the government has decided that the costs of smoking exceeds the benefits of smoking on flights. In 1988, the United States banned smoking on domestic flights under two hours. In 1990, the ban on smoking included all domestic flights under six hours. And in 2000, the smoking ban extended to all domestic and international flights. Benefit/cost analysis is useful, and in the case of smoking, the government has determined that the benefits of smoking on flights are less than the cost that is incurred for nonsmokers.

Public and Private Goods

Whether Goods are Rival or Excludable

A **rival good** is an item that can be consumed by only one individual at a time. A cheeseburger is a rival good. If I order an In-N-Out cheeseburger, no one else can simultaneously eat that burger with me. A rival good necessarily means that my eating a cheeseburger prevents another person from partaking of that particular food item. All food items are mutually exclusive.

A **nonrival good**, on the other hand, is a good that can be consumed jointly. A freeway, for example, is a nonrival good. Having multiple cars on the freeway does not take away the benefit that an individual in a car might derive from using the freeway. But what about traffic? If there is traffic, a freeway would be a good example of a typically nonrival good that becomes rival when traffic enters the picture.

Disneyland would be another example of a nonrival good. A theme park can be enjoyed simultaneously by families around the world. The problem of traffic on freeways exists to a similar extent to Disneyland enthusiasts. When too many people crowd Disneyland, what is typically nonrival becomes rival with the added wait individuals must face when trying to get on Space Mountain.

Although it may be possible to create a situation in which a nonrival good somehow becomes rival, it is the exception rather than the rule. Parks are nonrival. National defense is nonrival. Class lectures are nonrival. Nonrival items are things that can be consumed over and over again by one individual without taking away from another individual. One cannot do that with rival goods. You and your neighbor cannot eat the same slice of pizza. Nonrival food is simply not possible.

An **excludable good** is one in which providers can prevent nonpayers from having access to the good or service. A **nonexcludable good**, on the other hand, is one in which providers simply cannot prevent nonpayers from taking part in it. Cable television is an excludable good. Cable TV providers simply deny access to individuals who choose not to pay for its services. National defense, on the other hand, is the classic example of a nonexcludable good. The government cannot decide to protect only taxpayers from the threat of a nuclear attack. It is simply not possible with today's technology to divert a nuclear attack toward the houses of those who refuse to pay taxes.

Nature of Rival and Excludable Goods

There are four categories of goods: **private goods** (rival and excludable), **public goods** (nonrival and nonexcludable), **artificially scarce goods** (nonrival and excludable), and **common resources** (rival and nonexcludable).

Most goods are private goods: hamburgers, haircuts, pillows, baseballs. The free market is best suited for private goods. If Elise is hungry and wants to eat steak at a fancy restaurant, there is relatively little to prevent Elise from indulging in a nice meal. However, she cannot share the steak with her father, J. Daniel. If Elise gives one-third of her steak to her dad, then Elise can only consume two-thirds of the original steak. In addition, the restaurant can choose not to serve Elise the meal if she does not have the money to pay for the meal or is not properly dressed to eat at the fancy restaurant; steak is excludable. Of course, Elise is the CEO of Penelope Park Enterprises, so she can most definitely afford to buy steak for herself and her father, J. Daniel. And the following week, J. Daniel will gladly take Elise to McDonalds, another rival and excludable restaurant, to purchase two Happy Meals.

Public goods are generally goods that the government tends to become involved with. A **market failure** exists when there is an inefficient allocation of goods and services if left to the "invisible hand" of the free market. Most people agree that fire services, for example, are best left for the government to control. If firefighters agreed to fight fires only if individuals prepaid for fire prevention services, then many fires would never be quenched, as they would ignore fires from nonpayers.

The nature of selling private goods fundamentally differs from selling artificially scarce goods. If, for example, an entrepreneur decided to sell cutlery to help pay for his college tuition at Claremont McKenna College in the summer of his freshman year, then he would have to continually replenish his supply of goods. Each sale necessitates stocking up on inventory. That dilemma does not exist for selling gym memberships. A top gym membership salesman can sell one hundred memberships in a day without any of the memberships taking away from the other ninety-nine. Individuals who work out at the gym can enjoy workouts together but can clearly be prevented from entering into the facilities. In other words, the gym owner incurs very little to no marginal cost when signing up new members. Incidentally, this is one principal reason why gyms prefer signing up customers to yearly plans rather than monthly plans; it makes more sense to sell lengthier plans because when you're selling nonrival goods, you are selling something that you can immediately sell again.

Common resources are both rival and nonexcludable. The **tragedy of the commons** occurs when individuals act in their own self-interest at the expense of all others. Let's imagine that there are one hundred fish in a public lake. An individual fisherman would have no incentive to preserve any of the fish in the lake. He would only seek to maximize his own situation and take as many fish from the lake as possible. In the long run, it would be best for all fishermen to collectively decide to fish only a certain amount to control how many fish are removed from the lake and preserve the fish for posterity. The problem is that people do not think collectively. Individuals are motivated by self-interest, which is why it would make sense for the government to intervene and perhaps require permits for individuals wanting to fish at the local lake.

Healthcare is another example of a common resource. When one individuals sees a doctor for a condition, the service is rival. Doctors do not normally see patients in groups. The doctor-patient relationship is rivalrous. On the other hand, the effects of healthcare are generally nonexcludable. If an individual is injured badly and in need of emergency services, hospitals are not going to deny certain life-saving procedures because a patient does not have health insurance. An individual who would prefer healthcare to be provided to all would emphasize the nonexcludable nature of the service, whereas a person who would prefer individual choice in determining healthcare would probably emphasize that it is rival.

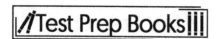

Effects of Government Intervention in Different Market Structures

Government Policy Interventions in Imperfect Markets

Effect of Per-Unit Taxes and Subsidies

A **per-unit tax** is a tax on every single quantity of good produced and serves to decrease the marginal amount of goods that a company produces. If a per-unit tax is added to an item, then the marginal cost increases (or marginal revenue decreases). Similarly, a **per-unit subsidy** is a subsidy on every single quantity of good produced and serves to increase the marginal amount of goods that a company produces. If a per-unit subsidy is added to an item, then the marginal cost decreases (or marginal revenue decreases). Governments tend to levy per-unit taxes on negative externalities (i.e., smoking, alcohol) whereas they might provide per-unit subsidies for what they perceive to be positive externalities (i.e., college, immunizations).

Effect of Lump-Sum Taxes and Lump-Sum Subsidies

Lump-sum taxes are taxes that are assessed regardless of the amount of goods produced and therefore do not affect the marginal behavior of individuals or companies. Christopher Reed is the CEO of Millennium Enterprises, a company that provides vacation tours in Europe. If Mr. Reed is assessed a lump-sum tax of $1,000 on his business, the number of individuals he signs up would be independent of the lump-sum tax, as it does not affect his marginal behavior. The lump-sum tax is essentially a sunk cost. The lump-sum tax increases the Average Total Cost (ATC) and decreases the company's profit but because it's part of the fixed cost, the Average Variable Cost (AVC) is unaffected. The lump-sum nature of a tax simply does not change a business owner's marginal decision making in the short-run. Mr. Reed still operates under the $MR = MC$ principle of profit maximization; it's just that he will be $1,000 less profitable.

Lump-sum subsidies are fixed amounts of money that are given to all firms within an industry. Lump-sum subsidies do not affect the marginal behavior of individuals or companies. Let's say that Christopher Cole is the CEO of Woodworks, a company that provides hand-crafted furniture to its clients. If Mr. Cole is given a lump-sum subsidy of $2,000 for providing beautifully hand-crafted furniture to his customers because of the value it provides to society, the output that he produces is not determined by the unexpected windfall that he has received. The lump-sum subsidy decreases the Average Total Cost (ATC) and increases the company's profit. However, the lump-sum nature of a subsidy does not change a business owner's marginal decision making in the short run; Mr. Cole is simply $2,000 richer.

An example of a lump-sum subsidy for an individual would be **universal basic income (UBI)**. If the government guarantees a monthly sum of $1,000 to every individual eighteen years or over, for example, the marginal behavior of a profit-maximizing individual would not change. They would still have the same incentive of making as much money as possible because UBI, a lump-sum subsidy, would have no effect on an individual's marginal decision to work; it merely adds to total income. Other forms of government-funded welfare, like unemployment insurance, do not function as a lump-sum subsidy. If, for example, Edward Beck is allotted $1,000 in biweekly unemployment benefits but is able to procure part-time labor as an extra for a television show that pays a total of $700 during the benefits period, then that amount would be subtracted from his paycheck. Edward would only receive $300. For all intents and purposes, the existence of unemployment benefits actually discourages labor, whereas UBI would not affect the desire to work for a profit-maximizing individual.

Could a lump-sum subsidy provided to all individuals eighteen years or older actually incentivize workers to leave the labor force in the long run? Possibly. In the case of a utility-maximizing individual, a lump-sum subsidy may actually discourage labor if income and leisure are viewed as substitutes. While the more typical case would be that the number of labor hours a household works would be unaffected, there may be some households that would take a lump-sum subsidy and reduce the total number of hours worked. A father may decide to quit his job and spend time with his family and utilize his $1,000/month lump-sum subsidy as a means of replacing his income rather than supplementing it. Another way of looking at this might be that the government is subsidizing the positive externality of a father spending time with his children.

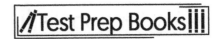

Effect of Binding Price Ceilings and Floors

A **binding price ceiling** is a price ceiling that is *below* the equilibrium price. Assume the market for apartments is perfectly competitive. If, for example, the equilibrium price of rent for an apartment in New York City is $2,000 and rent control of $2,500 is implemented, then there would be no impact on the equilibrium price or quantity. However, if rent control of $1,500 is implemented, then there would be a shortage of apartments.

In a monopoly, a binding price ceiling induces a monopolist to produce more of a product at the lower price. Because the monopolist can no longer charge the higher profit-maximizing price under free market conditions, the monopolist is now incentivized to produce more quantity than it otherwise would have in the absence of government intervention at the lower price of P_0, which is now the de facto marginal revenue curve. As seen in the graph that follows, a profit maximizing monopolist would produce at P* and Y*, which is allocatively inefficient and creates deadweight loss. With a binding price ceiling, however, a monopolist now produces at P_0 and Y_0. The monopolist can only continue to sell his product at P_0 at the point quantity demanded at P_0. Any quantity sold beyond Y_0 means that the original marginal revenue curve would prevail.

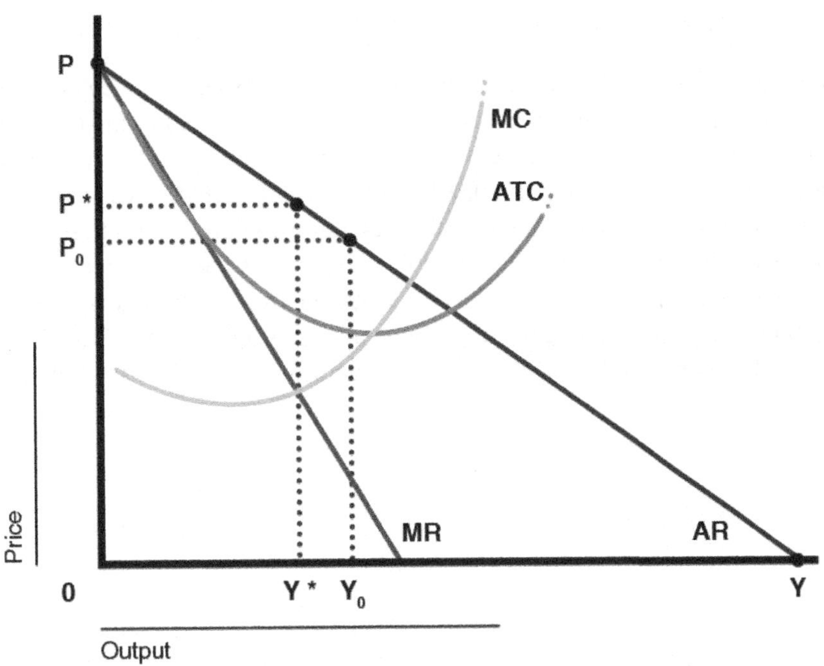

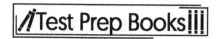

A **binding price floor** is a price floor that is *above* the equilibrium price. Assume the market for labor is perfectly competitive. If, for example, the equilibrium wage for a worker in Los Angeles is $10 per hour and minimum wage is set to $5 per hour, then there would be no impact on the equilibrium price or quantity. However, if minimum wage is increased to $15 per hour, then there would be a surplus of labor.

How Government Policies Can Alter Market Outcomes in Perfectly and Imperfectly Competitive Markets

In a monopsony, a binding price floor induces a monopsony to pay a higher wage to more of its workers. Because the monopsony can no longer pay the lower cost-minimizing (and therefore profit-maximizing) wage under free market conditions, the monopsonist is now incentivized to hire more workers than it otherwise would have in the absence of government intervention at the lower price, which would now be the de facto marginal factor cost curve. Left to market forces, the monopsonist is unwilling to do what's best for society. With a gentle push from the government, the monopsonist has the proper profit incentive to hire more workers than it would otherwise.

Effect of Government Intervention

If the government sets a price floor that is near the market price, the effect of intervention is the reduction of deadweight loss. More workers will be hired than would be hired in an unfettered free market. However, if the government sets the minimum wage significantly higher than the market wage, the impact of government intervention might mean that fewer workers would be hired than in the absence of government intervention.

Effect of Antitrust Policies

Antitrust policies aim to promote competition between firms in the economy. These policies regulate the ability of firms to coordinate prices, combine into a super company, and find ways to increase profit at the expense of the consumer.

The **Herfindahl-Hirschman Index (HHI)** is a measure that economists use to calculate the market shares that different firms have in a particular market. The HHI is calculated by squaring the market share of each individual firm and then adding up the sum of the squared shares. In a monopoly, because only one firm exists, the monopoly has an HHI total of 10,000. A high HHI Index indicates that there is a high level of market concentration in a few firms. The **Federal Trade Commission (FTC)** is the government organization primarily charged with examining possible mergers between companies. For example, if Coca-Cola and Pepsi somehow proposed the idea of a single, giant soda company called "Cokesi," the most likely outcome would be for the FTC to rule against allowing the merger. The FTC would probably argue that the merger between the two largest soda companies in the industry would serve to hurt market competition.

Calculate Changes in Market Outcomes

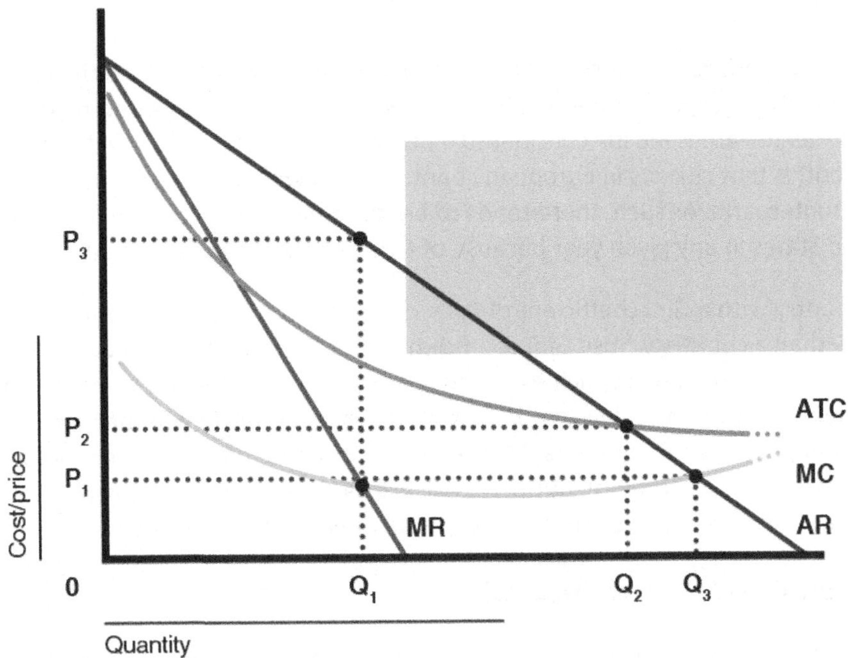

Natural Monopoly

Let's look at the graph above. In the case of a natural monopoly, an unregulated, profit-maximizing monopoly would set quantity at Q1 and charge P3. What is socially beneficial, although, would be for the monopolist to produce at Q3 and charge P1. However, in the long-run, this situation is untenable as it would mean that the monopolist would be incurring losses. Perhaps the government can step in and charge a "fair-return" or break-even price in which the business can continue to operate (at zero economic profit) by producing Q2, and charging P2. What is clear is that absent a government subsidy, the incentive for a natural monopoly to continue producing does not exist because each quantity produced incurs a per-item loss of profit.

Income and Wealth Inequality

Measures of Economic Inequality in Income and Wealth

Lorenz Curve and Gini Coefficient

The **Lorenz Curve** is a graph that depicts income inequality within a country. The horizontal axis measures the percentage of population while the vertical axis measures the aggregate wealth. For example, if the *x*-value is 35 and the *y*-value is 10, then it would mean that the bottom 35 percent of the population control 10 percent of the wealth. If the x-value is 99 and the y-value is 1, then those figures would indicate that the bottom 99 percent of the population control a measly 1 percent of the nation's wealth. And conversely, the top 1 percent of the population control 99 percent of the nation's wealth.

The Gini coefficient is one measure of economic inequality. The coefficient ranges from 0 to 1. A value of 0 corresponds to perfect equality while 1 represents perfect inequality. What a value of zero means is that 50 of the population own 50 percent of the nation's wealth whereas a value of 1 indicates the entire wealth of the nation resides in a single individual! Neither of these extreme coefficients represents actual countries. While it is theoretically possible for a country to have a Gini coefficient of 0 or 1, these two figures generally correspond with public policies within a country that either emphasize equality or efficiency.

Countries whose Gini coefficient is closer to the zero value typically favor policies that emphasize redistribution of wealth. European countries, for example, tend to have socialized medicine whereas in the United States, healthcare is mostly considered a private good that can be purchased on the open market. The tradeoff is that citizens in European countries, as a whole, are taxed at a higher rate than their American counterparts. As such, there tends to be more parity in income in Sweden, for example, than in the United States in any given year because of European government equality over efficiency.

For example, a country with a Gini coefficient of 0.5 would represent a country which has higher level of income inequality than a country whose Gini coefficient is 0.3. A socialist utopia would be a country whose Gini coefficient is zero and in which each and every citizen has the exact same level of wealth. This is an impossible situation to achieve, and many would even question whether such income parity should be the stated policy of governments. Most economists agree that countries should pursue policies that promote economic growth, but there exists less consensus regarding policies that reduce economic inequality because it may come at the expense of economic efficiency.

Sources of Income and Wealth Inequality

Since the end of the Great Recession in 2009, when unemployment peaked in the double digits, unemployment has precipitously dropped in the United States. The unemployment rate in January 2020 dropped to 3.6 percent and labor force participation was at 63.4 percent, which has trended consistently higher since the 1970s. Two-income households are now the norm rather than the exception, which can perhaps increase instances of income inequality. It's not uncommon for two high-income earners to get married, which serves to combine individuals with high-income earning capacity into one household. On the flip side, single-parent households have also risen since the 1970s, which has exacerbated income inequality as single parent households disproportionately tend to be poorer than their two-parent counterparts.

Another factor behind U.S. income inequality is the disparity between wages paid to unskilled and skilled workers. The rise of technology has automated away the need for certain types of unskilled labor. Those who have the education and human capital to succeed in today's global economy reap the benefits of increased demand for skilled labor. This winner-take-all economy, however, is not necessarily kind to laborers who lack higher levels of education. Andrew Yang, a Democratic candidate in the 2020 Presidential Election, has been an outspoken advocate for universal basic income as a way to combat the effects that a technology-based economy may have on certain segments of the labor force. His Freedom Dividend proposal calls for every adult living in the United States to receive a monthly check for $1,000 as a means to spread the wealth to all American citizens.

Differences in Tax Structures

One way that countries have attempted to reduce income inequality is through the implementation of the income tax. The Sixteenth Amendment to the United States Constitution, passed in 1913, established the right of Congress to impose a federal income tax. The U.S. income tax structure, like that of most countries, is a progressive tax structure. A **progressive tax structure** means that as income increases, the amount of money taxed is at a progressively higher rate. For example, let's assume there exists a nation called Zacharyland. In Zacharyland, the first $10,000 of gross income for a single individual is exempt from any taxation. Then, the amount between $10,000 and $40,000 is taxed at 10 percent, the amount between $40,000 and $70,000 is taxed at 12 percent, and the amount over $70,000 is taxed at 22 percent. The amount of tax gets progressively higher for individuals with high levels of income. Most countries have adopted this type of income tax system.

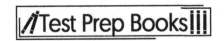

A **regressive income tax structure** means that as an individual's income increases, the amount of tax paid relative to his or her income decreases. For example, suppose that we have a country called Julietville. By fiat, Queen Juliet decrees that the country will have a regressive income tax structure. What would that mean for citizens in Julietville? The first $10,000 of gross income for a single individual is taxed at 22 percent. Then, the amount between $10,000 and $40,000 is taxed at 12 percent, while the amount between $40,000 and $70,000 is taxed at an even lower 10 percent. Finally, all income above $70,000 would be free from taxation. The amount of tax gets progressively lower and would therefore be considered regressive. No country has a regressive income tax, as most economists would argue that this type of tax structure unfairly places the tax burden on individuals with the least amount of disposable income.

A sales tax would be considered regressive because the amount of tax levied on an individual would be proportionately higher for lower income individuals than it would be for higher income individuals. If, for example, a worker who makes $50,000 a year purchases a car for $30,000 and pays $3,000 in sales tax, then the tax represents 6 percent of their income. In contrast, a worker who makes $150,000 a year who purchases that same model of car for $30,000 and pays $3,000 in sales tax only pays 2 percent of income toward the sales tax on the car. Regressive taxes disproportionately affect workers with lower income levels. In the United States, there have been some politicians who have called for the abolition of the current progressive tax system with calls to replace it with a national sales tax. For example, instead of paying federal income taxes directly from one's paycheck, individuals would pay an extra tax on the consumption of goods and services. There might be a 10 percent or 15 percent surcharge on a fast food order. While this shift in tax policy may be more efficient and encourage more labor, most economists would agree that this regressive tax would disproportionately benefit the wealthy.

Human Capital

The amount of **human capital** that an individual has determines (at least partially) their earning capacity. Skills and knowledge influence income. Human capital encompasses all the education, experience, and abilities of employees. Employers look for people who are capable of positively contributing to their respective companies. The free market tends to reward certain occupations over others and wages will rise for individuals when the demand for their labor increases or the supply decreases. The market for labor changes based on the supply and demand of skills and while preferences change over time, the undeniable fact is that those with high levels of human capital can adjust with the changes in the labor market much more readily than those with low levels of human capital.

Social Capital

Social capital is the idea that human interaction can lead to increased productivity or business performance. The advent of the internet has further magnified the importance of social capital. eBay relies on its social capital as part of its business model. An eBay seller with 2,290 reviews with a 99.9 percent positive rating will more likely garner the trust of a potential buyer than a seller with five reviews and a 40 percent positive rating. Companies such as Yelp and Uber rely on the feedback of their members as part of their business model.

Inheritance

Not all income is derived from individual labor. Sometimes, the source of household wealth is through a large **inheritance**. Part of wealth that is transferred from one generation to the next can be attributed to the transfer of human capital. Parents with high levels of human capital tend to transfer at least a portion of that human capital to their offspring. And, sometimes, people pass along large amounts of financial wealth from one generation to the next. Should the government play a role in limiting the amount of inheritance that children can receive from parents? Should inheritance be taxed? As with many normative economic questions, there does not exist a consensus as to how inheritance should be treated. Some people prefer economic equality and believe that wealth should not freely flow from one generation to the next. And so they would favor a high level of tax on inherited wealth. Others, however, emphasize the economic inefficiency that might result if the government instituted a burdensome estate tax and favor little or no tax on inherited wealth. As of 2020, the estate tax exemption is $11.58 million per individual. Any amount of assets above and beyond that amount is subject to a taxation rate of 40 percent. Most Americans are unaffected by the wealth tax, but the individuals in the upper echelon of wealth who are impacted by this "death" tax alter their behavior to avoid paying large amounts of money to the government.

Effects of Discrimination

Discrimination leads to an increase of deadweight loss because certain groups of people are paid less than their marginal revenue product. Firms that have monopsony power can choose to underpay their workers and receive more profits at the expense of workers. An example of an individual business exploiting racially discriminatory practices in the United States was the Dodgers' signing of Jackie Robinson to a Major League Baseball contract in April of 1947. Branch Rickey, the Dodgers President responsible for Jackie Robinson's signing, exploited the unwillingness of other baseball teams to sign black baseball players to their teams in order to improve his own club. Jackie Robinson's breaking of the color barrier in Major League Baseball had a tremendous social impact in the United States, but one cannot deny the Dodgers' economic motivation of exploiting the market inefficiency of racial discrimination.

Access to Financial Markets, Mobility, and Bargaining Power

Not all individuals have the same access to financial markets. In 2018, nearly 85 percent of all stocks owned by Americans belonged to the wealthiest 10 percent of households. This type of income inequality that exists in the United States makes it difficult for typical American households to benefit from gains in the financial markets. The lack of economic mobility can, at least in part, be blamed on the unequal distributions of wealth that comes from capital gains.

A **labor union** is an organization of workers that seeks to better their wages and working conditions by negotiating as a group rather than as individuals. This process of negotiations is sometimes referred to as **collective bargaining**. Labor union membership in the United States peaked in the United States in the 1950s with nearly 35 percent of American workers belonging to a labor union. Those numbers have consistently decreased in the latter half of the twentieth century and into the twenty-first century. Union membership in the United States today decreased to below 15 percent at the turn of the century, and the trend appears poised to continue indefinitely barring a seismic shift in how workers interact in the factor market.

Macroeconomics Practice Test

Multiple Choice

Economic Indicators and the Business Cycle

1. Using 2020 as the base year, if the nominal GDP in 2021 was $10 billion and the real GDP was $11 billion, which of the following must be true?
   a. The GDP deflator in 2021 was 110.
   b. The inflation rate in 2021 was 9 percent.
   c. The inflation rate in 2021 was 10 percent.
   d. The inflation rate in 2021 was negative.
   e. The real GDP per capita increased.

2. If the unemployment rate increased from 4.4 percent to 14.7 percent from April to May 2020, what can we definitively conclude has happened?
   a. The number of unemployed workers has increased.
   b. The labor force has increased.
   c. The labor force has decreased.
   d. The labor force participation rate has increased.
   e. None of the above

3. Ella took out a loan at an 8 percent nominal interest rate from Bank of America because the expected rate of inflation was 4 percent. The actual inflation rate ended up being 2 percent. Which of the following statements is true?
   a. Ella gains because the real interest rate is now 2 percent lower than expected.
   b. Ella loses because the real interest rate is now 2 percent higher than expected.
   c. The real interest rate is now 6 percent because the actual inflation rate was 2 percent lower than the expected inflation rate.
   d. The real interest rate is now 10 percent because the actual inflation rate was 2 percent lower than the expected inflation rate.
   e. Bank of America loses because the inflation rate ended up being 2 percent lower than expected.

4. Which of the following is an example of structural unemployment?
   a. A retired teacher who offers to provide volunteer tutoring services for the underprivileged
   b. A restaurant worker who loses his job because of recession
   c. A college student who works 10 hours at the local mall
   d. A successful real estate attorney who recently quit her job and is actively searching for a new career as an actress
   e. A grocery cashier whose job is replaced by a self-service kiosk

	Steak		Chicken	
	Price	**Quantity**	**Price**	**Quantity**
2020	$10	20	$5	60
2021	$5	20	$10	60

5. Assume that an economy produces just steak and chicken, as shown in the table above. If 2020 is the base year, what is the consumer price index (CPI) in 2021?
   a. 75
   b. 100
   c. 125
   d. 140
   e. 175

Total Population	**2,000,000**
Employed	900,000
Frictionally Unemployed	50,000
Structurally Unemployed	25,000
Cyclically Unemployed	25,000
Discouraged Workers	50,000

6. The table above shows the population and labor market data for an economy. What is the unemployment rate for the economy?
   a. 5 percent
   b. 9.5 percent
   c. 10 percent
   d. 15 percent
   e. 16.7 percent

7. Which of the following actions is most likely to be included in the nation's gross domestic product (GDP)?
   a. Zachary gives used earphones to his little sister, Juliet.
   b. Susan makes a steak dinner for her family.
   c. Penny buys a new car.
   d. Peter buys stock in a technology company.
   e. Danny barters with his neighbor, John, giving him a yellow sweater in exchange for a green jacket.

8. Which of the following statements is true in regard to the circular flow diagram?
   a. Households sell land, labor, and capital in the factor market, and businesses sell final goods and services in the product market.
   b. The physical flow refers to the monetary transactions that take place in the factor and product markets.
   c. Businesses sell land, labor, and capital to households in the factor market.
   d. Businesses own the factors of production, and households are the resource processors.
   e. The income that households receive from businesses in the factor market is called *factor payments*.

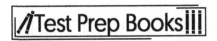

9. Which of the following is generally considered the best measure in determining a nation's standard of living?
   a. Nominal GDP
   b. Consumer price index
   c. Real GDP
   d. Real GDP per capita
   e. Unemployment rate

10. Which of the following situations is most consistent with an economy that has entered into the contraction phase of the business cycle?
   a. There is no cyclical unemployment.
   b. The actual unemployment rate is higher than the natural unemployment rate.
   c. Only frictional unemployment exists in the economy.
   d. There are fewer discouraged workers and part-time workers in the contraction phase than the expansion phase of the business cycle.
   e. Inflation tends to be rampant and ultimately leads to a recession.

National Income and Price Determination

1. Which of following will cause the short-run aggregate supply (SRAS) curve to shift to the left?
   a. A decrease in personal income taxes
   b. A sudden spike in the price of oil
   c. A decrease in inflation expectations
   d. An increase in labor productivity
   e. A decrease in the price level

2. Which of the following fiscal policy measures is the most appropriate action for the government to take if the economy is in an inflationary gap?
   a. Decrease government spending.
   b. Decrease income taxes.
   c. Increase the money supply.
   d. Increase government transfers.
   e. Increase the unemployment rate.

3. Which of the following indicates an increase in economic growth?
   a. An increase in the aggregate demand curve
   b. A decrease in the aggregate demand curve
   c. An increase in the long-run aggregate supply curve
   d. An inward shift of the production possibilities curve
   e. An increase in the supply curve

4. If an economy is in a recession and the government chose not to intervene in fiscal matters, which of the following would occur?
   a. The SRAS curve would shift to the left.
   b. The AD curve would shift to the right.
   c. The AD curve would shift to the left.
   d. The LRAS curve would shift to the left.
   e. Wages would decrease.

5. Assume that the marginal propensity to consume is 0.8. If the government decides to increase government spending by $100 million while also raising taxes by $100 million, which of the following will result?

a. The real GDP will increase by $100 million.
b. The real GDP will increase by $500 million.
c. The real GDP will decrease by $100 million.
d. The real GDP will decrease by $500 million.
e. The real GDP will remain the same.

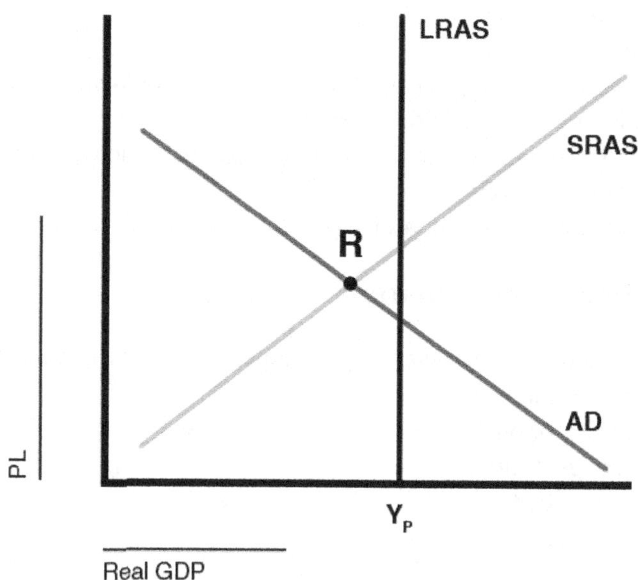

6. If an economy's short-run equilibrium is at point R and the government decides to use expansionary policy to close the recessionary gap, which of the following will occur?

a. The SRAS curve will shift to the right.
b. The SRAS curve will shift to the left.
c. The AD curve will shift to the right.
d. The AD curve will shift to the left.
e. The LRAS curve will shift to the right.

7. Assume the MPC is 0.75. If there is a recessionary gap of $20 million, which of the following measures will return the economy back to its long-run equilibrium?

a. Increase government spending by $4 million.
b. Increase government spending by $5 million.
c. Increase government spending by $10 million.
d. Decrease taxes by $5 million.
e. Decrease taxes by 10 million.

8. Imagine that an economy is at its long-run equilibrium and the government decided to increase government spending. What would happen to the equilibrium output and price level in the long run?
   a. Equilibrium output and price level would both increase.
   b. Equilibrium output and price level would both decrease.
   c. Equilibrium output would increase, but the price level would remain unchanged.
   d. Equilibrium output would remain unchanged, but the price level would increase.
   e. Equilibrium output and price level would both remain unchanged.

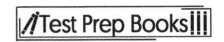

9. Assume that an economy is in long-run equilibrium. If there is a positive demand shock, which of the following will occur in the short run?
   a. The price level and unemployment rate will both increase.
   b. The price level and unemployment rate will both decrease.
   c. Inflation will increase, and unemployment will decrease.
   d. Inflation will decrease, and unemployment will increase.
   e. The price level will increase, but the real output will remain the same.

10. Which of the following typically occurs during a recession?
   a. Cyclical unemployment increases.
   b. Demand-pull inflation increases.
   c. Real GDP increases.
   d. The natural rate of unemployment increases.
   e. The government implements contractionary fiscal policy.

11. The short-run aggregate supply (SRAS) curve would shift to the left when which of the following occurs?
   a. There is a surge of exports due to a depreciated currency.
   b. The money supply decreases.
   c. The price of oil increases drastically.
   d. The government has passed a law eliminating the minimum wage.
   e. The government has decreased income tax rates.

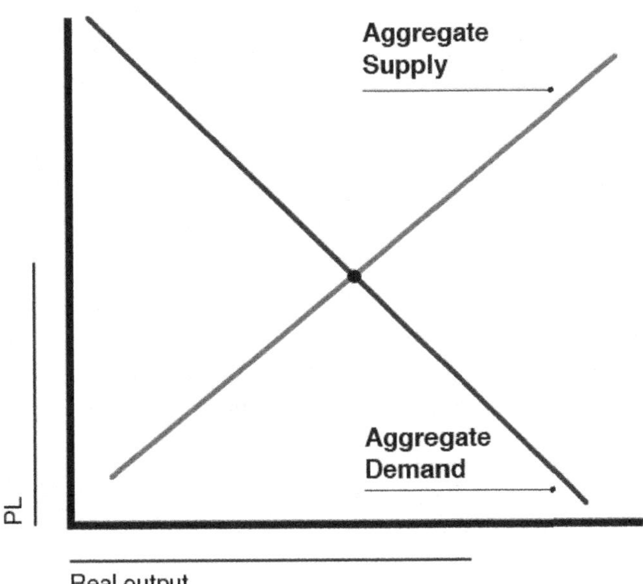

12. Given the aggregate supply and aggregate demand graph above, if the government's goal is to increase the level of real output and decrease the price level, what would be the best course of action?
    a. Increase the aggregate demand only.
    b. Decrease the aggregate demand only.
    c. Increase the aggregate supply only.
    d. Decrease the aggregate supply only.
    e. Increase the aggregate demand and decrease the aggregate supply equally.

13. During a recession, which of the following is most likely to happen?
    a. There will be an increase in aggregate demand.
    b. There will be an increase in government transfer payments.
    c. The long-run aggregate supply (LRAS) curve will increase.
    d. There will be fewer discouraged workers in the economy.
    e. The unemployment rate will decrease as previously full-time workers become part-time workers.

14. How do most economists generally view a push to require a balanced budget amendment?
    a. Economists generally favor a balanced budget amendment because it allows policymakers to incur a budget deficit during recessions.
    b. Economists generally favor a balanced budget amendment because it gives too much fiscal policy discretion to policymakers.
    c. Economists are generally against a balanced budget amendment because it would prevent the government from increasing spending during recessions.
    d. Economists are generally against a balanced budget amendment because it would give the government too much power in implementing monetary policy.
    e. Economists are generally against a balanced budget amendment because the government would have too much power to increase government spending during recessions.

Financial Sector

1. If an investment was originally made for $500, but is now currently worth $600, what is the rate of return on the investment?
    a. 20 percent
    b. 100 percent
    c. 10 percent
    d. 0.2 percent
    e. 50 percent

2. What will happen to the price of previously issued bonds if interest rates increase?
    a. The price of the bonds will increase.
    b. The price of the bonds will decrease.
    c. The price of the bonds will stay the same.
    d. The price of the bonds will reach their max value.
    e. There is no way to tell how the bonds' price will change.

3. If current inflation is at 2 percent, what would be the real interest rate on a loan with a nominal interest rate of 10 percent?
   a. 12 percent
   b. 20 percent
   c. 5 percent
   d. 8 percent
   e. 10 percent

4. Which of the following would NOT be described as a function of money?
   a. Medium of exchange
   b. Unit of account
   c. Storage of value
   d. Basis of credit
   e. Conductor of open market operations

5. Which of the following is NOT included in calculating measures of money using the monetary aggregate M2?
   a. M1
   b. Savings deposits
   c. Mutual funds
   d. Federal reserve holdings
   e. Cash

6. If a bank has total deposits of $10,000, and the reserve ratio is 10 percent, how much of its deposits can the bank loan back out?
   a. $9,000
   b. $1,000
   c. $10,000
   d. $9,990
   e. $100,000

7. How can a country's central bank increase the money supply without directly printing more currency?
   a. Increase required reserves
   b. Decrease required reserves
   c. Increase interest rates
   d. Sell bonds
   e. Wait for the market to change

8. In which of the following situations would the money supply need to be increased?
   a. There is an increase in the demand for loans.
   b. There is speculation that the interest rate will decrease.
   c. Wages are decreasing.
   d. Inflation increases.
   e. There is a surplus of money in the market.

9. If there is a shortage in the money supply, how will the nominal interest rate adjust to meet equilibrium?
    a. The rate will increase to increase demand of money.
    b. The rate will decrease to decrease demand of money.
    c. The rate will not change.
    d. The rate will increase to decrease demand of money.
    e. The rate will decrease to increase demand of money.

10. If the central bank wanted to increase the nominal interest rate, it could:
    a. Decrease the required reserve ratio
    b. Use expansionary policy to purchase bonds in the open market
    c. Print more money
    d. Increase the discount rate
    e. Purchase bonds from a foreign country

11. Which of the following might be an example of a monetary lag?
    a. The demand for money decreases because of high interest rates.
    b. The country's demand for money increases because of higher wages.
    c. The supply of money is increased to match a perceived increase in demand, but instead it creates a surplus.
    d. The demand for money increases because a new technology is available for purchase, resulting in an increase in supply from the central bank.
    e. Reserve requirements are lowered to increase the money supply in the market.

12. In an open economy, the central bank can increase the amount of loanable funds to decrease interest rates by:
    a. Switching to a closed economy to prevent foreign investments
    b. Purchasing bonds from another country
    c. Selling bonds to another country
    d. Declaring war
    e. Switching currency

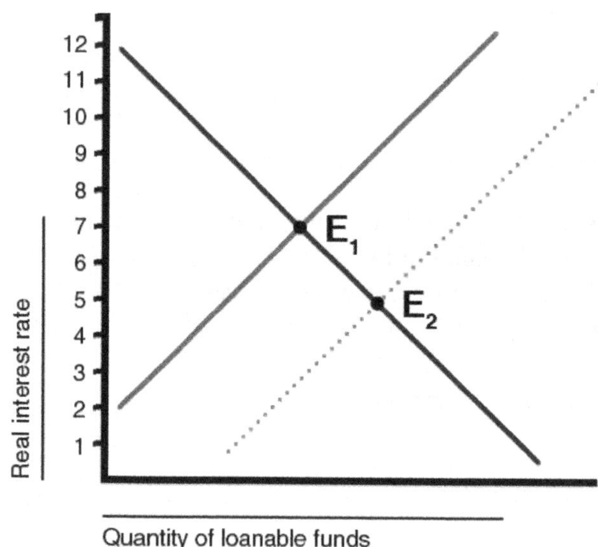

13. The graph above shows the loanable funds market with an equilibrium interest (E-1) rate of 5 percent. If the supply of loanable funds is increased as shown on the graph, what will be the equilibrium interest rate be at E-2 to meet demand?

a. 4 percent
b. 9 percent
c. No change
d. 2 percent
e. 7 percent

Open Economy

1. During a recession, which of the following generally occurs with tax revenues and government spending?

a. Tax revenues increase and government spending increases.
b. Tax revenues decrease and government spending decreases.
c. Tax revenues increase and government spending decreases.
d. Tax revenues decrease and government spending increases.
e. Tax revenues and government spending both decrease.

2. According to the quantity theory of money, a 20 percent decrease in the money supply will change the aggregate price level in the long run by which of the following?

a. 0 percent
b. Less than 20 percent
c. 20 percent
d. 50 percent
e. More than 50 percent

3. Which of the following equations accurately reflects what the money supply equals according to the quantity theory of money?

a. $M = V \div PY$
b. $M = PY \div V$
c. $M = VP \div Y$
d. $M = PV \div Y$
e. $M = VP \div Y$

4. A movement from a point on the production possibilities curve (PPC) to a point below the PPC represents which of the following?

a. Economic expansion
b. Economic recession
c. Increased employment
d. Increased efficiency
e. Long-run economic growth

5. Crowding out is most likely to occur with which of the following changes?

a. Increase in government spending
b. Increase in budget surplus
c. Decrease in budget deficit
d. Increase in taxes
e. Increase in the discount rate

6. Which of the following will happen if a country's government increases business taxes?
   a. The short-run Phillips curve will shift to the left.
   b. The short-run aggregate supply curve will shift to the right.
   c. The long-run aggregate supply curve will shift to the right.
   d. The aggregate demand curve will shift to the left.
   e. The demand curve for loanable funds will shift to the right.

7. If real output is $27,000 and price level is 2, and the velocity of money is 3, then the money supply is which of the following?
   a. $3,000
   b. $4,500
   c. $6,000
   d. $18,000
   e. $27,000

8. If policy makers use fiscal policy to reduce unemployment, which of the following will MOST likely happen in the short run initially?
   a. The nominal interest rate will decrease.
   b. The inflation rate will increase.
   c. The real interest rate will decrease.
   d. The money demand will increase.
   e. Frictional unemployment will decrease but cyclical unemployment will increase.

9. Which of the following transactions would increase the current account surplus in Italy's balance of payments accounts?
   a. An Italy-based company sells roasted coffee to Spain.
   b. Mario, an Italian investor, buys stocks in an Italian company.
   c. Teemu, a Finn, buys stocks in an Italian company.
   d. An Italian-based company buys a new computer from Mexico.
   e. Joon-ho, a Korean citizen, works at an Italian company in Paris.

10. In the short run, contractionary monetary policy will MOST likely cause which of the following?
   a. A decrease in the interest rate and a decrease in prices
   b. A decrease in the interest rate and an increase in private investment
   c. A decrease in prices and an increase in private investment
   d. An increase in the interest rate and an increase in private investment
   e. An increase in interest rate and a decrease in private investment

11. If real interest rates in the United States fall relative to real interest rates in South Korea, which of the following will occur?
   a. South Korean investors will buy more United States securities.
   b. South Korean exports to the United States will increase.
   c. The supply of dollars will decrease.
   d. United States investors' demand for the South Korean won will decrease.
   e. The South Korean won will appreciate relative to the dollar.

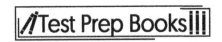

12. Assume that Jibinville and Zachland are trading partners. If the average income in Jibinville increases, which of the following will occur in the foreign exchange market?
   a. The demand for Jibinville's currency will increase, and Jibinville's currency will appreciate.
   b. The demand for Zachland's currency will increase, and Jibinville's currency will depreciate.
   c. The demand for Zachland's currency will increase, and Jibinville's currency will appreciate.
   d. The supply of Jibinville's currency will decrease, and Jibinville's currency will appreciate.
   e. The supply of Zachland's currency will increase, and Zachland's currency will depreciate.

13. Which of the following is a monetary policy tool that will decrease the nominal interest rate in the money market?
   a. Raising taxes
   b. Raising the discount rate
   c. Raising the federal funds rate
   d. Buying bonds on the open market
   e. Lowering taxes

14. If a sharp rise in inflation occurs in Julietville, which of the following will occur in the money market?
   a. The money supply will decrease and nominal interest rates will decrease.
   b. The demand for money will increase and nominal interest rates will decrease.
   c. The demand for money will increase and nominal interest rates will increase.
   d. The demand for money will decrease and nominal interest rates will decrease.
   e. The opportunity cost of holding money will decrease.

15. If the central bank of Country C wishes to decrease the value of its currency on foreign exchange markets, it can do which of the following?
   a. Sell the currencies of other countries
   b. Decrease the domestic money supply in Country C
   c. Increase interest rates in Country C
   d. Decrease interest rates in Country C
   e. Increase government transfer payments in Country C

16. Which statement is MOST consistent with supply-side economic theory?
   a. It is the government's responsibility to stimulate the economy by spending when the private sector's investment spending is down.
   b. The Laffer Curve shows us that raising taxes will ultimately stimulate the economy because it will responsibly balance the budget.
   c. An increase in money supply will have no long-term impact on long-term economic growth.
   d. Because the spending multiplier is higher than the tax multiplier, the government should first increase spending before reducing taxes.
   e. Reducing the tax burden on businesses will increase the supply of goods and lead to economic growth.

17. Which of the following statements is TRUE regarding the national debt and deficits?
    a. The national debt is the total amount of money owed, whereas the deficit refers to the payments on the national debt.
    b. The national debt increases during times of budget surpluses but decreases during times of budget deficits.
    c. The national debt increases during times of budget deficits but decreases during times of budget surpluses.
    d. The United States has never had a budget deficit in its history and paid off its national debt at the end of World War II.
    e. If a country incurs a budget deficit in a year following a budget surplus, the national debt will neither increase nor decrease.

18. Which of the following will occur based on the foreign exchange market graph shown below?

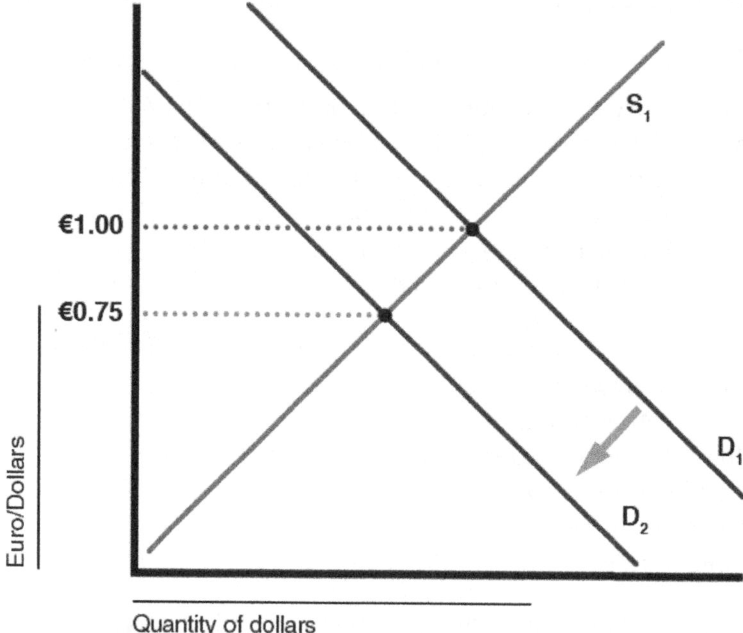

    a. The dollar will appreciate in value relative to the euro and therefore exports will increase.
    b. The dollar will appreciate in value relative to the euro and therefore exports will decrease.
    c. The dollar will depreciate in value relative to the euro and therefore exports will increase.
    d. The dollar will depreciate in value relative to the euro and therefore exports will decrease.
    e. The dollar will appreciate in value relative to the euro and therefore imports will decrease.

Questions 19 and 20 refer to the following loanable funds graphs:

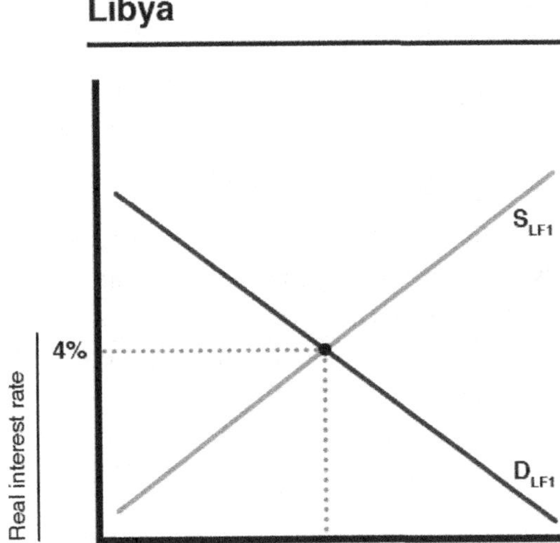

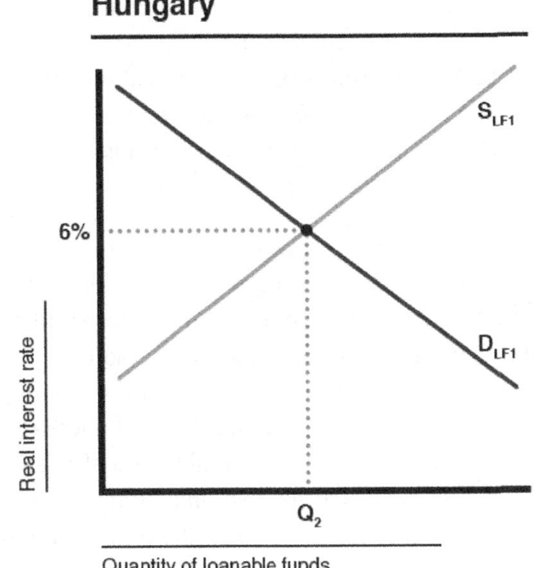

19. Which of the following will occur given the difference in interest rates between Libya and Hungary?
    a. Capital inflows into Hungary
    b. Capital inflows into Libya
    c. Capital outflows from Hungary
    d. Capital outflows from Libya
    e. Both A and D

20. In the long run, what will happen to interest rates in Hungary and Libya?
    a. Interest rates in Hungary and Libya both increase.
    b. Interest rates in Hungary and Libya both decrease.
    c. Interest rates in Hungary increase, and interest rates in Libya decrease.
    d. Interest rates in Hungary decrease, and interest rates in Libya increase.
    e. There would be no change in interest rates in either country.

21. The Big Mac Index, which is the nominal exchange rate at which a Big Mac is priced in various countries, describes which of the following?
    a. Appreciation of currency
    b. Depreciation of currency
    c. Real GDP per capita
    d. The balance of payment on the current account
    e. Purchasing power parity

22. Assume that vaccinations are a positive externality. Assume that the companies were left to produce at a point where the marginal private benefit equals the marginal cost. Which of the following can be used to reach the socially optimal point in the market for vaccinations?
   a. A per-unit subsidy for vaccinations
   b. A lump-sum subsidy for vaccinations
   c. A per-unit tax for vaccinations
   d. A lump-sum tax for vaccinations
   e. A price ceiling for vaccinations

23. Suppose that a new presidential administration completely eliminates government welfare and also replaces the current progressive taxation system with a lump-sum tax to all its citizens regardless of income level. This elimination of welfare and changing of a progressive tax system to an implementation of a regressive tax system will most likely:
   a. increase income inequality and efficiency.
   b. increase income inequality and decrease efficiency.
   c. decrease income inequality and efficiency.
   d. decrease income inequality and increase efficiency.
   e. decrease income inequality and not affect efficiency.

Free Response

Question 1

The information below includes macroeconomic data for the nation of Parkland using 2020 dollars in the year 2020.

Consumption	$700,000
Investment	$200,000
Exports	$250,000
Imports	$150,000
Taxes	$200,000
Government Spending	$200,000

Population	30,000
Employed	15,000
Unemployed	5,000

GDP Deflator (2020)	120

a. Calculate each of the following measures. Show your work.

- i. 2020 Nominal GDP
- ii. 2020 Real GDP
- iii. 2020 Real GDP per capita

b. Jibrin is a citizen in Parkland who currently lives abroad in Conquerorville where he runs a bobblehead business. Is the output produced by Jibrin's bobblehead company included in Parkland's GDP data? Explain.

c. The GDP deflator for Parkland in 2019 was 240.

- i. Did inflation or deflation occur in 2020? Explain.
- ii. What was the inflation rate in 2020? Show your work.

d. Was the number of discouraged workers in Parkland greater than, equal to, or less than the number of unemployed workers, or is the number indeterminate? Explain.

Question 2

In Switzerland, the actual rate of unemployment is currently greater than the natural rate of unemployment.

a. Using a correctly labeled graph of aggregate demand (AD), short-run aggregate supply (SRAS), and long-run aggregate supply (LRAS), graph the short-run equilibrium price level and short-run equilibrium output level, labeled as P_L and Y_L, respectively, and the long-run output as Y_F.

b. What is the appropriate fiscal policy measure required to get the economy back to equilibrium? Explain.

c. What is the amount of government spending change required to close a $250 billion gap if the marginal propensity to consume (MPC) is 0.8?

d. If the government decides to alter the income tax rate instead of changing the amount of government spending to close the gap, would the amount of the tax increase or decrease be greater than, smaller than, or equal to the change in government spending? Explain.

e. If Switzerland received an influx of highly skilled immigrants from neighboring countries, what would happen to the LRAS curve? Explain.

Question 3

The United States is an open economy that is in the midst of a severe recession.

a. Correctly draw an aggregate demand/aggregate supply graph including the LRAS, SRAS, and AD curves. On the graph, answer the following questions.

- i. What is the equilibrium output and price level in the current recession?
- ii. What is the full employment output level?

b. The central bank decides to use monetary policy to close the output gap.

- i. What open market operation would the central bank use?
- ii. On a properly labeled money market graph, show the impact of the open market operation you chose in (i), and the direction of the interest rate.

c. As a result of the interest rate change in b. (ii), will capital flow into or out of the United States? Explain.

Macroeconomics Answer Explanations

Multiple Choice

Economic Indicators and the Business Cycle

1. D: The formula for GDP deflator is:

$$Nominal\ GDP \div Real\ GDP \times 100 = GDP\ deflator$$

Because we know both the nominal and real GDP in 2021, we can find the GDP deflator in 2021:

$$\$10\ billion \div \$11\ billion \times 100 = 91$$

Because the GDP deflator in the base year is always 100, we know the inflation rate is negative because:

$$(91 - 100) \div 100 \times 100 = -9\%$$

Another way to determine that deflation, or a negative rate of inflation, has taken place is that the nominal GDP is less than the real GDP following a year in which nominal GDP and real GDP were equal. Real GDP per capita is real GDP divided by the population, and no data on population is given.

2. E: Each of the scenarios is possible, but without further information, we cannot definitively conclude that any of them have actually happened. The number of unemployed workers increasing is usually the reason why the unemployment rate increases. However, there could have been people who dropped out of the labor force, meaning that the number of unemployed workers would have decreased. So, the labor force could have increased or decreased. The labor force participation rate might have increased, although that situation is highly unlikely. The labor force participation rate probably decreased because with such a huge increase in the unemployment rate, it is likely that some people dropped out of the labor force; however, we do not know for sure without additional data.

3. C: $Real\ interest\ rate = Nominal\ interest - Inflation$. Because the expected rate of inflation is 4 percent and the nominal rate of interest was 8 percent, the expected real interest rate was 4 percent ($8\% - 4\% = 4\%$). However, the actual rate of inflation was only 2 percent. In cases in which the actual rate of inflation is lower than the expected rate of inflation, the lender "wins" and the borrower "loses." The real interest rate is now 6:

$$8\%\ (nominal\ interest\ rate) - 2\%\ (actual\ inflation\ rate) = 6\%\ (real\ interest\ rate)$$

4. E: Structural unemployment refers to unemployment created by technology, which creates a mismatch between skills employees have and skills demanded in the economy. A retired teacher who volunteers to tutor is no longer part of the labor force. A laid-off restaurant worker is a victim of cyclical unemployment. The college student is unemployed and not part of the work force. Any individual is considered to be employed as long as he or she was gainfully employed for 1 hour in the previous week. A successful real estate attorney who has decided to switch careers is frictionally unemployed.

5. D: $Consumer\ price\ index\ (CPI) = Cost\ of\ market\ basket\ in\ the\ current\ year \div Cost\ of\ market\ basket\ in\ the\ base\ year$

In the base year, this means the CPI will always be 100, so the CPI in 2020 is 100. In 2021, the cost of the market basket in the current year is:

$$(\$5 \times 20) + (\$10 \times 60) = \$100 + \$600 = \$700$$

The cost of the market basket in the base year is:

$$(\$10 \times 20) + (\$5 \times 60) = \$200 + \$300 = \$500$$

Thus, the CPI in 2021 is:

$$\$700 \div \$500 \times 100 = 1.4 \times 100 = 140$$

Inflation has increased by 40 percent from 2020 to 2021.

6. C: The unemployment rate is the:

$Number\ of\ unemployed \div Labor\ force$, or $Number\ of\ unemployed \div (Unemployed + Employed)$

The three types of unemployment are frictional unemployment, structural unemployment, and cyclical unemployment. Discouraged workers have dropped out of the labor force, so they are not counted as being unemployed. Therefore, the unemployment rate is:

$(50{,}000 + 25{,}000 + 25{,}000) \div (100{,}000 + 900{,}000) = 100{,}000 \div 1\ million = 10\%.$

7. C: Gross domestic product (GDP) is the sum total of all goods and services a country produces. When an individual purchases a new car, it counts as part of GDP. A donation of used goods that involves no monetary transaction is not part of GDP. Making food for one's family is not part of GDP, and stock purchases are not GDP transactions. In addition, barter is not included in any GDP transactions.

8. A: In a circular flow diagram, households sell land, labor, and capital to businesses in the factor market and businesses sell final goods and services to households in the product market. The monetary flow (not physical flow) refers to the monetary transactions that take place in the factor and product markets. Households sell land, labor, and capital to businesses in the factor market because households own the factors of production and businesses are the resource processors.

9. D: A nation's real GDP per capita is considered to be the best measure in determining a nation's standard of living. Real GDP per capita is found by dividing the country's real GDP by the nation's population. Nominal GDP numbers measure a nation's economic activity but do not adjust for inflation. The consumer price index measures a country's rate of inflation, not necessarily a country's standard of living. Although real GDP does measure a country's economic growth, no adjustment is made for population. A high unemployment rate usually means an economy is struggling, whereas a low unemployment rate typically means a nation is experiencing economic progress. However, the unemployment rate itself is a poor proxy of a country's standard of living.

10. B: When the economy is in the contraction phase of the business cycle, the actual unemployment rate is higher than the natural unemployment rate. Recall that the natural unemployment rate is $Frictional\ unemployment + Structural\ unemployment$. When the actual unemployment rate is higher than the natural unemployment rate, frictional, structural, and cyclical unemployment all exist. Although not necessarily an ironclad rule, there would probably be more discouraged workers and part-time workers during contractions than during expansions because of the less robust workforce that exists in a recessionary climate. Also, deflation, not inflation, usually portends a recession.

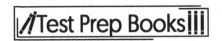

National Income and Price Determination

1. B: A sudden spike in the price of oil will shift the SRAS curve to the left. There are three reasons why the SRAS curve shifts to the left: increased wages, increased price of inputs (such as oil), and increased inflations expectations. A decrease in personal income taxes will shift the aggregate demand curve to the right because of the increase in consumption expenditures. A decrease in inflation expectations and an increase in labor productivity increases the SRAS curve. A price level decrease, in and of itself, will not shift the SRAS curve; there will only be a movement down the SRAS curve.

2. A: If the economy is an inflationary gap, the government can use contractionary fiscal policy to close the gap. There are three things the government can do: Decrease government spending, increase income taxes, or decrease government transfer payments. Decreasing income taxes or increasing government transfers are examples of expansionary fiscal policy and will exacerbate inflation. An increase of the money supply is an example of expansionary monetary policy, not fiscal policy. And finally, the government does not unilaterally increase or decrease the unemployment rate; a higher unemployment rate is an unfortunate byproduct of the government's use of contractionary fiscal policy.

3. C: An increase in the long-run aggregate supply (LRAS) curve indicates that the economy has experienced economic growth. The aggregate demand (AD) curve is represented by the equation:

$$Y = C + I + G + NX$$

If there is an increase in AD, the AD curve shifts to the right; if there is a decrease in AD, the AD curve shifts to the left. An inward shift of the production possibilities curve indicates a decrease in economic growth. A shift to the right of the supply curve represents an increase in supply of an individual product, not the economic growth of an economy.

4. E: If the economy is in a recession, the SRAS curve would shift to the right because wages would decrease. When the economy's short-run equilibrium is below the long-run equilibrium level, the economy will self-equilibrate, with the SRAS curve shifting to the right. The aggregate demand will remain unchanged. If the government decided to implement fiscal policy measures, there are three expansionary measures that could be used to get the economy back to its long-run equilibrium: Increase government spending, increase government transfers, or decrease income taxes. In order for the LRAS curve to shift to the left, there would have to be a decrease in capital formation or mass emigration from a country that would deplete the economy's level of human capital.

5. A: If the marginal propensity to consume is 0.8, the spending multiplier is:

$$1 \div (1 - MPC) = 1 \div (1 - 0.8)$$

$$1 \div 0.2 = 5$$

The tax multiplier is:

$$MPC \div (1 - MPC) = 0.8 \div 0.2 = 4$$

When the government increases spending by $100 million, the resultant increase is:

$$\$100\ million \times 5 = \$500\ million$$

When taxes increase by $100 million, the decrease in real GDP is:

$$-\$100\ million \times 4 = -\$400\ million$$

Therefore, the combined impact would be a real GDP increase of $100 million.

6. C: Expansionary fiscal policy will shift the aggregate demand (AD) curve to the right. If the government did absolutely nothing, wages would decrease, and the short-run aggregate supply (SRAS) curve would shift to the right. The SRAS curve would shift to the left in an inflationary gap (assuming the government took a hands-off approach). The AD curve would shift to the left if the government implemented contractionary fiscal policy measures and would worsen the recession. The LRAS would shift to the right if there was an increase in economic growth through an increase in capital stock or human capital.

7. B: If the MPC is 0.75, the MPS is 0.25. The spending multiplier is:

$$1 \div MPS = 1 \div 0.25 = 4$$

Because the recessionary gap is $20 million, the amount of government spending required to close the gap is $\$20\ million\ \div\ multiplier\ =\ G$, so:

$$\$20\ million\ \div\ 4\ =\ \$5\ million$$

In order to close the gap through a decrease in taxes, the requisite amount required would be $\$20\ million\ \div\ tax\ multiplier\ =\ T$, in which T represents the change in tax. The tax multiplier is $MPC\ \div\ (1 - MPC)\ =\ 0.75\ \div\ (1 - 0.75)\ =\ 0.75\ \div\ 0.25\ =\ 3$, so the government would have to reduce taxes by:

$$\$20\ million\ \div\ 3\ =\ \$6.7\ million$$

8. D: If the government decides to increase spending, the aggregate demand curve would shift to the right and the equilibrium output and price level would both increase in the short run. However, in the long run, the SRAS would shift to the left as wages would increase, input prices would increase, or inflation expectations would increase. As a result, the equilibrium output would decrease back to its original level, and the price level would increase.

9. C: If there is a positive demand shock, both the price level and real output will increase in the short run. An increase in the price level means that inflation will increase and unemployment will decrease because there is a positive correlation between a higher real GDP output and lower unemployment. In the long run, the price level will increase, and the output will remain the same because the SRAS curve would shift back to the left; however, that is not the case in the short run.

10. A: During a recession, aggregate demand decreases, so the price level and real output both decrease. Demand-pull inflation occurs when aggregate demand increases. A recession will decrease the level of real GDP in the short run. The natural rate of unemployment will stay the same because cyclical unemployment is not part of the natural rate. In addition, the government would typically implement expansionary fiscal policy, not contractionary fiscal policy, during a recession.

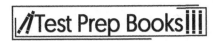

11. C: When the price of an input such as oil increases, the SRAS curve shifts to the left, leading to cost-push inflation. If there is a surge of exports as a result of a depreciated currency, the aggregate demand would increase because exports are a component of aggregate demand. If the money supply decreases, aggregate demand would decrease. If the government passes a law eliminating the minimum wage, the SRAS curve would decrease and the price level would decrease. And finally, a decrease in income taxes would shift the aggregate demand to the right.

12. C: If the government's goal is to increase real output while decreasing the price level, increasing the aggregate supply is the best course of action. Increasing the aggregate demand will increase the real output and the price level. Decreasing the aggregate demand will decrease both the real output and price level. Decreasing the aggregate supply will increase the price level and decrease the real output. Increasing the AD curve and decreasing the AS curve will definitely increase the price level, but the real output would be indeterminate.

13. B: During a recession, there will be an increase in government transfer payments because unemployment payments increase. These welfare payments are called *automatic stabilizers* because the government "stabilizes" the economy during contractionary phases. The government will typically go into a budget deficit during recessions while theoretically being in a budget surplus during expansions. The LRAS curve remains the same in a recession. The number of discouraged workers during a recession is more likely to increase than decrease, although that is not certain. In addition, when full-time workers become part-time workers, the unemployment rate stays the same.

14. C: A balanced budget amendment's purpose is to prevent the government from spending excessively in any given year. However, most economists generally are against passing a balanced budget amendment because it would effectively prevent the government from increasing spending during times the economy needs the most help. Automatic stabilizers, such as unemployment benefits, are designed to increase during recessionary times. A balanced budget amendment would effectively prevent the government from providing fiscal stimulus, which would worsen a recession.

Financial Sector

1. A: The rate of return on an investment is a percentage based on the amount of earnings made or lost on a loan; it can be found by subtracting the original amount of the loan from the current amount, dividing that number by the original amount, and then multiplying by 100. Using the numbers provided by the question, the formula can be set up as $[(600 - 500) \div 500] \times 100$. This gives a rate of return of 20 percent, Choice *A*.

2. B: The price of previously issued bonds and interest rates have an inverse relationship because the amount of return received on a bond depends on how high its interest rate is. If a bond is purchased at one interest rate, and then interest rates increase, the previously issued bond will not carry as much interest as bonds issued after the increase. The bond will then have to be sold at a lower value because it is not worth as much as current bonds in the market. Therefore, the correct Choice then is Choice *B*, the price of bonds will decrease if the interest rate was to increase.

3. D: Unlike the nominal interest rate, the real interest rate takes into account inflation. The equation for finding the real interest rate is to subtract a loan's nominal rate from the inflation rate at the time. In this case, a loan with a nominal interest rate of 10 percent at 2 percent inflation can be expressed as: $10\% - 2\% = 8\%$. This makes Choice *D* the correct Choice.

4: E: Money is a form of exchange that gives value to goods and services, meaning it is a medium of exchange, a storage of value, a unit of account, and a basis of credit. It does not however, conduct open market operations itself, as this is the responsibility of a country's central bank, and is not directly determined by money alone.

5. D: M2 is a way to calculate money measures that includes all liquid assets circulating in the economy, expressed as M1, as well as assets that are not as liquid in an economy, like savings deposits and mutual funds. Cash is also a part of the M2 calculation because it is used in M1, and M2 includes all the money accounted for in M1. However, M2 does not include federal reserve holdings, Choice *D*, because it only measures money that can be used more immediately in the market and is not intended to account for amounts to be used for long-term savings like federal reserve holdings, which will not be circulating in the economy.

6. A: The reserve ratio is determined by a country's central bank to set a required reserve amount of deposits a bank must keep on hand. If the reserve ratio is at 10 percent, this means that 10 percent of the bank's deposits cannot be lent back out for profit. In this example, 10 percent of $10,000 is $1,000, meaning the bank must keep $1,000 on hand, allowing it to loan back out $9,000 of its total deposits, Choice *A*.

7. B: Choice *B*, decrease the reserve requirement, is the only choice that will increase the money supply; the remaining choices will either cause the money supply to decrease or not change. Increasing required reserves means less money will go back out into the economy because banks will have to keep more savings on hand. Increasing interest rates will make more people want to save because they can get a higher return, decreasing the money supply. Selling government bonds will also decrease the money supply by taking money from the market, and waiting for changes will not have a determinable effect.

8. B: When interest rates are low, the demand for money will increase, leading to the need for more supply. Higher interest rates mean more demand for loans, while lower interest rates mean more demand for money. A country's central bank controls the money supply to reach equilibrium in the money market, where supply equals demand. Wages decreasing, inflation, and a surplus in the money market all lead to less demand, and thus more supply will not be needed, making only Choice *B* correct.

9. D: A shortage in the money supply occurs when there is not enough money to meet what is demanded. The nominal interest rate will adjust itself based on the shortage in order to decrease demand, so that the amount of money in the market goes back to equilibrium. This is done by the nominal interest rate increasing, creating more demand for loans and less demand for money, Choice *D*.

10. D: Expansionary policy is used to increase the money supply in the market, resulting in lower nominal interest, which all the choices except Choice *D* are an example of. If a country's central bank increases the discount rate at which banks can borrow from them, however, it will in turn raise nominal interest rates and decrease demand for money, because banks will also be able to charge more interest on loans made overnight to each other in order to meet reserve requirements.

11. C: Monetary lag occurs when changes in the market are not reacted to quickly enough to have the desired effect. Choice *C* presents an example of reacting too late to a change in demand, and its effects create a surplus in the market because of the lag. The other choices reflect more natural outcomes of monetary policy that are not a result of monetary lag.

12. C: An open economy describes an economy that opens its borders to foreign investment and trade. A country can increase its supply of loanable funds by selling bonds to other countries. In an open economy, only the central bank can control the supply of money on its own. Choice *C* is correct because it explains how an open economy is used to increase the funds in the loanable funds market.

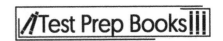

13. D: When the supply of loanable funds is increased in the market, the real interest rate will decrease to make loans less in demand and fix any surplus in the market. On the graph shown, the interest rate drops 3 percent from its original position at 5 percent, resulting in a new equilibrium of 2 percent, Choice *D*.

Open Economy

1. D: During a recession, the actual GDP is less than the potential GDP. In other words, the government will collect relatively less amounts of tax revenue because of the reduced economic activity. In addition, the increase in unemployment will create a situation of more government spending to combat the economic downturn. Tax revenues will therefore decrease and government spending will increase.

2. C: According to the quantity theory of money, the equation $MV = PY$ shows the relationship that money supply has to the aggregate price level. Monetarists believe that the velocity is fixed. Therefore, a change in the money supply will proportionately affect PY, or nominal GDP. Hence, if the money supply decreases by 20 percent, the nominal GDP will also drop by 20 percent. Because real output is unaffected by the money supply, it is the price level that drops by 20 percent.

3. B: During the 1960s and 1970s, most monetarists believed that a steady growth of the money supply was the optimal way to ensure steady growth in spending and GDP. The velocity equation is $MV = PY$. Rewritten, the equation is $M = PY \div V$, meaning that the money supply is the nominal GDP (PY) divided by the velocity (V), which is a measure of the number of times the average dollar bill in the economy circulates within the course of a year.

4. B: A point on the production possibilities curve represents efficiency and means that all factors of production (land, labor, and capital) are utilized in the economy. While this is unlikely to happen in the real world, a point on the PPC does represent this state of efficiency. If a point on the PPC moves below the PPC, then that movement represents an economic recession. A point below the PPC represents underutilization of resources, which means that there is unemployment. And unemployment is a characteristic of an economic recession.

5. A: An increase in the budget deficit will increase the aggregate demand curve to the right, which will induce the crowding-out effect such that higher interest rates crowd out private investment. Because there is no answer choice of "increase in the budget deficit," we know that an increase in government spending is the equivalent of an increase in the budget deficit. Both increasing the budget surplus or decreasing the budget deficit would entail shifting the demand for loanable funds to the left, which is the opposite of crowding out. An increase in taxes would also shift the demand for loanable funds to the left. An increase in the discount rate would shift the money supply to the left on the money market graph.

6. D: If the government increases business taxes, there will be a leftward shift of the aggregate demand curve. The short-run Phillips curve would definitely not shift to the left as that would reduce both inflation and unemployment. The short-run aggregate supply curve would shift to the left, not to the right. In addition, increased business taxes would reduce the budget deficit and so shift the demand for loanable funds to the left.

7. D: Monetarists hold that it's the quantity of money that spurs inflation and adheres to the $MV = PY$ equation in which M = money supply, V = velocity, P = price level, and Y = real output. Because the real output and price level are given, we calculate the two numbers, which equals $54,000, or the nominal GDP. As money supply and velocity multiplied together equals $54,000 and the velocity is 3, we know the money supply is $18,000.

8. B: The two ways the government can reduce unemployment via expansionary fiscal policy are by reducing income taxes or increasing government spending. When either or both of these policies are implemented, the demand for loanable funds will increase and shift to the right. The real interest rate will increase. However, because that is not an answer choice, it is also true that the AD curve will shift to the right, increasing both the real GDP and price level (inflation), so the inflation rate will increase.

9. A: An export would be counted as part of the current account surplus in a country's balance of account. If a native investor purchases stock in their native country, then there is no impact on the balance of accounts. When a foreigner purchases stock within Italy, this transaction would count toward the financial account surplus. An Italian company purchasing a computer from Mexico would contribute toward a current account deficit. In addition, income from a foreigner within Italy counts toward a financial account surplus and therefore increases Italy's current account deficit.

10. E: Contractionary monetary policy would typically be used when the Federal Reserve wants to control inflation by shifting the AD curve to the left. There are three traditional monetary policy tools: lowering the discount rate, decreasing the required reserve ratio, and selling government securities. When any of these three tools are used, the money supply curve (on the money market graph) will shift to the left and the nominal interest rate will increase. This will lead to a decrease in private investment as $Y = C + I + G + NX$ because when interest rates increase, private investment (I) will decrease as a result.

11. E: If real interest rates in the United States fell relative to real interest rates in South Korea, then South Korean investors will have less of an incentive to invest in American assets. Hence, the demand for the U.S. dollar will decrease and the dollar will depreciate. Therefore, the South Korean won will appreciate relative to the dollar. South Korean investors will buy fewer U.S. securities, and South Korean exports to the United States will decrease. The supply of dollars will increase and U.S. demand for the South Korean won will increase.

12. B: When average income in Jibinville increases, the aggregate demand shifts to the right because there is an increase in consumption. $Y = C + I + G + NX$, and C will increase. The real output, but more importantly for this problem, the price level, goes up. Inflation in Jibinville will hurt its currency in the open market and the demand for Jibinville money decreases (and therefore its currency depreciates), which means the demand for Zachland's currency will increase as a result.

13. D: Buying bonds on the open market will increase, or bloat, the money supply. The money supply will increase and lower the nominal interest rate in the money market. Raising the discount rate and raising the federal funds rate will shift the money supply curve to the left and increase the nominal interest rate. Lowering taxes will increase the real interest rate in the loanable funds market and raising taxes will decrease the real interest rate in that same loanable funds market.

14. C: Inflation makes money relatively worth less, not necessarily worthless, just *worth* less. So, it goes to reason that if inflation takes hold in Julietville, there will be an increase in demand for money in the money market. The money demand curve shifts to the right, and because the money supply is vertical, the nominal interest rate goes up. The money supply does not change. The opportunity cost of holding money decreases as you move along the money demand curve to the right as interest rates decrease.

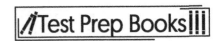

15. D: If the central bank of Country C decreases interest rates, it is utilizing expansionary monetary policy. On the money market graph, the money supply curve shifts to the right, and the nominal interest rate will decrease. Investors in other countries will have a decreased demand for currency in Country C, and Country C's currency will naturally depreciate in value. A country would buy the currencies of other countries if it wanted to artificially depreciate the value of its currency, not sell them.

16. E: Supply-side economics stands in stark contrast to Keynesian economics. Supply-side theory focuses on reducing the tax burden on businesses as a way of increasing the supply of goods and increasing economic growth. The Laffer Curve shows that lowering the tax rate can actually increase tax revenue. Critics, however, point to the lack of empirical evidence supporting supply-side theory and pejoratively refer to it as either "trickle-down" economics or "voo-doo" economics.

17. C: The national debt increases when there is a budget deficit and decreases if there is a budget surplus. In 2020, the national debt continued to increase with no signs of decreasing in the near future. Politicians disagree as to whether reducing the national debt, which would require reducing the budget deficit, should even be a priority for the government.

18. B: The dollar will appreciate in value relative to the euro and therefore exports will decrease, and imports will increase. When the demand for currency increases, the currency (or the dollar in this case) will appreciate in value. While this is good for domestic travelers, this increase in currency value is not good for domestic businesses that export because exports will decrease and therefore imports will increase. As a result of increased currency value, the GDP will decrease because $Y = C + I + G + NX$, and NX decreases when exports go down.

19. E: In high-interest Hungary, there will be capital inflows because the relatively higher interest rate in Hungary will cause Libyan investors to invest in Hungary. There will also be capital outflows from low-interest Libya until the interest rate in both countries equalizes. Capital will tend to flow out of countries that have a high interest rate into countries that have a low interest rate.

20. D: The interest rates in Hungary originally started at 6 percent while the interest rates in Libya started at 4 percent. When capital flows out of Hungary and into Libya, the interest rates should equalize to 5 percent. Hence, the interest rates in Hungary decrease from 6 percent to 5 percent while the interest rates in Libya increase from 5 percent to 6 percent. The country with the capital outflow will see a decrease in interest rates while the country with the capital inflow will see an increase in interest rates.

21. E: The purchasing power parity between two countries shows the nominal exchange rate by measuring a comparable basket of goods found in both countries. *The Economist* uses just one product, McDonald's Big Mac, to rank the purchasing power parities of all countries that sell a Big Mac. While the Big Mac Index was created initially as a "fun" way to measure purchasing power parity, the Index has become a very useful measure in serving as a proxy for the purchasing power parity for all good and services.

22. A: A tax would discourage behavior, whereas a subsidy would encourage behavior. In addition, a lump-sum subsidy has no effect on marginal behavior, whereas a per-unit subsidy does have an effect on marginal behavior. A per-unit subsidy properly incentivizes individuals to get more vaccinations.

23. A: The elimination of government welfare and replacing of a progressive income tax with a regressive tax would most likely serve to increase income inequality. However, there would be less deadweight loss with a lump-sum tax because work behavior would not be affected by the lump-sum nature of the tax. Therefore, efficiency increases.

Free Response

Question 1

1. a. i.

The nominal GDP equation is $Y = C + I + G + NX$.

$$Y = \$700{,}000 + \$200{,}000 + 200{,}000 + (\$250{,}000 - \$150{,}000)$$

$$Y = \$1.1\ million + 100{,}000 = \$1.2\ million$$

1. a. ii.

Real GDP uses constant prices, and nominal GDP uses current prices. One can find the real GDP as well by using the GDP deflator equation:

$$GDP\ Deflator = Nominal\ GDP \div Real\ GDP \times 100$$

$$120 = \$1.2\ million \div Real\ GDP \times 100$$

$$Real\ GDP = \$1.2\ million \div 120 \times 100$$

$$Real\ GDP = \$1\ million$$

1. a. iii.

$$Real\ GDP\ per\ capita = Real\ GDP \div Population$$

$$Real\ GDP\ per\ capita = \$1\ million \div 30{,}000 = \$33.33$$

1. b.

Because Jibrin has produced the bobbleheads in Conquerorville and not Parkland, Jibrin's bobblehead output is not included in Parkland's GDP data. The location where an item is produced is important.

1. c. i.

Deflation occurred because the GDP deflator decreased from 240 to 120.

1. c. ii.

The inflation rate is $GDP\ Deflator\ (new) - GDP\ Deflator\ (old) \div GDP\ Deflator\ (old) \times 100$.

$$Inflation\ rate = (120 - 240) \div 240 \times 100 = -120 \div 240 = -50\%$$

The inflation rate was –50%, or deflation was 50%.

1. d.

The number of discouraged workers could be greater than, less than, or equal to the number of unemployed workers. Therefore, the answer is indeterminate. We know that the number of unemployed workers is 5,000 and that there are 15,000 employed workers. In addition, 10,000 people are classified as not in the labor force, but that figure includes retired individuals, children, and other categories of individuals who do not work but are not unemployed. There could be zero discouraged workers, 10,000 discouraged workers, or somewhere in between. We simply do not have enough information.

Question 2

2. a.

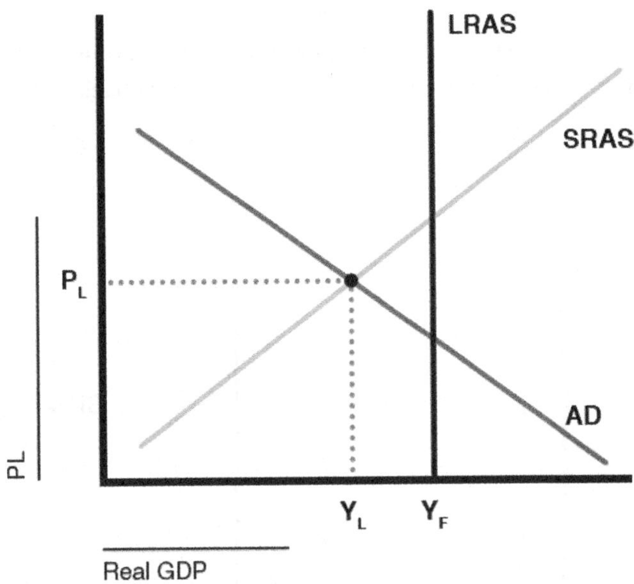

2. b.

There are three different types of expansionary fiscal policy measures the government can implement in order to get the economy out of a recession: Increase government spending, decrease income taxes, or increase government transfer payments. Any of these three fiscal policy tools will increase the real output and price level and get the economy closer to its long-run equilibrium output.

2. c.

The spending multiplier is:

$$1 \div (1 - MPC) = 1 \div 0.2 = 5$$

The equation is the $G \times Multiplier = Change\ in\ GDP$. We know that the multiplier is 5 and the desired change in GDP is $+\$250\ billion$, so $G \times 5 = \$250\ billion. G = \$50\ billion.$

An increase in government spending of \$50 billion will close the \$250 billion recessionary gap.

2. d.

The tax multiplier is:

$$MPC \div (1 - MPC) = 0.8 \div 0.2 = 4$$

The equation is the $T \times Multiplier = Change\ in\ GDP$. We know that the multiplier is 4 and the desired change in GDP is $+\$250\ billion$, so $T \times 4 = \$250\ billion.\ T = \$62.5\ billion.$

A decrease in taxes of $62.5 billion will close the $250 billion recessionary gap.

Therefore, the tax decrease will be a greater amount than the increase in government spending because the spending multiplier is greater than the tax multiplier.

2. e.

The long-run aggregate supply (LRAS) will shift to the right because there is an increase in quantity and quality of labor. The country's stock of human capital increases and causes the LRAS to shift to the right.

Question 3

3. a.

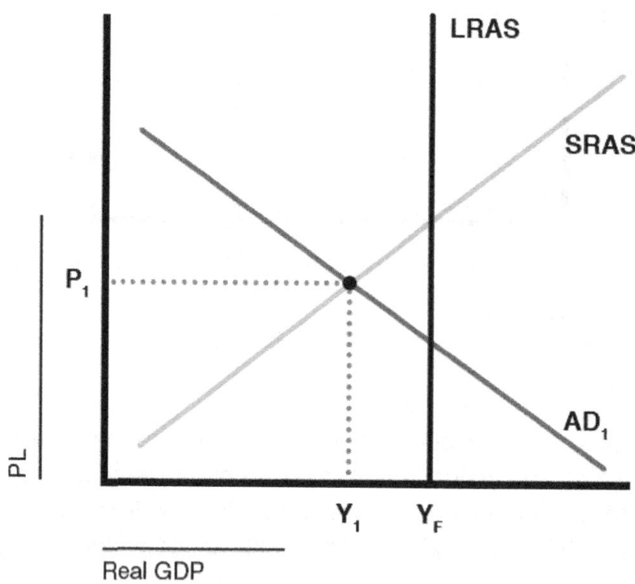

3. b. i.

Buy government bonds because that will increase (or bloat) the money supply and shift the aggregate demand to the right, increasing the real GDP.

3. b. ii.

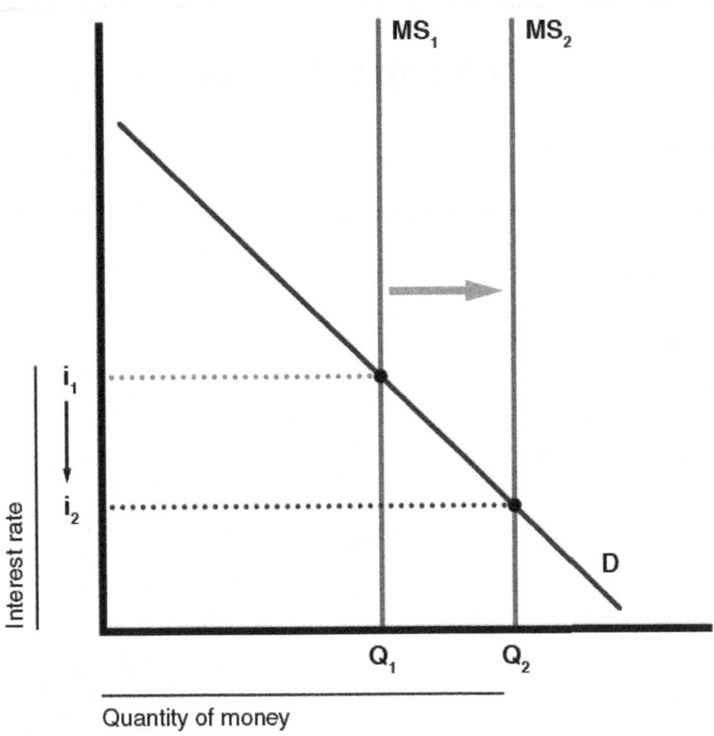

3. c.

Capital will flow out of the United States because the decrease in interest rates will make investment less attractive in the United States and more attractive elsewhere.

Microeconomics Practice Test

Multiple Choice

Supply and Demand

Use the following graph to answer questions 2 and 3:

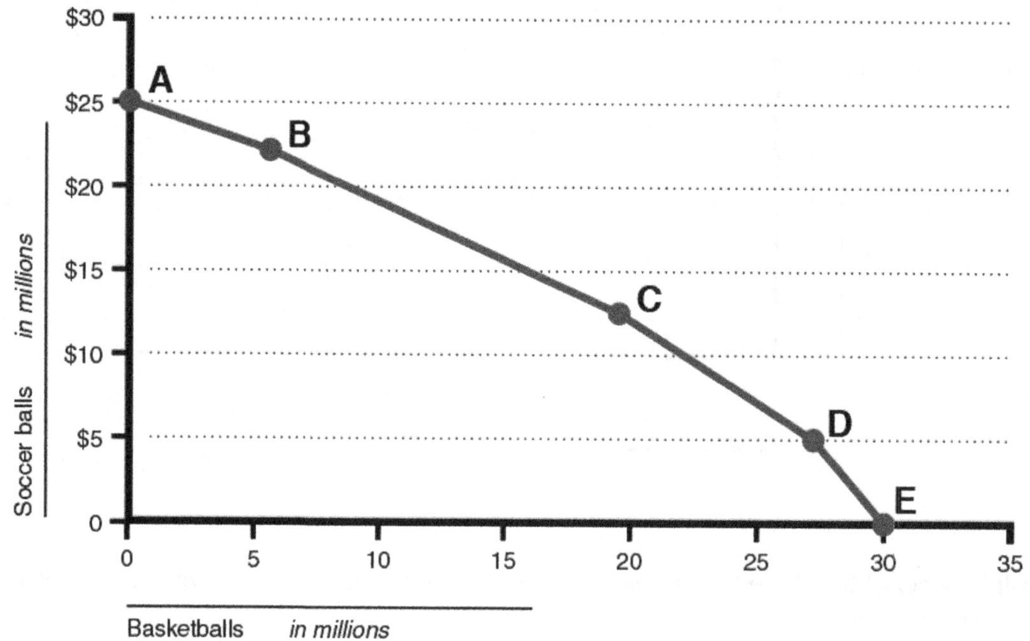

1. When compared to market economies, why do command economies generally fail to produce as efficiently as market economies?
   a. They most often haven't had the luxury of abundant natural resources.
   b. They are unfairly limited by the principles of scarcity in at least one factor of production.
   c. Command economies fail to allow economic players to respond to positive or negative incentives.
   d. The invisible hand prevents a laissez-faire economy from guiding the marketplace.
   e. Command economies unfairly allow business owners to profit from the consumer's ignorance.

2. Select the choice that properly interprets the production possibility curve.
   a. Point B demonstrates a business producing 22 million basketballs and 7 million soccer balls.
   b. Point A represents a business producing 25 million soccer balls and 25 million basketballs.
   c. Point D represents a business producing 27 million basketballs and 27 million soccer balls.
   d. Point E represents a business producing 30 million basketballs and zero soccer balls.
   e. Point C represents a business producing 12 million basketballs and 12 million soccer balls.

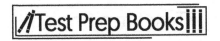

3. Which of the following trade-offs would cause the business to lose the most soccer balls?
   a. Moving from point A to point B
   b. Moving from point B to point C
   c. Moving from point C to point D
   d. Moving from point D to point E
   e. Moving from point C to point E

4. Which of the following concepts should a nation calculate if they are trying to determine whether trading is in their best interest?
   a. Production possibility curve
   b. Absolute advantage
   c. Comparative advantage
   d. Marginal utility
   e. Total utility

5. Which choice would give an advantage to a domestic producer compared to a foreign producer of a particular good or service?
   a. A tariff
   b. A domestic regulation
   c. A floating interest rate
   d. An elastic demand
   e. An inelastic demand

6. If Diane experiences less satisfaction from consuming a third cup of tea than from her second cup of tea, which of the following did she experience?
   a. Negative marginal utility
   b. Diminishing marginal utility
   c. Positive marginal utility
   d. Diminishing marginal return
   e. Negative marginal return

7. Charles was given a substantial raise and as a result demanded more of good A but less of good B. Which of the following is true about goods A and B?
   a. A is a complement to B.
   b. B is a substitute for A.
   c. A is an inferior good, and B is a normal good.
   d. A is a normal good, and B is an inferior good.
   e. A and B are both normal goods.

8. If technology advances help producers lower the cost of production, what will happen to supply?
   a. It will remain unchanged.
   b. The entire supply curve will shift left (inward).
   c. The entire supply curve will shift right (outward).
   d. The supply curve will not change, but the demand curve will increase.
   e. The supply curve will not change, but the demand curve will decrease.

9. What relationship do two goods have if their cross-price elasticity is positive?
   a. Inferior goods
   b. Superior goods
   c. Normal goods
   d. Substitutes
   e. Complements

10. If the producer of a good absorbs the majority of the burden for an excise tax, which of the following is true?
   a. The supply of the good is more elastic than the demand.
   b. The demand of the good is more elastic than the supply.
   c. Supply and demand are equally elastic.
   d. The excise tax was levied in conjunction with a subsidy to consumers.
   e. The excise tax was unfairly levied on the producer.

11. If consumer and producer surplus rapidly decrease in a short period of time, which of the following may have occurred?
   a. Positive demand shock
   b. Negative demand shock
   c. Price ceiling
   d. Price floor
   e. Increase in scarcity

12. What type of impact will a tariff have between foreign and domestic competition?
   a. It gives an advantage to foreign competitors because they can charge less for their product as a result of the tariff.
   b. It gives an advantage to foreign competitors because it is a tax that must be paid by domestic producers.
   c. It gives an advantage to domestic competitors because it is additional money they receive from the government to outproduce their foreign competitors.
   d. It gives an advantage to domestic competitors because it is an additional tax that foreign companies must pay to sell a product in another nation, making their product more expensive.
   e. It does not give an advantage to foreign or domestic companies because a tariff equally affects both types of producers by charging them both a tax that must be added to the product's cost.

13. Which of the following will a company most closely watch if they decide to change the price of a good or service they are producing?
   a. Surplus
   b. Shortage
   c. Total revenue
   d. Marginal revenue
   e. Measure of unit elasticity

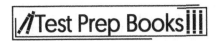

14. Amber was willing to sell a car for $4,000, but she sold it for $4,500. Greg bought the car for $4,500 but was willing to pay $5,500 for the car. Which of the following choices is correct?
  a. Amber has a $500 producer surplus, and Greg has a –$500 consumer surplus.
  b. Amber has a $500 consumer surplus, and Greg has a $1000 producer surplus.
  c. Amber has a $500 producer surplus, and Greg has a $4500 consumer surplus.
  d. Amber has a $500 consumer surplus, and Greg has a $500 producer surplus.
  e. Amber has a $500 producer surplus, and Greg has a $1000 consumer surplus.

15. If a small increase in the price of a good or service results in a significant decrease in the demand for the good or service, it is safe to assume which of the following?
  a. There are few substitutes for the good or service.
  b. There are many substitutes for the good or service.
  c. The good or service is inferior.
  d. The good or service is unit elastic.
  e. The good or service has a tariff that increased the price unnecessarily.

16. What form of measurement is used when determining the optimum amount of pleasure derived from the consumer choice theory?
  a. Demand
  b. Supply
  c. Utils
  d. Revenue
  e. Elasticity

17. Joseph is able to produce twelve fishing hooks and eight lures per hour. James is able to produce seventeen fishing hooks and four lures per hour. Which of the following is true?
  a. Joseph has an absolute advantage in both lures and hooks over James.
  b. James has an absolute advantage in both lures and hooks over Joseph.
  c. James has an absolute advantage in lures.
  d. Joseph has an absolute advantage in hooks.
  e. James has an absolute advantage in hooks, and Joseph has an absolute advantage in lures.

18. A publisher sells 90 percent of a particular book at $25. Which of the following choices is an accurate description of the publisher's situation?
  a. The publisher is at a state of equilibrium.
  b. The publisher should have produced more of the book.
  c. The publisher is at a state of disequilibrium.
  d. The publisher must be selling an inferior good.
  e. The publisher should have published 10 percent less of the book to maximize the total revenue.

19. If a producer wants to produce 40 million books and 10 million magazines, which of the following must happen?
  a. They must produce at point A.
  b. They must maximize the use of their current resources.
  c. They must add additional factors of production to reach those amounts.
  d. They must produce at points B and E.
  e. They must decrease the amount of variables they are using.

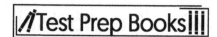

Production, Cost, and Perfect Competition

1. The quantity of radios and the corresponding total cost of radios is given in the chart below. What is the average fixed cost of 4 radios?

Quantity of Radios	Total Cost of Radios
0	$300
1	$350
2	$375
3	$425
4	$600
5	$750

a. $75
b. $100
c. $150
d. $200
e. It cannot be determined from the information given.

2. Which of the following must be true if at the 42nd unit of output, marginal cost (MC) is $13 and average total cost (ATC) is $15?
a. The ATC of producing the 41st unit is more than $15.
b. The ATC of producing the 41st unit is less than $15.
c. The MC of producing the 41st unit is more than $13.
d. The average variable cost of producing the 42nd unit is more than $15.
e. The average variable cost of producing the 42nd unit is equal to $2.

3. Which of the following statements is true regarding average fixed cost (AFC)?
a. The average total cost (ATC) will always be less than the AFC.
b. The marginal cost will always intersect the AFC at its minimum point.
c. The AFC will always decrease and never intersect with the x-axis.
d. As production increases, the AFC will decrease initially and then increase.
e. The vertical distance between the ATC and the marginal cost (MC) equals the AFC.

Questions 4 and 5 refer to the table below, which shows the short-run production function of a perfectly competitive firm, Carrots, Inc. The firm produces carrots using labor as its only variable input.

Number of Workers	Number of Carrots Produced
0	0
1	50
2	110
3	180
4	220
5	230
6	225

4. The hiring of which worker represents the beginning of diminishing marginal product of labor for Carrots, Inc.?
   a. 1st worker
   b. 2nd worker
   c. 3rd worker
   d. 4th worker
   e. 5th worker

5. The hiring of which worker represents the beginning of negative marginal product of labor for Carrots, Inc.?
   a. 3rd worker
   b. 4th worker
   c. 5th worker
   d. 6th worker
   e. Negative marginal product of labor never occurs for Carrots, Inc.

6. If a lump-sum tax is imposed on a monopoly, which of the following statements is true?
   a. The ATC will decrease.
   b. The marginal revenue will increase.
   c. The AVC will increase.
   d. The marginal cost will increase.
   e. The profit-maximizing point will remain the same.

7. The table below shows some of the different types of costs for a firm. Only two numbers are filled in. Based on the information in the table, what is the average variable cost (AVC) of producing the second unit?

Quantity	Total Cost	Average Fixed Cost	Average Variable Cost	Average Total Cost
0	$50			
1				
2				$32

a. $5
b. $6
c. $7
d. $8
e. $10

8. If the marginal cost of producing the first widget is $15, the marginal cost of producing the second widget is $20, and the marginal cost of producing the third widget is $40, what is the average variable cost of producing 3 units?

a. $5
b. $10
c. $20
d. $25
e. $50

9. A marginal cost tends to slope upward with increased production because of the effects of which of the following?

a. Increasing marginal product
b. Diminishing marginal product
c. Diseconomies of scale
d. Economies of scale
e. Diminishing marginal utility

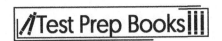

Questions 10 and 11 refer to the data in the table below. A perfectly competitive firm operates with a fixed amount of capital. Labor is the only variable input. The table below shows the daily output of clock radios with each additional worker hired.

Number of Workers Hired	Quantity of Output (Units)
0	0
1	100
2	300
3	550
4	725
5	800
6	850

10. What is the marginal product of the 4th worker?
    a. 75
    b. 100
    c. 175
    d. 200
    e. It cannot be determined from the information given.

11. The firm experiences negative marginal returns of labor with the hiring of which worker?
    a. 3rd worker
    b. 4th worker
    c. 5th worker
    d. 6th worker
    e. The firm does not experience negative marginal returns.

12. At the current quantity that Jibby's Strawberries is selling strawberries, the firm has a marginal revenue of $100 and marginal cost of $105. Which of the following is true (assuming an upward sloping marginal cost curve)?
    a. The firm is not maximizing profit.
    b. The firm's profits would increase if they increased the quantity sold.
    c. The firm is losing money and should therefore shut down.
    d. The firm earns negative economic profit.
    e. The firm earns $0 accounting profit.

13. The table below shows some of the different types of costs for a firm. Only three numbers are filled in. Based on the information in the table, what is the marginal cost (MC) of producing the second unit?

Quantity	Fixed Cost	Variable Cost	Total Cost	Marginal Cost
0	$20			
1		$22		
2			$50	

    a. $4
    b. $6
    c. $7
    d. $8
    e. $10

14. When the marginal cost curve lies above the average total cost curve, which of the following statements is true?
  a. The marginal cost is decreasing.
  b. The fixed cost is increasing.
  c. The average fixed cost is increasing.
  d. The average total cost is increasing.
  e. The average variable cost is decreasing.

15. The table below shows a firm's total cost of producing different levels of output. What is the average variable cost (AVC) of producing 2 units?

Quantity (Units)	Total Cost
0	\$50
1	\$59
2	\$64
3	\$71
4	\$85

  a. \$5
  b. \$7
  c. \$14
  d. \$32
  e. It cannot be determined from the information given.

Imperfect Competition

1. Which of the following is FALSE regarding a profit-maximizing monopolist in the long run?
  a. Monopolists earn economic profit.
  b. Price is greater than marginal cost.
  c. Monopolists will always produce on the inelastic portion of the demand curve.
  d. Monopolists will produce at an inefficiently low quantity.
  e. Deadweight loss is created when monopolists produce at the profit-maximizing quantity.

2. Which of the following must be true in a two-player game theory scenario in an oligopoly?
  a. No firm has a dominant strategy.
  b. Only one firm has a dominant strategy.
  c. Both firms must have a dominant strategy.
  d. Either one firm or both firms have a dominant strategy.
  e. None of the above

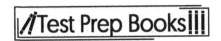

Questions 3 and 4 refer to the game theory matrix below. Marvel is the x-player, and DC Comics is the y-player.

		DC	
		Superman	Batman
Marvel	Ironman	A ($150 million, $120 million)	B ($50 million, $150 million)
	Thor	C ($200 million, $55 million)	D ($88 million, $96 million)

3. Which of the following statements is true regarding the dominant strategy for Marvel and DC Comics?
   a. Marvel has a dominant strategy of Ironman; DC Comics has no dominant strategy.
   b. Marvel has a dominant strategy of Thor; DC Comics has a dominant strategy of Superman.
   c. Marvel has a dominant strategy of Thor; DC Comics has a dominant strategy of Batman.
   d. Marvel has no dominant strategy; DC Comics has a dominant strategy of Superman.
   e. Marvel has no dominant strategy; DC Comics has a dominant strategy of Thor.

4. Which of the following statements is accurate regarding prisoner's dilemma and Nash equilibrium for Marvel and DC Comics?
   a. This is a prisoner's dilemma, and the Nash equilibrium is Marvel choosing Ironman and DC Comics choosing Superman (box A).
   b. This is a prisoner's dilemma, and the Nash equilibrium is Marvel choosing Thor and DC Comics choosing Batman (box D).
   c. This is not a prisoner's dilemma, and the Nash equilibrium is Marvel choosing Ironman and DC Comics choosing Superman (box A).
   d. This is not a prisoner's dilemma, and the Nash equilibrium is Marvel choosing Thor and DC Comics choosing Batman (box D).
   e. This is a prisoner's dilemma, and the Nash equilibria are Marvel choosing Ironman with DC Comics choosing Superman (box A) and Marvel choosing Thor and DC Comics choosing Batman (box D).

5. If the three largest firms in the marketplace produce 92 percent of total output, the market is which of the following?
   a. Perfectly competitive
   b. An unregulated monopoly
   c. Monopolistic competition
   d. An oligopoly
   e. A monopsony

6. A firm that competes in a perfectly competitive market produces 100 units of output and sells the product for $50 per unit. At this level of output, the average total cost is $40, the average variable cost is $30, and the marginal cost is $37. What should this firm do to maximize short-run profits?
   a. Increase output until price equals average total cost.
   b. Increase output until price equals marginal cost.
   c. Leave output unchanged.
   d. Decrease output to 99 units.
   e. Shut down because the price is greater than the average variable cost.

7. Which of the following is true in a monopolistically competitive market?
   a. All firms sell products at the productively efficient point.
   b. All firms sell products at the allocatively efficient point.
   c. Firms sell at a price that is higher than the marginal cost.
   d. Firms sell at the revenue-maximizing quantity.
   e. Collusion usually takes place because there are so few companies in a monopolistically competitive market structure.

8. Compared to a monopoly with the same demand and cost curves, a firm in a perfectly competitive industry's price and output will be which of the following?

Price	Output
a. Higher	The same
b. Higher	Higher
c. The same	Higher
d. Lower	The same
e. Lower	Higher

9. Which of the following is true when a firm engages in perfect price discrimination?
   a. Companies divide customers into distinct groups (i.e., young or old).
   b. Firms charge where the price equals the average total cost (ATC).
   c. All customers end up paying a price that is lower than the initial market price.
   d. Total consumer surplus increases.
   e. Producer profits increase.

10. Which of the following is true of firms in a monopolistically competitive market structure in the long run?
   a. Price equals marginal cost.
   b. Products are differentiated.
   c. Firms attempt to maximize revenue, not profit.
   d. Firms earn economic profit.
   e. Products are homogeneous.

11. If individual firms in a perfectly competitive market are incurring economic losses, the number of firms and the price of the product, in the long run, will change in which of the following ways?

Number of Firms	Price
a. Decrease	Increase
b. Decrease	No change
c. Decrease	Decrease
d. Increase	Decrease
e. Increase	No change

12. What is the area of economic profit for the profit-maximizing monopolist on the graph below?

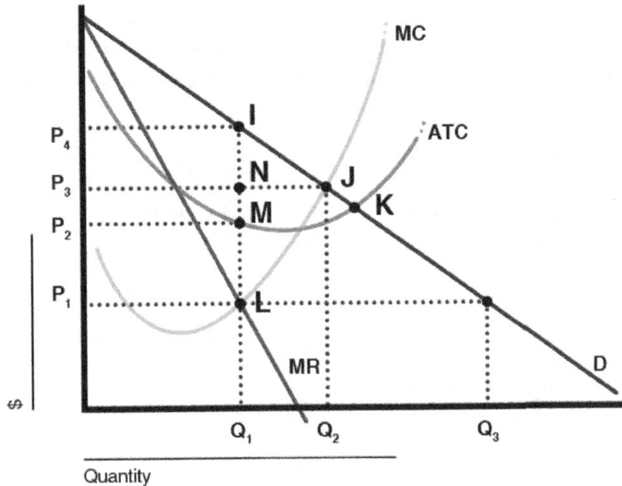

a. $0P_1LQ_1$
b. P_1P2ML
c. P_1P_3NL
d. P_2P_3NM
e. P_2P_4IM

13. Two firms (firm A and firm B) are deciding whether to charge a high price or a low price in a two-person game theory model. If firm A employs a dominant strategy of charging a high price, which of the following must be true?
a. Firm B has a dominant strategy of charging a high price.
b. Firm B has a dominant strategy of charging a low price.
c. Firm B has no dominant strategy.
d. Firm B has a dominant strategy of either charging a low price or high price.
e. None of the above

14. As an unregulated monopolist, Edco Trash Services is earning positive economic profits. If Edco decided to make $0 economic profit rather than maximize profit, Edco would decide to set a price that is equal to which of the following?
a. Marginal cost
b. Marginal revenue
c. Average variable cost
d. Average total cost
e. Average fixed cost

15. Which of the following is a true statement regarding how firms behave?
a. Firms in both monopoly and perfect competition make economic profit in the long run.
b. Collusion is mostly likely to take place in perfect competition because there are so few firms in the marketplace.
c. Firms are "price takers" in perfect competition because of their inability to affect market price.
d. Advertising is critical for firms in perfect competition because products are differentiated.
e. In an oligopoly, one firm has complete control of the market output.

Market Failure and Role of Government

1. Assume that workers making clocks are in a perfectly competitive labor market and work for a wage of $100 per day. What is the optimal number of workers that a clock producer will hire if the clock sells for $8?

Number of Workers	Total Daily Output of Clocks
0	0
1	25
2	55
3	75
4	90
5	100

a. 1 worker
b. 2 workers
c. 3 workers
d. 4 workers
e. 5 workers

2. In a monopsonistic labor market, which of the following would serve to reduce deadweight loss associated with a firm that has hired workers at the profit-maximizing point of labor?
a. Tax the laborers
b. Tax the company
c. Institute a binding price ceiling
d. Institute a binding price floor
e. Set a quota for number of workers hired

3. Which of the following will shift a factor's demand curve to the left?
a. A decrease in the price of the good being produced
b. An increase in the price of the good being produced
c. A technological advance that increases the MPL
d. An increase in the demand for the good being produced
e. An increase in the minimum wage

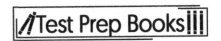

Questions 4–5 refer to the table below, which shows the short-run production function of a perfectly competitive firm, Paper Bags R Us. The firm produces brown paper bags using labor as its only variable input.

Number of Workers	Number of Paper Bags Produced
0	0
1	100
2	250
3	340
4	400
5	430
6	440

4. The hiring of which worker represents the beginning of diminishing marginal product of labor for the brown paper bag company?
   a. Third worker
   b. Fourth worker
   c. Fifth worker
   d. Sixth worker
   e. The company never experiences diminishing marginal product of labor.

5. Assume that brown paper bags sell for $0.50 and that workers are paid $15 an hour in a perfectly competitive labor market. What is the profit-maximizing number of paper bags that Paper Bags R Us will make?
   a. 100 paper bags
   b. 250 paper bags
   c. 340 paper bags
   d. 400 paper bags
   e. 430 paper bags

Use the graph below to answer Questions 6–7:

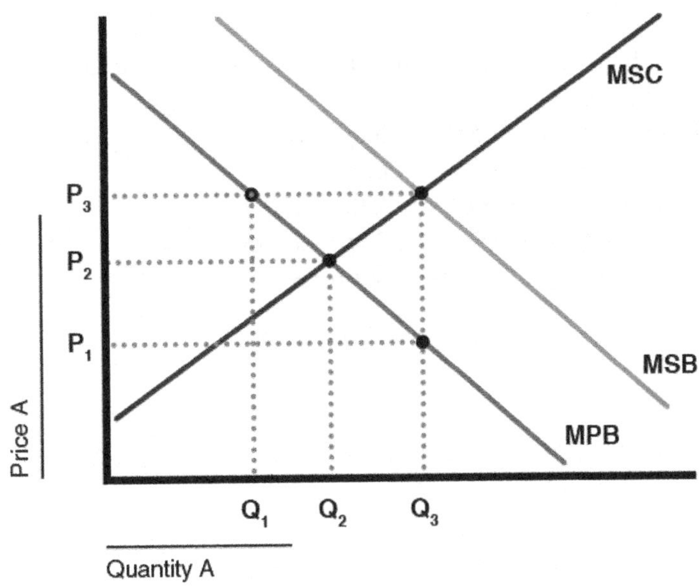

6. The socially optimal quantity and the per-unit subsidy that will achieve the socially optimal quantity are which of the following?

Socially Optimal Quantity	Per-Unit Subsidy
a. Q1	P3 – P1
b. Q2	P3 – P2
c. Q3	P3 – P1
d. Q2	P3 – P1
e. Q3	P2 – P1

7. Based on the location of the marginal social benefit (MSB) curve, which of the following statements is most likely TRUE for Good A?
   a. Production of Good A creates a negative externality.
   b. Production of Good A creates a positive externality.
   c. Q2 is the socially optimal point of production for Good A.
   d. The free market will overproduce Good A.
   e. It would be better to offer a lump-sum subsidy to producers rather than a per-unit subsidy.

8. If positive externalities exist in the market for college education, which of the following is most likely to be TRUE?
   a. Taxing college education will lead to the socially efficient level of output.
   b. Subsidizing college will decrease the amount of deadweight loss.
   c. If the government provides financial aid to students, a large amount of deadweight loss will result.
   d. The socially optimal quantity of college students is less than the optimal quantity of college students at the free market equilibrium point.
   e. Quotas will increase the level of social efficiency.

9. Which of the following is an example of a pure private good (rival and excludable)?
   a. National defense
   b. Netflix
   c. Pizza
   d. Public park
   e. Disneyland

10. Country A has a Gini coefficient of 0.6, and Country B has a Gini coefficient of 0.4. Which statement must definitely be TRUE?
   a. Country A has lower average income than Country B.
   b. Country B has lower average income than Country A.
   c. There is more income inequality in Country A than in Country B.
   d. There is more income inequality in Country B than in Country A.
   e. Country A has more deadweight loss than Country B.

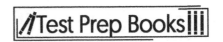

11. Which of the following is TRUE when there are positive externalities associated with the production of a good?

a. Marginal social benefits will exceed marginal private benefits, so the good will be underproduced when left to market forces.
b. Marginal private costs will exceed marginal social costs, but the government can correct the problem by taxing the company.
c. Producers should be taxed so that they will produce less of the good.
d. Consumers should be taxed so that they will consume less of the good.
e. The market will adjust automatically to ensure marginal social costs and marginal social benefits are equal.

Free Response

Question 1

Norway and Sweden are trying to determine whether it would be beneficial for them to trade with each other.

- i. Fill out the chart below and give an absolute advantage (under the "With Trade" column) to Norway for both beef and chicken.
- ii. Give a comparative advantage to Norway producing beef and Sweden producing chicken.
- iii. Describe the effect a trade quota could have on one or both of the countries.

Number (in millions of pounds)		Without Trade		With Trade		Gains from Trade
		Production	Consumption	Production	Consumption	
Norway	Beef					
	Chicken					
Sweden	Beef					
	Chicken					

Question 2

As the only restaurant in a small town in Jarden, Texas, Mr. Cluck's Chicken has a local monopoly on the sale of chicken sandwiches. Mr. Cluck's Chicken is currently incurring an economic loss.

a. Draw a correctly labeled graph for Mr. Cluck's Chicken and label the following points.

- i. Mr. Cluck Chicken's profit-maximizing price and quantity, labeled P_1 and Q_1, respectively
- ii. A correctly placed average total cost (ATC) curve
- iii. Mr. Cluck Chicken's socially optimal price and quantity, labeled P_s and Q_s, respectively
- iv. The revenue-maximizing quantity, labeled Q_R

b. Assume that Mr. Cluck's Chicken has been declared an "essential" business by the governor of Texas and is provided a lump-sum subsidy to help make the business profitable.

- i. What happens to the profit-maximizing quantity? Explain.
- ii. What happens to Mr. Cluck's Chicken's economic profit? Explain.

c. Assume the demand for chicken sandwiches decreases because the price of steak sandwiches has dropped drastically.

- i. What must be true for Mr. Cluck's Chicken to continue to operate in the short run?
- ii. What happens to Mr. Cluck's Chicken's profit-maximizing quantity and price in the short run assuming the firm continues to operate?

Question 3

Southland is a small town in which there is only one employer, Casey Steel. Casey Steel is monopsonist in the labor market and competes in a perfectly competitive steel market. Assume that labor is the only variable input.

a. Identify the profit-maximizing quantity of labor for Casey Steel.

b. Identify the wage Casey Steel pays to hire the profit-maximizing quantity of labor.

c. Find the socially optimal quantity of labor for Casey Steel.

d. If the government imposes a minimum wage of $30, does the amount of deadweight loss increase, decrease, or stay the same? Explain.

Microeconomics Answer Explanations

Multiple Choice

1. C: Because command economies are controlled by a government, the individual citizens who actually produce the goods are not allowed to make decisions based on the demand of the product or the profit they might gain from producing more. These individuals cannot respond to their situation, positive or negative, and therefore command economies do not produce at their maximum capacity of efficiency. Choice *A* is incorrect because the amount of resources has historically had very little to do with a nation's success in efficiently distributing them. Choice *B* is incorrect because every nation's resources are always scarce. Choice *D* is incorrect because the invisible hand actually helps to guide the economy more efficiently. Choice *E* is incorrect because the government is in control of the majority of the economy; it has nothing to do with the behaviors of producers and consumers.

2. D: The company would produce 30 million basketballs and zero soccer balls. The other choices show a combination of soccer balls and basketballs being produced up until point A, wherein all resources are being used to produce soccer balls and none are dedicated to producing basketballs.

3. E: If the company decided to move from point C to point E, it would lose 12 million soccer balls. All of the other choices cause the business to lose even fewer soccer balls. From point A to B (Choice *A*) would lose 3 million soccer balls. From point B to C (Choice *B*) would lose 10 million soccer balls. From point C to D (Choice *C*) would lose 7 million soccer balls. From point D to E (Choice *D*) would lose 5 million soccer balls.

4. C: If a nation is trying to determine whether it is most beneficial to trade with a neighboring nation, knowing who has the comparative advantage when producing goods and services will best help them determine a beneficial trade. The nation with the lowest opportunity cost when producing this product has a comparative advantage over their counterpart. If both nations have a comparative advantage over one another in a given area, it would be beneficial to trade. Choice *A* is incorrect because a production possibility curve illustrates the realities of production but does not show whether trade is beneficial. Choice *B* is incorrect because an absolute advantage does not give you enough information to make this decision. Choices *D* and *E* are incorrect because marginal utility and total utility are not concepts that relate to trade.

5. A: A tariff is a tax imposed on an import. Because this tax is not imposed on a domestic producer, it gives the domestic producer an advantage. Choice *B* is incorrect because a domestic regulation would harm the domestic producer, not the foreign producer. Choices *C, D,* and *E* are incorrect: A floating interest rate, elastic demand, and inelastic demand don't have an adverse effect on one or the other because both are affected by them equally.

6. A: Negative marginal utility means that a person experiences less overall satisfaction from consuming an additional unit of something than if they had not consumed an additional unit at all. This is what Diane experienced. Choice *B* cannot be correct because diminishing marginal utility means Diane experienced more satisfaction when an additional unit was added, but the level of satisfaction did not increase as much as it did when the previous unit was added. Positive marginal utility means that if a unit was added, she would experience more satisfaction, which means Choice *C* cannot be correct. Satisfaction is measured in utils (or utility), which means Choices *D* and *E* cannot be correct.

7. D: If a person's wage increases and they demand more of a good, it is a normal good. If they demand less of a good, it is an inferior good. Without more information, we don't know if goods A and B are complements (Choice *A*) and/or substitutes (Choice *B*) to one another. Choice *C* cannot be accurate because good A is desired more, and an inferior good means an increase in Charles's wage would make him demand less. Choice *E* cannot be true because if they were both normal goods, he would desire more of each of them after his income rose.

8. C: Because technology is allowing producers to supply more of a good or service at a lower cost, the entire supply curve shifts outward. Choice *A* is not correct because it is easier to produce something with more advanced technology, and therefore an advance in technology will have an effect on the supply side. Choice *B* is not correct because if the supply curve moved inward, it means producers are supplying less of something after technology makes it easier. This doesn't make sense. Choices *D* and *E* cannot be correct because the eventual effect it will have on demand cannot be determined until it first shifts the supply curve.

9. D: When goods have a positive cross-price elasticity, they are substitutes for one another. Choices *A* and *C* are not correct because there is no way to determine whether they are inferior or normal goods based on the information given. Choice *B* is not correct because a superior good is not a term used in economics. Choice *E* is not correct because a negative cross-price elasticity means they are complements for one another.

10. B: When demand is more elastic than supply, producers bear more of the cost for the tax. If Choice *A* was true, it would mean that supply is more elastic than demand because under these circumstances, consumers bear more of the cost for the tax. Supply and demand are not equally elastic (Choice *C*) because the supplier is bearing the majority of the cost, which means one or the other is more elastic. Choices *D* and *E* are a matter of judgment, not mathematically determined by the elasticity of supply and demand.

11. B: A negative demand shock is when the quantity demanded of a good or service has decreased drastically due to an unexpected economic event. This causes the producer and consumer surplus to decrease because they must lower the price of the good or service, which means they will see less profit. Choice *A* is not correct because a positive demand shock would lead to an increase in producer and consumer surplus. Choices *C* and *D* are not correct because a price ceiling and price floor are not due to a sudden, drastic economic event but rather a policy decision by government. Option *E* is not correct because scarcity is not something that relates to a sudden decrease in consumer and producer surplus.

12. D: A tariff is a tax levied on foreign companies wanting to sell a good or service in another country. This benefits domestic producers because they don't have to pay the tax, which means the cost of production is lower. It cannot give an advantage to foreign companies (Choices *A* and *B*) because the foreign company has to pay the additional tax. Choice *C* is incorrect because a tariff is not money received by a domestic company (that would be a subsidy) but money paid by a foreign company to the government. Choice *E* is incorrect because domestic companies do not pay the tax.

13. C: The most important variable companies watch is total revenue. The total revenue is what a company earns from selling its goods and services. If that number decreases substantially, it could affect the survivability of the company. Choices *A* and *B* are not correct because, although a surplus and shortage are important to a company, they only help to determine the price. They are not as important as the total revenue. Choice *D* is not correct: Although the marginal revenue is important because it shows how much money they made after selling an additional unit of a good or service, it is not as important as knowing how much total revenue the company generates. Choice *E* is not correct because the measure of unit elasticity is not something that will impact the overall pricing of a good or service.

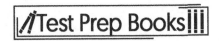

14. E: A producer surplus is the amount of money above what a producer is willing to sell a good or service for, whereas a consumer surplus is the amount of money beneath what a consumer was willing to pay for a good or service. Because Amber was willing to sell it for $500 less than what she sold it for, she made a $500 producer surplus. Greg bought it for $1,000 below what he was willing to pay for the product, and therefore he made a $1,000 consumer surplus. Choice *A* confuses what Greg has with a negative consumer surplus, which is not possible. Choice *B* confuses the terms *consumer surplus* and *producer surplus*. Choice *C* lists the total amount she sold it for, not the consumer surplus for Greg. Choice *D* confuses the terms *consumer surplus* and *producer surplus*.

15. B: If a good or service is elastic, that means there will be a substantial impact on the quantity demanded if the price increases. One reason for the substantial impact in a price change is the availability of substitutes. If there are a lot of substitutes, people will purchase the substitutes rather than the good or service they most prefer. Choice *A* is the opposite of that, so it cannot be true. Choices *C, D,* and *E* cannot be known based on the limited information in the question.

16. C: Utils measure the optimum level of enjoyment or satisfaction a person receives from consuming goods or services. The consumer choice theory is the study of how people maximize their satisfaction when choosing combinations of goods and services. Choices *A* and *B* are incorrect because demand and supply measure the quantity of something, not satisfaction. Choices *D* and *E* are incorrect because revenue measures money and elasticity measures how much of one variable changes when another variable is altered.

17. E: An absolute advantage is when somebody can produce more of something than someone else. James produces seventeen fishing hooks, and Joseph only produces twelve fishing hooks. James has an absolute advantage when producing fishing hooks. Joseph produces eight lures to James's four. Joseph has an absolute advantage producing lures. Choice *A* is incorrect because Joseph does not have an absolute advantage in hooks. Choice *B* is incorrect because James does not have an absolute advantage in lures. Choice *C* is incorrect because Joseph, not James, has an absolute advantage in lures. Option *D* is incorrect because Joseph has an absolute advantage in lures, not hooks.

18. C: Disequilibrium means there is either a shortage or surplus of goods unsold at a given price. In this particular case, 10 percent of the books are unsold, which means there is a disequilibrium. Choice *A* is incorrect because equilibrium means there is no more quantity demanded and there are no books left over. This scenario does not meet that criteria. Choice *B* is incorrect: The publisher should not produce more of the book because there are already too many available at the price. Choice *D* is incorrect because there is no way to know whether the good is inferior based on the information in the question. Choice *E* is incorrect because the total revenue is not impacted by the number of books that are not yet sold.

19. C: Because no point on the production possibility curve allows for the possibility of producing that many books and magazines, more resources must be added to reach that level of production. Point A (Choice *A*) will not allow them to produce more of anything. Choice *B* is not correct because any point on the line has them maximizing their resources. To extend beyond it, one must add resources. Choice *D* is incorrect because production possibility curves don't work by adding together the points. Choice *E* is not correct because if they maximize their current resources, they cannot reach the amount they desire.

Production, Cost, and Perfect Competition

1. A: The average fixed cost (AFC) is $75 because the fixed cost is $300 and the quantity is 4. $AFC = fixed\ cost \div quantity$, or $\$300 \div 4\ =\ \$75$. It might be tempting to assume there is not enough information to answer the question because the fixed cost is not directly listed in the problem. However, because the total cost is $300 when the quantity is zero, the fixed cost is $300. Another common mistake might be to incorrectly take the quantity of 4 radios and apply $600 as the fixed cost when $600 is actually the total cost. The average total cost (ATC) is $150 because $\$600 \div 4 = \$150$, but the AFC is $75.

2. A: The ATC of producing the 41st unit would be more than $15 because if the marginal cost (MC) is below the ATC, the ATC will decrease. Because $13 (MC) is less than $15 (ATC), it goes to reason that the previous item's unit had an ATC of greater than $15. Recall that the ATC and MC cross at the minimum point of the ATC. If the MC is less than the ATC, the ATC is decreasing. If the MC is greater than the ATC, the ATC is increasing. The average variable cost (AVC) is not known because the average fixed cost (AFC) is not given.

3. C: The average fixed cost (AFC) will always decrease and never intersect with the x-axis because, by definition, fixed cost occurs before any quantity is produced. Variable cost is independent of fixed cost. As more and more quantity is produced, the AFC gets smaller and smaller but never reaches $0. The average total cost (ATC) will always be greater than the AFC (assuming the existence of a positive AFC) because $ATC = AFC + AVC$. The ATC and marginal cost (MC) intersect at the minimum point of the ATC (not the AFC). And the vertical distance between the ATC and AVC (not MC) equals the AFC.

4. D: The 4th worker represents diminishing marginal product of labor. The 1st, 2nd, and 3rd workers produce 50, 60, and 70 carrots, respectively. The 4th and 5th workers both represent diminishing marginal product of labor with 40 and 10 carrots, respectively. However, because the question is asking when diminishing MPL *begins*, the correct answer is with the 4th worker.

5. D: The 6th worker represents negative marginal returns because total production decreases from 230 carrots to 225 carrots, and therefore the marginal product of labor (MPL) of the 6th worker is –5 carrots. The difference between diminishing MPL and negative MPL is that diminishing MPL increases the total product (MPL is positive) for diminishing MPL, whereas total product decreases for negative MPL (MPL is negative).

6. E: If a lump-sum tax is imposed on a monopoly, the output will remain the same because the marginal cost (MC) is unaffected. Hence, the profit maximizing point ($MR = MC$) will remain the same. The average total cost (ATC) will increase. The marginal revenue (MR) will remain the same because the amount of money collected by the monopoly will be unchanged. The average variable cost (AVC) also will remain unchanged because a lump-sum tax is added to the fixed cost and not the variable cost. The marginal cost remains the same, and so the MC curve remains unmoved.

7. C: The average variable cost (AVC) is $7. The first step in finding the answer is figuring out the average fixed cost (AFC). Even though the fixed cost is not a given, the fixed cost is $50 because the total cost is $0 when no quantity is produced. From there, it is possible to find the AFC when the quantity is 2: $\$50 \div 2 = \$25$. The equation for finding the average total cost (ATC) is:

$$AFC + AVC = ATC$$

$$\$25 + AVC = \$32, \text{ so } AVC = \$7$$

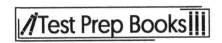

8. D: The average variable cost (AVC) of producing 3 units is \$25 because the variable cost is the summation of the previous marginal costs, or $\$15 + \$20 + \$40 = \$75$, and so $\$75 \div 3 = \$25$. Another method of finding the AVC is if the average fixed cost (AFC) and the average total cost (ATC) are known. Because $AFC + AVC = ATC$, if two of the variables are known, it is simply a matter of plug and chug to find the third variable.

9. B: A marginal cost curve tends to slope upward with increased production because of the effects of diminishing marginal product. When firms hire more and more workers, diminishing marginal product of labor eventually takes place. The amount of marginal product from each worker will decrease. Increasing marginal product will increase the marginal product from the hiring of each worker and thus be correlated with the downward sloping portion of the marginal cost curve. Economies of scale and diseconomies of scale refer to production as it relates to the average total cost (ATC) curve. Diminishing marginal utility refers to the fact that marginal utility decreases and is related to consumption, not production.

10. C: The marginal product of labor (MPL) of the 4th worker is 175. The formula for finding the MPL of the nth worker is by taking the total product (TP) of the nth worker and subtracting the TP of the $(n - 1)$th worker:

$$MP_n = TP_n - TP_{n-1}$$

11. E: The firm does not experience negative marginal returns. The marginal product of the 1st, 2nd, and 3rd workers is 100, 200, and 250, respectively, and represents increasing marginal product of labor. The 4th, 5th, and 6th workers represent diminishing marginal returns of labor with an MPL of 175, 75, and 50, respectively. It is possible that if the firm continues to produce clock radios, negative marginal returns of labor will take place but, given the numbers in the table, negative MPL does not take place.

12. A: The firm is not maximizing profit because a firm maximizes profit where $MR = MC$. The marginal cost at the current level of production is \$105, whereas the marginal revenue is \$100, so MC has exceeded MR. Increasing the quantity sold will incur more of a per-product loss. There is not enough information to determine if the firm should shut down or not. If P < AVC, Jibby's Strawberries should shut down, but that information has not been given. In addition, there is no data on the economic profit because total numbers are not given. The firm is earning a positive accounting profit.

13. D: The correct answer is \$8. In order to find the marginal cost of the second unit, one must find the total cost of the second unit and subtract the total cost of the first unit, or:

$$MC_2 = TC_2 - TC_1$$

The total cost of two units is \$50, and the total cost of one unit is \$42 because:

$$the\ fixed\ cost\ (\$20) + the\ variable\ cost\ (\$22) = \$42$$

$$\$50 - \$42 = \$8$$

14. D: When the marginal cost curve lies above the ATC, the ATC is increasing. The ATC curve and the MC curve will always intersect at the minimum point of the ATC curve. If the MC is below the ATC, the ATC is decreasing. If the MC is above the ATC, the ATC is increasing. A firm's fixed cost stays constant no matter the output, and the AFC continues decreasing as output increases. If the MC is above the AVC, the AVC is increasing.

15. B: The average variable cost (AVC) is \$7. The total cost of making zero units is \$50, so the fixed cost of production is also \$50. Because the total cost of making two units is \$64 and the fixed cost of making two units is \$50, the variable cost is \$14: $the\ variable\ cost\ =\ total\ cost - fixed\ cost$. Therefore, the $AVC\ =\ \$7$ because $variable\ cost \div quantity\ =\ AVC$, or $\$14 \div 2\ =\ \$7$.

Imperfect Competition

1. C: Profit-maximizing monopolists will always produce on the elastic portion of the demand curve. Where $MR = 0$ on the demand curve, the demand is unit elastic. On the left-hand (or upper portion) side of the demand curve, the demand is elastic. This is the portion of the demand curve that monopolists of the profit-maximizing variety will produce on. They will never produce on the right-hand (or lower portion) side of the demand curve because the marginal revenue is negative when the MR curve passes the x-axis. Monopolists earn economic profit, charge a price that is greater than marginal cost, and produce at an inefficiently low quantity (and high price, for that matter) while creating deadweight loss.

2. E: In a game theory matrix, it is possible that no firm has a dominant strategy. It is also possible that one firm has a dominant strategy. It is also possible that both firms have a dominant strategy. And it is possible that either one firm or both firms have a dominant strategy. However, none of the situations are necessarily a prerequisite in a game theory model.

3. C: Marvel has a dominant strategy of Thor; DC Comics has a dominant strategy of Batman. If DC Comics chooses Superman, Marvel has an option of Ironman (\$150 million) or Thor (\$200 million). Because \$200 million > \$150 million, Thor is the better of the two options. If DC Comics chooses Batman, Marvel has an option of Ironman (\$50 million) or Thor (\$88 million). Because \$88 million > \$50 million, Thor is the better of the two options. Therefore, Marvel has a dominant strategy of Thor. If Marvel chooses Ironman, Batman (\$150 million) beats Superman (\$120). If Marvel chooses Thor, Batman (\$96 million) still beats Superman (\$55 million). Thus, DC Comics has a dominant strategy of choosing Batman.

4. B: This is a prisoner's dilemma, and the Nash equilibrium is Marvel choosing Thor and DC Comics choosing Batman (box D). The dominant strategy for Marvel is Thor, and the dominant strategy for DC Comics is Batman. When those two strategies are played, the Nash equilibrium lands in box D. If Marvel and DC Comics collude at box A, the profits for both companies are maximized collectively. However, they both individually have incentives to "cheat" with Marvel choosing Thor and DC Comics choosing Batman, which makes this particular game theory situation a prisoner's dilemma.

5. D: When two to four firms dominate the market, they operate in an oligopoly. Three firms comprising 92 percent of total output definitely qualifies as being oligopolistic. In an unregulated monopoly, one firm produces all the output. In perfectly competitive and monopolistically competitive markets, there are large numbers of sellers in which each individual seller has very little market share. A monopsony is a situation in which there is only one buyer.

6. B: The firm should increase output until the price equals the marginal cost. As it stands, the marginal cost is only \$37, whereas the price is well above that amount at \$50. Keep in mind that in a perfectly competitive market structure, the marginal revenue doubles as the price. Because the marginal cost is below the price, a profit-maximizing firm will continue to produce until $MR = MC$. At its current output, the firm is underproducing output.

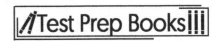

7. C: Firms sell at a price that is higher than the marginal cost in a monopolistically competitive firm. When $P > MC$, firms do not produce at the allocatively efficient level, which is when $P = MC$. In addition, firms in monopolistically competitive firms are not productively efficient because that is when firms produce at the minimum of ATC. Firms in any market structure, including monopolistically competitive firms, produce at the profit-maximizing point ($MR = MC$) and not the revenue-maximizing point, which is where $MR = 0$. In addition, collusion is unlikely to take place in monopolistic competition because collusion usually takes place in oligopoly.

8. E: A perfectly competitive industry's price and output will be lower and higher, respectively. A monopoly will purposely limit output and charge a higher price in order to maximize profit. A perfectly competitive firm also attempts to profit maximize, but it does so by producing the allocatively efficient amount, which just happens to coincide with its profit-maximizing amount.

9. E: Perfect price discrimination means that a company is able to charge *exactly* what a consumer is willing to pay for an item. Hence, producer profits increase. Total consumer surplus will most assuredly decrease, not increase. Most customers will end up paying a price that is higher than the price before perfect price discrimination. If firms charged where the price equals average total cost (ATC), producer profits would decrease because there would be no economic profit. When companies divide their customers into different groups, this is referred to as *third-degree price discrimination*.

10. B: Products are differentiated in a monopolistically competitive market. Price equals marginal cost in perfect competition, but price is greater than marginal cost in monopolistic competition, just like in a monopoly. Firms in monopolistic competition attempt to maximize profit, not revenue. In the long run, there is no economic profit for monopolistically competitive firms, and products are definitely not homogeneous.

11. A: Economic losses will drive out firms. On a supply-and-demand graph, the existence of economic losses will cause exit of suppliers, so the supply will shift to the left and create a situation of $0 economic profit. As a result, in the market, the equilibrium price will increase and the equilibrium quantity will decrease.

12. E: The economic profit is represented by the rectangular area, P_2P_4IM. The economic profit is the area below the price but above the average total cost (ATC). Another way of calculating the profit is by taking the total revenue, or $0P_4IQ_1$, and subtracting the total cost, or $0P_2MQ_1$. Another method of calculating economic profit is by calculating the price by the quantity, or $(P_4 - P_2) \times Q_1$.

13. E: None of the statements must be true. Although the details of the game theory matrix are not provided, the answer does not require knowledge of any specific numbers. Firm B *could* have a dominant strategy of charging a high price or a low price, or it could have no dominant strategy. Whether or not firm B has dominant strategy is independent of the existence of firm A's dominant strategy. For any of the answer choices to be correct, firm A's having a dominant strategy must imply that firm B either has a dominant strategy or does not have a dominant strategy, and this is not the case.

14. D: A profit-maximizing monopolist will produce where $MR = MC$ just as firms would produce in any market structure. Setting the price at marginal cost might be allocatively efficient but would most likely result in economic loss for the monopolist. Setting the price at marginal revenue would also lead to economic loss because the MR is below the demand curve. In addition, setting the price to AFC would not be advisable because the AFC is a curve that continues to slope downward.

15. C: Firms are "price takers" in perfect competition as opposed to their counterparts in monopoly who are "price makers" because of their ability to set the market price. In a monopoly, firms make economic profit in the long run; firms in perfect competition do not. Collusion does not take place in perfect competition because there are too many firms for a collusive agreement to take place. Collusion most likely occurs in an oligopoly. Advertising is most beneficial for forms in monopolistic competition, not perfect competition. Perfectly competitive firms sell commodities, not differentiated products. A firm has complete control of market output in a monopoly, not an oligopoly.

Market Failure and Role of Government

1. D: The optimal number of workers to hire is 4 because the MPL at 4 workers is 15 and the resultant MRP is $15 \times 8 = \$120$ while the daily wage rate is \$100. The fifth worker, however, produces an MRP of $10 \times 8 = \$80$. Because the MRP is below the MFC (wage), it is not advisable to hire the fifth worker. Because the MRP does not equal the MFC at any single worker, the rule is to hire the worker in which the MRP is above the MFC but before the MRP dips below the MFC. Hence, the optimal number of workers to hire is 4.

2. D: Institute a binding price floor because a minimum wage (binding price floor) would mean that the new marginal factor cost is the minimum wage, so the monopsonist is now incentivized to hire more workers closer to the socially optimal point and thus reduce deadweight loss. Without the minimum wage, a monopsonist would prefer to restrict the number of hires and pay the lower wage rate to a fewer number of workers in order to maximize his or her profit.

3. A: If the price of a good decreases, then the MRP decreases because the equation for MRP is $MRP = MPL \times Price$. So, if the price of the product goes down, the MRP (factor demand) will shift to the left. A second way in which the MRP could shift to the left is if the MPL decreases.

4. A: The third worker represents diminishing marginal returns. The first worker represents 100 additional paper bags. The second worker adds an additional 150 paper bags, which represents increasing marginal returns. The third worker increases the total to 340, but the marginal rate of production drops to 90. Hence, the third worker represents the beginning of diminishing product of labor. The fourth, fifth, and sixth workers all continue the trend that the third worker began.

5. E: The wage rate is \$15 per hour and the $MRP = MPL \times Price$, so at the fifth worker, the MPL is 30 because the number of brown paper bags increases from 400 to 430.

$$MRP = 30 \times 0.50 = \$15$$

Because the fifth worker represents the point at which $MRP = MFC$, the fifth worker should be hired, which means the total output will be 430 paper bags.

6. C: The correct answer is Q3, Socially Optimal Quantity and P3–P1, Per-Unit Subsidy. The graph is a positive externality graph. The socially optimal quantity is Q3 but the market quantity is Q2. To get to the socially optimal point of Q3, a per-unit subsidy the distance between the MPC and MBC is necessary, which is P3–P1.

7. B: The production of Good A creates a positive externality. Because the MSB is above the MPC, there exists an external benefit, which means that this is a positive externality graph. The existence of the MSB generally indicates that the graph is a positive externality graph. A negative externality graph will typically have an MSC curve above the MPC curve.

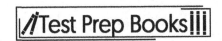

8. B: Left to the unregulated free market, society will "underproduce" positive externalities. Therefore, subsidizing positive externalities will create more quantity of college education, and thus decrease deadweight loss. When it is determined that something generates positive externalities, it is generally prudent for the government to subsidize that particular activity in order to reach the socially optimal output.

9. C: All food is rival and excludable. Only one person can eat a slice of pizza; it is necessarily rivalrous. When someone consumes a slice of pizza, no one else is enjoying its benefits. It's also excludable, meaning that a pizza company can prevent nonpayers from enjoying a delicious slice of pizza.

10. C: The higher Gini coefficient (0.6) means that there is more wealth relatively concentrated in a smaller group of individuals. A Gini coefficient of 1 means the entirety of a country's wealth is in one person's hands, whereas a Gini coefficient of zero means that country has reached a state of perfect socialism where there are no more millionaires and billionaires. Therefore a Gini coefficient of 0.6 represents more income inequality than does a Gini coefficient of 0.4.

11. A: The MSB curve will be above the MPB curve in a positive externality graph. Therefore, individuals, left to the free market, will produce less than at the socially optimal quantity.

Free Response

1. i.

The specific numbers could vary, but Norway should have a higher number in production for both beef and chicken under the "With Trade" column.

1. ii.

The specific numbers will vary, but the opportunity cost Sweden will experience should be lower for producing one of the goods than the other. A sample is below:

Number (in millions of pounds)		Without Trade		With Trade		Gains from Trade
		Production	Consumption	Production	Consumption	
Norway	Cookies	100	100	0	120	+20
	Pies	100	100	200	100	0
Sweden	Cookies	280	280	400	300	+20
	Pies	90	90	0	100	+10

1. iii.

If a trade quota was set by one of the countries or both of them, the amount of beef or chicken that could be traded would be decreased. The most significant impact would be seen in the "Gains From Trade" column. If the amount allowed to be traded was lowered significantly, it would no longer be beneficial for a trade to occur.

Question 2

2. a.

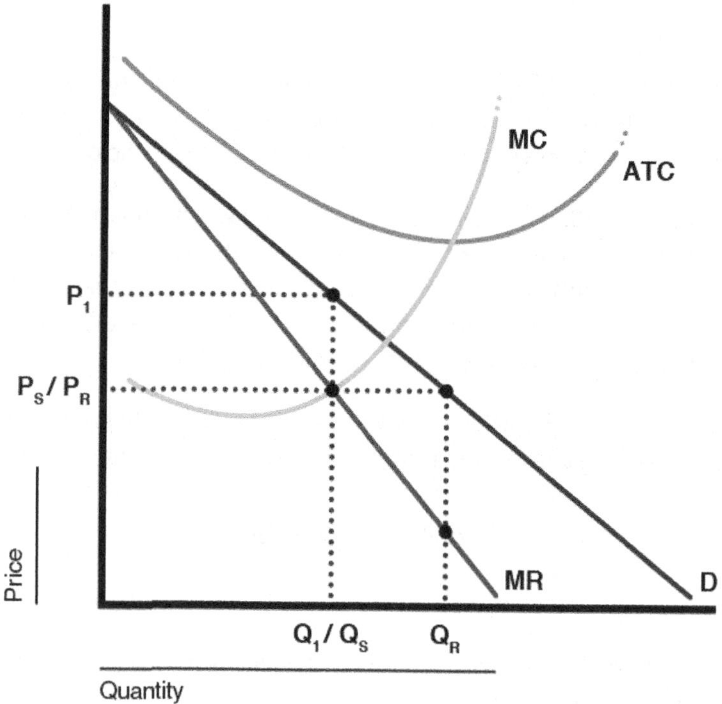

2. b. i.

The profit-maximizing quantity does not change because a lump-sum subsidy does not affect the marginal cost (or marginal revenue). A lump-sum subsidy will only reduce the average total cost (ATC) and increase profitability.

2. b. ii.

Mr. Cluck's Chicken's economic profit will increase (or Mr. Cluck's Chicken's economic loss will decrease). The lump-sum subsidy will not affect the MC (or MR) but will affect fixed cost, which will reduce the average total cost (ATC).

2. c. i.

The price must be greater than the average variable cost (AVC) in order to continue operating in the short run. If the price is less than the AVC, each additional item that is produced will incur a per-output loss, and so it would be better to shut down than to produce.

2. c. ii.

Both the profit-maximizing quantity and price will decrease because the demand for chicken sandwiches will decrease (as well as the marginal revenue). The new profit-maximizing point will be to the left of the original profit-maximizing point.

Question 3

3. a.

200

3. b.

$40

3. c

400

3. d.

The amount of deadweight loss will decrease because the minimum wage now serves as the marginal factor cost (MFC), so the company is now incentivized to produce where the (new) $MFC = MRC$, which would be 400 workers. Because that is the socially optimal point, there is no deadweight loss. Hence, the DWL decreases (to zero).

Index

Dear AP Economics Test Taker,

We would like to start by thanking you for purchasing this study guide for your AP Economics exam. We hope that we exceeded your expectations.

Our goal in creating this study guide was to cover all of the topics that you will see on the test. We also strove to make our practice questions as similar as possible to what you will encounter on test day. With that being said, if you found something that you feel was not up to your standards, please send us an email and let us know.

We would also like to let you know about other books in our catalog that may interest you.

AP Chemistry

This can be found on Amazon: amazon.com/dp/1628457090

AP European History

amazon.com/dp/1628459425

SAT

amazon.com/dp/1628459654

We have study guides in a wide variety of fields. If the one you are looking for isn't listed above, then try searching for it on Amazon or send us an email.

Thanks Again and Happy Testing!
Product Development Team
info@studyguideteam.com

FREE Test Taking Tips DVD Offer

To help us better serve you, we have developed a Test Taking Tips DVD that we would like to give you for FREE. **This DVD covers world-class test taking tips that you can use to be even more successful when you are taking your test.**

All that we ask is that you email us your feedback about your study guide. Please let us know what you thought about it – whether that is good, bad or indifferent.

To get your **FREE Test Taking Tips DVD**, email freedvd@studyguideteam.com with "FREE DVD" in the subject line and the following information in the body of the email:

a. The title of your study guide.

b. Your product rating on a scale of 1-5, with 5 being the highest rating.

c. Your feedback about the study guide. What did you think of it?

d. Your full name and shipping address to send your free DVD.

If you have any questions or concerns, please don't hesitate to contact us at freedvd@studyguideteam.com.

Thanks again!